W9-ARK-314

PRAISE FOR
FED, WHITE, AND BLUE

"Part travelog, part culinary adventure, this breezy tome will satisfy many."

—*Library Journal*

"The dangerously obsessive, staggeringly knowledgeable, provocative and opinionated Simon Majumdar knows his shit. No question about it. . . . Plus—the bastard can write."

—ANTHONY BOURDAIN, AUTHOR OF *Kitchen Confidential* AND *Medium Raw*

"I have crisscrossed this country a dozen times by car, by motorcycle, by train and light aircraft. I've eaten a thousand meals, from the glaciers of Alaska to the bars of Key West. And if Simon Majumdar asked me to join him on a journey across that same edible landscape tomorrow, I'd go without hesitation, because every mile (and meal) would be new again."

—ALTON BROWN, CREATOR OF *Good Eats* AND HOST OF *Cutthroat Kitchen*

"The Indiana Jones for the foodie set."

—ANDREW FRIEDMAN, CO-EDITOR OF *Don't Try This at Home*

"Reading about Simon Majumdar's American food adventures makes me prouder than ever of our stars and stripes cuisine. . . . His palate is second to none. . . . I should know: I've been on the wrong side of his critics' table on *Iron Chef America* many times."

—BOBBY FLAY, IRON CHEF AND RESTAURATEUR

"I would trust few people as much as Simon to find the story and the human connection behind many American cooking traditions. *Fed, White, and Blue* is the perfect way for readers to explore his deep connections to food and the heart, beginning with an ever-healing family dal recipe and extending all the way to his love of martinis and barbecue alike."

—ALEX GUARNASCHELLI, IRON CHEF AND AUTHOR OF *Old-School Comfort Food*

"This is a remarkable book. A rich and deeply personal account of food in America as seen from the other side of the pond. Full of wonderful stories and delicious thoughts. I never imagined that I would learn so much."

—GEOFFREY ZAKARIAN, IRON CHEF

"I know very few people who have the passion for food and the thirst to learn more about it than Simon. You are going to love living this journey with him as he makes his way through the country, experiencing some classic and unique American flavors for the first time."

—MICHAEL SYMON, IRON CHEF AND CO-HOST OF *The Chew*

"Passion changes everything, and Simon Majumdar is definitely passionate about getting a true sense of what America is. Journey along with him as he explores America's culturally diverse kitchens and sheds new light on the old saying, 'You are what you eat.'"

—ANTHONY MELCHIORRI, CREATOR AND HOST OF *Hotel Impossible*

"The traveler's essay has been essential in understanding our country since de Tocqueville was first published two hundred years ago. Now comes Simon Majumdar, who nails us in all our inelegant glory. *Fed, White, and Blue* is an insider's look from an outsider's perspective on the nature of eating and living in America. . . . Funny, smart, and instructive, Majumdar gets us as only he can."

—ANDREW ZIMMERN, CREATOR, HOST, AND CO-EXECUTIVE PRODUCER OF *Bizarre Foods with Andrew Zimmern*

"As an American, I have explored my own country and learned a great deal, but Simon brings his unique perspective colored by his European and Indian background to create an exploration of my native land with the clarity few natives could, and takes even a seasoned American traveler like myself on a witty, eye-opening food journey almost as fun as saying his last name. Try it! *Majumdar*."

—ADAM RICHMAN, TV FOOD AND TRAVEL HOST

FED, WHITE, AND BLUE

Finding America with My Fork

★ ★

SIMON MAJUMDAR

AVERY
an imprint of Penguin Random House
New York

This book is dedicated to Baba, Mum, Robin, Auriel, Jeremy, Matt, Evan, and Biba, the family who made me. It is also dedicated to Luz and Pering, the family who accepted me. Most of all, it is dedicated to my beautiful and patient wife, Sybil, without whom none of this would have happened.

an imprint of Penguin Random House LLC
375 Hudson Street
New York, New York 10014

Previously published in hardcover by Hudson Street Press
First trade paperback edition 2016
Copyright © 2015 by Simon Majumdar

Penguin supports copyright. Copyright fuels creativity, encourages diverse voices, promotes free speech, and creates a vibrant culture. Thank you for buying an authorized edition of this book and for complying with copyright laws by not reproducing, scanning, or distributing any part of it in any form without permission. You are supporting writers and allowing Penguin to continue to publish books for every reader.

Most Avery books are available at special quantity discounts for bulk purchase for sales promotions, premiums, fund-raising, and educational needs. Special books or book excerpts also can be created to fit specific needs. For details, write SpecialMarkets@penguinrandomhouse.com.

ISBN 978-1-10198-289-1 (paperback)

Printed in the United States of America
1   3   5   7   9   10   8   6   4   2

Book design by Alissa Theodor

While the author has made every effort to provide accurate telephone numbers, Internet addresses, and other contact information at the time of publication, neither the publisher nor the author assumes any responsibility for errors, or for changes that occur after publication. Further, the publisher does not have any control over and does not assume any responsibility for author or third-party websites or their content.

Penguin is committed to publishing works of quality and integrity.
In that spirit, we are proud to offer this book to our readers;
however, the story, the experiences, and the words
are the author's alone.

CONTENTS

CONTENTS

LIST OF IMAGES

LIST OF IMAGES

Page 177: Bill Esparza, my expert guide to the Mexican culinary delights of Los Angeles.

Page 189: With Cynthia Sandberg and my new friends at Love Apple Farms. (Image © Tana Butler)

Page 201: With Skip Madsen and his brewing manager, Dan, enjoying a pint of fantastic beer from the American Brewing Company.

Page 213: With Dr. Terry Simpson, just after our plane landed at Cook Inlet, Alaska. Thankfully no bears in sight. (Image © Katherine Gottlieb)

Page 225: Farmer Matt Romero showing me why New Mexican chiles are the best in the world.

Page 237: At my first University of Texas Longhorns game. I probably shouldn't have worn blue.

Page 251: Helping in the food pantry at Williams Memorial Methodist Church during my visit to Texarkana.

Page 265: Hunting down in the Delta. No animals were harmed in the taking of this photograph. (Image © Jeff Chao Chao Photography LLC)

Page 279: Riding the pig-mobile with my chum Chef Michele Ragussis as we head to feed the crew of Richard Petty Motorsports (thankfully the beard did not last long).

Page 299: Flying the flag. I may now be a citizen of the United States, but the journey continues. Any ideas?

FOREWORD

Simon Majumdar and I met on the set of a program called *Next Iron Chef* back in . . . well, quite a while ago. When the producers first suggested him as a judge for the series, I had to admit I'd never heard of the guy, so off to the webbernetter I ran. Interesting fellow, I thought. I discovered that he'd had a serious career in publishing, then went "off-res," so to speak, to eat everything on the planet. He'd written a book about it called *Eat My Globe*, so I figured I'd give it a read. After all, what red-blooded male can resist a man/suitcase love story?

Turns out *Eat My Globe* wasn't a travelogue or a gastro-journal but something much better. This Simon guy went looking for answers, and big ones at that. He was trying to figure out who the hell he was and where he fit in on planet Earth, using his stomach to mine the mysteries. By the time we met on set I'd already decided he was a kindred spirit. The only problem was that he's so much smarter than me it was all I could do to keep up. Our first conversation, which, if I recall correctly, concerned the intricate history of chicken tikka masala, solidified my respect for him. Since that big globe head of his seems to retain every fact his being stumbles across, and those jug ears capture every word spoken in a thousand-foot range, Simon is something of an encyclopedia of edibilia. And yet instead of coming across as a know-it-all (nobody likes a know-it-all), he has evolved into an evangelist, a kind of Johnny Appleseed hell-bent on spreading the word of world cuisine.

However, Simon's not just about the food. Sure, he's developed the palate of a world-class food critic, and his sharp wit and voluminous vocabulary (not to mention that damned accent) have made him the darling of culinary competition show producers everywhere, but what he really digs are the people behind the food. Simon sees cuisine as the connective tissue that holds humankind together, and he's dedicated himself to traveling the planet in an attempt to map that tissue. In doing so, he's collected enough passport stamps to join the exclusive club to which only the Bourdains and Zimmerns of the world belong. And yet his greatest challenge was still to come, because this citizen of the world has decided to become an American.

Even though he hates pizza.

We'll have to work on that.

Being Simon, he figured that if he was going to join our star-spangled club he should take a little road trip and discover his new country the way he has the rest of the planet: with his stomach. And he came up with an interesting and thoroughly modern way of doing it. Through his website and social media (and good old word of mouth), he invited people to tell him where to go and what to eat. And it turns out plenty of people were willing to tell Simon where to go. The following months had Simon crisscrossing the country, stitching together a fantastical culinary quilt. This book is the story of that journey. Whether hanging out with fishermen, learning the truth of American meat production, roasting chilies, tailgating in Texas (wish I could have seen that), making beer, or freezing his butt off for barbecue, Simon has done here what he does best: eat, talk, write, repeat. In that order.

Did he come back with a better understanding of what it is to be American? To be honest, I think not. I think he came back an American.

Welcome, brother Simon.

Now, about that pizza.

Alton Brown
June 2014

Green Card, Green Light

"What is the purpose of your visit?"

The stocky man seated in the immigration booth wore the dark blue uniform of the Department of Homeland Security and a tag on his lapel that declared his name to be Gonzalez. He didn't crack a smile as he leafed through my documents. The people who greet you at immigration seldom do. I guess it is part of the training, to make people nervous enough to give away clues to their bad intentions. It worked. I stammered through my answer even though I had nothing to hide.

"Er, um, er, I live here," I replied, pointing to the much-coveted green card that had slipped from between the pages of my passport and onto the desk before him.

He grunted and looked up, giving me a cold, hard stare that convinced me he suspected I was harboring a dozen Indian relatives in my small backpack, intending to free them the moment I stepped through customs.

"So, how long have you lived here?" he asked sharply, adding quickly, "Are you planning to become a U.S. citizen?"

The first part was easy enough to answer. I had moved to the United States in 2010, when I decided that uprooting myself from my beloved London and moving six thousand miles across the globe was a tiny price to pay for the chance to live with the most amazing woman I had ever met. The second part, however, was trickier to answer. I am very proud to be British, and the notion of changing allegiance in my middle years had actually never crossed my mind.

"Er," I stuttered again, adding, "I've never even really thought about it." It wasn't the in-depth answer he may have been hoping for, but it seemed to do the trick. He stamped my customs form, thrust my prized burgundy European passport back at me with another grunt, and waved me through to baggage claim to endure the inevitable tortuous wait for a reunion with my bags.

My wife, Sybil, was waiting for me as I emerged blinking into the bright lights of the arrival hall, and after a quick hug we made our way to the parking lot. As we pulled out of the lot and onto the freeway, she turned to me and asked, "Why so quiet, honey?" She was right; apart from a few words when we met, I had barely said a word since I had passed through immigration.

I made some excuse about jet lag and stared out the window, engrossed in my own thoughts and the traffic that was clogging Los Angeles's notorious I-405. I realized that the immigration officer's question had struck a nerve, and although it had never even been an issue until that moment, at the back of my mind the first seed had been planted on what exactly it might mean if I did ever decide to become an American citizen.

That night over supper, I explained to Sybil why I had been sucking on such a thoughtful tooth all the way from the airport. Moving to the United States had been challenging enough—if I was actually going to become an American it would be another matter altogether. I was not even sure what that process might entail, practically or emotionally.

I'll be honest with you, my loving spouse's initial response to my question, "How does one become an American?" was not as helpful as I would have hoped. She smirked at me over the top of a large glass of good red wine and said, "Well, the first thing you are going to have to do is have an operation to remove that British stick from up your ass." I sighed and rolled my eyes, but persevered.

This was a serious matter. Did becoming an American mean I would have to stop being British? That would never do. I was far too proud of the country of my birth to ever relinquish fully my claims on being a UK citizen, and that burgundy passport had proved useful enough in my travels around the world that I was loath to ever give it up.

Did becoming an American mean I would have to be subjected to American sport? (By the way, even if you were to lay me down on a bed of hot coals and have Butterbean do the Lambada on my chest I shall always insist on saying "maths" and "sport," not "math" and "sports.") I really hoped not. Baseball was the only game on earth I could imagine to be duller than cricket. I could live any number of lifetimes before I began to understand American football, and I certainly did not spend my formative years in the industrial heartland of Yorkshire supporting my local team through thin and thinner to demote my beloved "proper" football to a game called "soccer" that is seemingly only played by eight-year-old schoolgirls.

Did it mean I was going to have to change the way I talked? It was already hard enough trying to persuade Sybil that "schedule" should be pronounced "schedule" and NOT "schedule" (that doesn't come out on the page quite as well as I had hoped, but if we ever meet, I will explain to you what I mean), and there was just no way I was ever going to ask for the "check," require "aluminum" foil, or ever, ever, so help me God, ever say "to-may-to" without a gun being placed against my temple.

As she reached out to spear the last survivor of a pile of thick pork chops that had been our reunion supper, Sybil finally added something constructive. "If you want to know what it means to become an American, honey, you should go and meet some." I smiled back at her for two reasons. One was that, as usual, her advice was bang on the button. The second was that, as always, she had used our dinner discussion as a diversionary tactic to ensure she took more than her fair share of food from the serving plate. All I could do was nod in admiration. If I had been quicker or smarter, I would have done the same thing.

Our mutual love of food was one of the many reasons I had fallen in love with Sybil in the first place. She was smart, funny, and beautiful, but most of all she shared my almost pathological obsession with food, a passion she had displayed during our first meal together, after I met her in Brazil, when I tried to take an extra portion from a platter of grilled chicken. She did not even look up as she grabbed my hand and said with cold steel in her voice, "Touch that piece and I will cut you." I could tell that this was not a joke, and I knew then that I wanted to get to know this woman even more.

Fast-forward to eighteen months of a long-distance relationship that had involved regular commutes from London to Sybil's apartment in Los Angeles, and I was certain that I wanted to spend the rest of my life with her. I proposed one afternoon in New York's Central Park. Almost inevitably, the proposal came after a large lunch and, as we sat in the park basking in the glow of the summer sun and our new commitment, our first discussions were of what food we would serve at the wedding. I knew that it was a perfect match.

My own love of food is one that I inherited from my family. I come from a mixed parentage of Bengali father and Welsh mother, the combination of which not only provided amazing smells from the family kitchen most hours of the day, but also an interest in food that many people have told me borders on an illness. It is an obsession not just for me but also for the rest of the Majumdar clan, who spend most of our time together talking about what we have eaten, are eating, and will be eating in the future. If you doubt the level of our devotion, I offer up in evidence the response of my older brother, Robin, to the text telling him that Sybil and I had just become engaged. His reply simply read, "Good. How was lunch at Jean Georges?" (For the record: It wasn't great.)

My long-held desire to "go everywhere, eat everything" became so overwhelming that, in 2007, I left my career of more than twenty years in publishing and spent a year and my life savings visiting more than thirty countries to follow my dream. That's how I ended up first in Brazil, and now in Los Angeles, staring at an empty plate while my beloved happily sucked the last scraps of flesh from the bones of a pork chop.

Sybil wiped her lips with a napkin and turned her attention to a plate of cheese and crackers I had just laid before her. "It's always about the food with you, honey," she said as she sliced into a particularly whiffy slab of Reblochon. "You should ask Americans to tell you about their food." Even though her voice was muffled by crackers and dairy, what she said made absolute sense—and so the idea for the book you are now reading was planted very firmly in my mind.

As Sybil turned her attention towards doing the dishes, I flopped down on our comfortable sofa to do what I always do when an idea takes hold of me and won't let go. I took out my battered old notebook and began to write. I scribbled the word "AMERICA" in bold letters at the top of the page and, under it, began to place keywords that I thought might help my thought process.

I have had a love affair with America and Americans for as long as I can recall, formed during my early childhood while watching imported TV shows and cemented during my teenage years as songs about cars and girls flowed through the tinny speakers of my Hitachi music center.

America seemed like a magical, mystical place, and I longed to visit as soon as I could. I was fortunate enough that my career in publishing gave me plenty of opportunities to do so, as I took business trips to cities like Los Angeles, Chicago, Boston, and, of course, New York. Added to which, every time I pondered on where to spend my few weeks of hard-earned vacation each year, it was nearly always towards a large map of the United States that I turned for inspiration. It never ever let me down, sending me to places as far afield as Graceland in Memphis, the vineyards of the Napa Valley, the dazzling craziness of Las Vegas, and the French Quarter of New Orleans.

Sybil's suggestion made sense. If I really wanted to go and find out more about America and Americans, food was the best—in fact the only—way I should do it. I knew from all my previous travels that the moment you talk to people about the food they eat or, better still, ask to eat with them, they open up not only their kitchens but also their lives, allowing you to experience a side of them that you might never normally be allowed to see. I was certain that if I asked people to show me what it means to become one of them by allowing me to share their food experiences, the invitations would come flooding in. I began to make a list of what I was looking for.

I knew for certain that I wanted to spend time with those who grow, produce, sell, and cook the food that feeds the United States' population of nearly three hundred million, from those who marshal the vast herds of cattle that satisfy the American love for beef to those who sell heirloom tomatoes at the growing number of farmers' markets that are appearing all over the nation. From those who dedicate their lives to crafting extraordinary beer, wine, and spirits to those who brave the roughest seas to bring some of the very best fish and seafood to our tables.

I also knew that if I was going to become the United States' most unlikely (who said most unlikable?) immigrant, I should go and meet some other communities of immigrants and find out what they were having for dinner. I made notes to reach out both to those who had been in the United States for generations, like the Germans and Italians, and also to the new wave of immigrants that have made America the melting pot of culinary creativity that it is, like the Filipino community that spawned my wife's family and the Mexican community that provides the engine room for so many of America's cities (and without whom the restaurant industry would probably have to shutter its doors).

And, if I was going to write about immigrants, then I should certainly try and meet with the community that was here before everybody else. That led me to Native Americans, without whose help the first settlers would never have survived. I had heard that many groups within this particular community had become revitalized over the last few decades and would have some great stories and some great food to share.

There were others. I knew that America is a nation that was built on the ability of its people to hunt and fish. So much so, in fact, that you could argue that without such skills America as we know it now would not exist. I wanted to meet the people who still call the outdoors their office, who hunt deer and game to fill their own larders and those of others. I didn't just want to meet them, I wanted to hunt with them, prepare meals from what we caught, and share it with them.

Americans love to compete, and when they compete, they love to win. This is as true when it comes to food as it is to all other aspects of life. I should know—I spend a large percentage of my life judging some of the most competitive chefs in the country. I knew that there were entire circuits devoted to competitive eating and competitive cooking. I wanted to meet with the people who took part in these events, see what motivated them, and join them in their efforts to be the best in class.

If there are thousands of people who cook for a living in the United States, then there are millions who cook simply for the joy of it, and I wanted to meet them too. Those people who spend hours in the kitchen preparing wonderful meals for their families, not for any gain but for the simple quality time they get to spend together while eating great food. I was hoping that as I traveled around the country on my adventure, people would offer me the chance to share real American meals with real American people, whatever their religion or political persuasion.

Finally, I knew that I would also have to see the dark side of the American food industry. Although this country produces some of the best food on the planet, it also wastes more of its food resources than any other nation on earth. This is particularly striking when you see how many people, including the elderly and small children, are among the number struggling to find enough to eat every day of their lives. I knew that for me to get a true "warts and all" picture of America, I would need to spend time with the people who give their time to run homeless shelters, food banks, and programs aimed at feeding needy children.

An hour or so later, when Sybil came to find me, I was still sitting on the sofa and still scribbling furiously into my notebook.

"So, baby"—she smiled as she sat next to me and nestled her head on my shoulder—"what did you decide?"

I smiled back. "I decided that I am going to go and look for America."

"Cool," she responded, adding, "bring me back something good to eat."

I knew I would. Like I said, it's a perfect match.

Masarap: Delicious

Sybil is Filipino American and, among the many other benefits of being married to such an incredible woman (and, no, she is not dictating this) is the opportunity her heritage has given me to indulge my passion for what I believe is one of the most underrated cuisines of Asia. It's an indulgence that is made even more available by the fact that Los Angeles is home to one of the biggest communities of Filipinos in the United States.

My deep affection for Filipino cuisine began before I met Sybil, during my first visit to Manila. It is fair to say that, despite the fact that I spent only a short time in the country, I immediately fell in love with the people and the food. Indeed, if I were ever pressed to choose the best meal of my entire life, I might well pick a lunch prepared for me by noted Filipino artist, writer, and gourmand Claude Tayag, at his home in Angeles in the province of Pampanga. As we sat in his "Bale Dutung," or wooden house, he presented me with course after course of food so astonishing that it totally redefined my limited expectations for Filipino food. I can still recall every bite—it remains a meal that lingers in my memory both for the amazing tastes and the incredible hospitality. When it came time for me to leave the country, I promised myself that this would only be the first of many visits to the Philippines, and I am delighted to say that I was right.

Much more important, this newfound love was cemented when

I met Sybil during a short stay in Salvador de Bahia, Brazil. It wasn't long before we were bonding over a mutual devotion to pork. By the time it came for me to say good-bye and continue on with my travels around the world, I was pretty certain that this was the woman with whom I wanted to spend the rest of my life.

I pursued her with laudable determination, and in 2010 we married in a small but beautiful outdoor ceremony in Los Angeles. It was at the reception, as I fought my way through a crowd of her relatives intent on molesting a whole roasted pig, that I realized, along with a beautiful new bride, I had gained an entirely bonkers and entirely wonderful coterie of Filipino in-laws. Over the last four years of marriage, my wife's relatives have made me feel incredibly welcome in my new family and have also taken such a delight in introducing me to Filipino food that I have become one of its biggest advocates—and gained twenty pounds.

In addition to force-feeding me on every possible occasion, my new family has also spoken with such pride about their heritage that I have become intrigued not only with the country but also with the fascinating but checkered history of Filipinos in America. It made sense that one of my first adventures on the Fed, White, and Blue journey should be to find out more about the food and culture of my adopted family and the Filipino community near Los Angeles.

Since the mid-1980s, the Philippines has ranked behind only Mexico as the source of most immigrants to the United States and as of now is behind only China as the country of origin for the most Asian Americans. There are currently more than 3.5 million Filipinos in the United States, yet, despite their numbers and their undeniable contribution, they often remain decidedly reticent about promoting their achievements, their culture, and their cuisine. In fact, so unwilling are they to blow their own trumpet that you will often hear them referred to as or even calling themselves "the invisible minority."

This, it would seem, runs far deeper than just food, and I have found a number of reasons that might help explain it. The first is that, above possibly any other immigrant group in the United States, Filipinos have been hugely successful at assimilating into American society. More than half of the arriving adults in the last twenty-five years had already earned bachelor degrees before coming to this country. Also, as English is a common language in the Philippines, most arrivals speak excellent English, making their entry into the skilled job market and general community that much easier.

The second reason has to do with the impact of nearly three hundred years of occupation on the Filipino psyche. Starting with the Spanish in the late 1500s and then continuing in 1898 with the United States after it bought the country in a job lot with Cuba and Puerto Rico for $20 million, occupation lasted until the Philippines declared independence in 1946.

The Spanish occupation, in addition to creating this reticence, resulted in the early arrival of Filipinos into what is now the United States. In the 1760s, AWOL "Manila men" who had labored in appalling conditions on Spanish galleons founded the town of Saint Malo in Louisiana, and in 1781, a gentleman with the rather impressive name of Antonio Miranda Rodriguez was one of the envoys sent by King Charles III of Spain to form what is now the city of Los Angeles, although illness caused Rodriguez to arrive later than his companions.

During the time of the American occupation, Filipinos arrived in great numbers into the United States, often brought over to provide cheaper labor than recently emancipated African Americans. They occupied the lowest rungs of society and were subject to a great deal of racial abuse and discrimination from those who believed that they were taking jobs from local people. The clamor to stop the immigration of Filipinos, as well as a general growing anti-Asian sentiment, resulted in the passing of the 1934 Tydings-McDuffie Act, which limited the number of immigrants from the Philippines to a mere fifty people a year.

Everything changed during World War II. Many Filipinos joined the U.S. Navy because of the large U.S. naval base in Subic Bay. They primarily carried out the menial tasks of cooking and cleaning and were repaid, after the conflict, with the repeal of the act in 1946. This saw numbers rise to almost twenty thousand new arrivals into the United States every year. Since that time, Filipinos have contributed massively to American society at all levels, and yet they still remain one of its least visible ethnic minorities. All aspects of their culture, including Filipino cuisine, have only recently begun to emerge from under the shadows of other Asian American communities.

I decided that I wanted to spend time in the kitchen of a Filipino restaurant and accepted an invitation from my friend Aldous Liongson, who is the head chef of Salo-Salo Grill in West Covina. I first met AJ, as he prefers to be known, during a now-infamous family meal where I lost the fierce "Battle of Crispy Pata" with my wife's eighty-four-year-old Auntie Minda. She emerged with the pork, and I was left with nothing but a wound on my left hand to show where she had stabbed me with a steak knife.

We had ordered a great deal of food that day, even by the standards of my family, and AJ had come out of the kitchen to see which table was putting such a strain on his line cooks during the hectic lunchtime service. As he introduced himself, he nodded approvingly at the assortment of empty plates that had accumulated on our table. Having just admitted defeat in the war for pork, I excused myself and stepped outside the restaurant to spend some time chatting with him as he took the opportunity to break for a cigarette.

AJ was born in Quezon City and moved to the United States in 1987 at the age of six. He attended culinary school on the West Coast and then headed east to develop his skills, spending six or seven years working in top-level kitchens in New York City before being asked by his father, Reggie, to move back to West Covina and take over as head chef at the restaurant he had opened in 2001.

It was a tough time, he explained. Both he and his partner, Liz, found the move from East to West Coast a huge lifestyle change. I could identify with that, as at the time I was struggling with my own move from London to Los Angeles. AJ wrestled in particular with his work because he had gone from the blisteringly creative cooking environment of one of the world's greatest eating cities to one where the cooking was rooted in tradition to the point where it could easily be accused of being old-fashioned.

"I am trying to change the menu a little, to lighten up some of the heavier dishes, so we can attract new customers," he told me between drags on his cigarette, "but it's a very slow process. My father has final say and we don't want to scare off our loyal customers by altering the food too much." He pointed back into the restaurant, filled almost entirely with older Filipino Americans, to make his point.

It was a conversation I'd had with many people before—and since—meeting with AJ. It's part of the balance chefs of all ethnic cuisines have to achieve in America as they try to respect the traditions of their culture while attempting to introduce their food to as wide an audience as possible. If you change the food too much, the old guard will soon let you know that what you are doing is not authentic. Leave it just as it is, and you risk consigning a wonderful but possibly challenging cuisine to a culinary ghetto, where its audience will decline over time.

AJ told me that, much as he respected his father and the regulars who had kept his restaurant going for over a decade, his time in New York had given him the hunger to take Filipino cuisine to the next level. Having just eaten his food, I had to agree that he had the skills to do it.

Before he went back to work, AJ suggested that I should come back and spend some time with him in the kitchen. He would show me how to make some Filipino classics as well as some of the newer dishes he was trying to persuade his father to add to the menu. When the idea for the book was born, I decided to take him up on the offer.

Not only would it give me the perfect opportunity to spend time with a young and talented chef who was also a Filipino immigrant, but anything I happened to pick up about preparing Filipino cuisine could only earn me plus points back on the home front. As we planned my visit, AJ upped the ante by suggesting we invite my relatives back for another meal on my last day in the kitchen so they could give their opinions on my culinary efforts.

A few weeks after we talked, I pulled into the parking lot of Salo-Salo at eight-thirty a.m., as requested, to find AJ waiting for me by the back door of the restaurant. Before we got down to work, he gave me a tour of the kitchen space. It was much smaller than I had expected but spotlessly clean, with food dated and stored properly in both coolers and walk-ins. "We are sticklers for detail here," he said as he pointed towards a number of notice boards with cleaning schedules, house recipes, and staff instructions pinned to them.

As more of the staff began to arrive, my attention wandered to two pots that were already bubbling on the stove. In one, large slabs of pork belly were simmering away in a broth flavored with onions, carrots, celery, and garlic. They had been brined first and after cooking would be cooled, dried in the oven, and then deep-fried to order to make the famous Filipino dish of lechón. "I add lemongrass to the brine too, to freshen up the flavors," AJ told me—just one of the small changes he had made to his father's traditional recipe.

In the next pot were pork knuckles that had also been brined and would be braised, oven-dried, and fried in a similar fashion to make the crispy pata that had so entranced Auntie Minda that she was prepared to draw my blood. The lechón would be served with Mang Tomas, a sauce made from pork liver, while the crispy pata would be accompanied by a sharp dip of palm vinegar and soy sauce.

"We don't like to waste much," AJ said when he saw me looking at the pots, adding that the braising stock would also be used. Some would go to a deliciously tangy soup called sinigang, which would be soured in the traditional way with tamarind, and the rest to the dish that we were just about to work on, kare-kare.

Kare-kare is one of my favorite things to eat. A stew traditionally made of oxtail that is thickened with ground toasted rice and ground roasted peanuts (for which, these days, peanut butter is often a regular substitute), it's a distinctively Filipino recipe.

First, AJ had me dry-roast short-grain rice on a low heat in a wok and then grind it to a fine powder in a hand-cranked mill before passing it through a sieve to clear out impurities. I then poured a small amount of oil into another large hot wok on the stove and added minced garlic and diced onions. "Filipino soffritto," AJ said with a laugh, referring to the base of onions, carrots, and celery so common in Italian cooking. "We use it as the base for just about everything."

Once the onions and garlic had begun to take on some color, I added the ground rice, a few ladles of the beautifully rich and fragrant pork stock from the bubbling pans of pata, some pungent patis (powerful Filipino fish sauce), a little achiote paste for the deep red color it brings to the final dish, and then the contents of two enormous jars of smooth peanut butter. It was an unlikely combination, and I have to be honest that at this point it looked very, very far from the appetizing dish that I have come to love so much over the years. However, once I began to stir the mixture together, the familiar smell of kare-kare soon began to fill the air.

AJ nodded at my efforts, and I continued stirring until the contents of the wok had become a thick golden brown paste that would form the base of the finished dish. We had enough for about twenty portions, and once it cooled, I spooned it into containers ready for the line chefs to use during service.

By the time I had finished preparing the sauce, the restaurant had opened and orders were already beginning to trickle in from the first few customers. I watched as one of the chefs grabbed one of my containers and added it to a wok with stir-fried eggplant, bok choy, onions, garlic, and more of that amazing pork broth to form a sauce. He added four glistening chunks of oxtail that had been braised until the meat was falling off the bone and left it to simmer for a few minutes, until the sauce formed a thick coating around the meat. Before the chef sent the order out from the kitchen, he passed me a spoon and motioned for me to take a taste.

One bite reminded me why this might well be one of my all-time favorite dishes. The meat was juicy and soft, the vegetables added crunch, the fish paste made it fragrant, and then there was the sauce from the paste I had made, which offered up layer upon layer of flavor that lingered on the tongue for minutes after I had stopped eating. Tastes have the ability, more than just about anything else, to take you back to other times and other places, and I was immediately transported back to my first night in Manila and a restaurant called Abe, enjoying my first-ever taste of kare-kare.

It was all AJ could do to stop me from finishing off the entire order, but I pulled myself away and watched as he plated up the kare-kare and sent it out to the customer with bagoong alamang, a traditional condiment made with fermented shrimp that added saltiness to the dish.

As service began in earnest, I stepped in to help AJ and his crew deal with the tickets that had begun to flow steadily. There are few things that I find more enjoyable than watching a well-oiled kitchen at work, and here it was obvious to see that everyone knew exactly what they were doing.

The backbone of Salo-Salo's crew was its coterie of Mexican line cooks. "These guys are amazing." AJ pointed with his chef's knife over at a colleague who was manning the sauté station and overseeing half a dozen orders without batting an eyelid. "We simply couldn't run the kitchen without them," he added. It is a story that could be told in any one of thousands of kitchens across the country.

Over the next two days, AJ and I worked on the dishes we would place before my in-laws for approval. We made Talangkanin, a stunning dish of rice laced with alique—fat from crabs that AJ had lightly poached in oil—and pinakbet, an eggplant dish heavily scented with bagoong. "They are Filipinos," AJ said, rolling his eyes slightly. "So they are bound to order a lot more than just three dishes. But if you prove you can make these, they'll at least consider you worthy to be an honorary Pinoy."

As we cooked, I was able to talk to AJ about his determination to bring Filipino food to the next level. The more I watched his terrific kitchen technique at play and listened to him talk about his heritage and cuisine with such passion, the more I began to suspect that Chef AJ Liongson might just be one of the new generation of Filipino chefs to take this cuisine forward.

On the one hand, he has enough respect for his father's recipes, his customers, and his heritage not to throw the baby out with the bathwater. But he's not so bound by these traditions that he's afraid to use the techniques he's learned to improve things where they need to be improved.

It had been, he acknowledged, a very hard struggle to get to this position.

"When I arrived back here from New York," he told me, "I was convinced I knew everything and I had a huge ego. But working with these guys"—he pointed again towards one of his Mexican line cooks—"soon knocked it out of me. I think they respect me now."

The next couple of days passed far too quickly. Although I was excited at the thought of feeding my family as my grand finale, I was also saddened by the fact that I would soon be leaving behind the camaraderie and good humor of AJ's kitchen. I had enjoyed my short time there, and I knew for a fact that we would remain friends, linked by our mutual desire to see this underrated cuisine deservedly brought to the attention of a wider audience.

At around six p.m. on my last day, Sybil and my in-laws arrived and commandeered a large table at the front of the restaurant. As AJ had prophesied, they laughed at the notion that three dishes of food would be enough, and the table was soon filled with so many platters that more than one of the line cooks made semi-joking suggestions that I contribute some overtime payment to their weekly checks.

The dishes we had made all received a thumbs-up, and AJ was thrilled with the positive reception from his Filipino audience. "Now," he told me, "we just have to get non-Filipinos to love it."

I shook his hand, looked him in the eye, and said, "AJ. That's my job."

You Heave, You Leave

As I have noticed in many years of visiting and a few short years of living in the United States, Americans don't just like to consume large amounts of food, they love to watch others do it too. Switch on the Travel Channel at any time and you'll often find Adam Richman screaming from the screen, "This is the biggest sandwich in Dayton, Ohio! Can I finish it?" Or turn to my own home on the Food Network and it won't be long before you can "enjoy" the sight of spiky-haired Guy "Flavortown" Fieri shoving a giant hot dog down his throat so quickly that it would make a porn star blush. Those two stars alone will confirm that watching others eat to excess in America has become something of a national obsession.

Even though I find the thought of people guzzling vast amounts of food for no other reason than because they can slightly odd, it does still have a uniquely "only in America" quality to it that made me want to investigate it further for this book.

I already knew a bit about eating competitions, of course. Back in the UK, on wintry weekends during the 1980s when our own sporting calendar was decimated by the weather, the sport magazine shows would often fill their schedules with clips of odd "sporting" events from the United States. They did this, I suspect, more out of desperation than any hope of drawing an audience, but as a bored student I loved watching them and actually began to look forward to the moments when the announcer would tell me, "Today, instead of the scheduled program of racing from Doncaster, we are going to bring you anvil-tossing from Iowa." They often showed some of the major competitive eating events in America, and I even began to recognize and follow some of the more well-known names on the circuit. However, it wasn't until I began my research for this book that I began to realize just how popular competitive eating had become.

Eating contests in America actually have their origins back in nineteenth-century rural county fairs. However, the "big bang" of competitive eating can really be traced to the very first of the legendary Nathan's Famous hot dog eating competitions in the early part of the twentieth century. The much-told story that it originated when four immigrants challenged one another to see who could prove their patriotism by inhaling the most encased meat has been debunked, but the competition itself still remains the most well-known and most highly attended challenge in the country, and previous winners such as Takeru Kobayashi have become eating legends in their own lifetimes.

There are now well over one hundred events, with hundreds of participants, held under the auspices of the Major League Eating federation as well as dozens of independent challenges that offer prize money ranging from a few hundred to tens of thousands of dollars. Some people compete part-time as a hobby, while others make close to a full-time living traveling across the country to take on any challenge offered.

My very first invitation for the Fed, White, and Blue journey came from a gentleman who makes a good deal of his living by eating more than other people do. Jamie McDonald from Hartford, Connecticut, had seen a post of mine on Twitter and sent me an e-mail saying, "Why don't you join my entourage at Wing Bowl?" I had never heard of Wing Bowl, but a few minutes of Internet research soon told me that this was one event that I absolutely had to attend—and that

Jamie "the Bear" McDonald was just the person I wanted to attend it with.

The first Wing Bowl event was held in 1993, in the lobby of the Wyndham Franklin Hotel in Philadelphia. The brainchild of two local radio DJs, Angelo Cataldi and Al Morganti, it was a response to the fact that the city's football team, the Philadelphia Eagles, were a bit crappy and had never made it to the Super Bowl. Naturally, the DJs decided to create their own version. It was an immediate hit, attended by more than a thousand people, and grew so popular that eventually it had to be moved to the Wells Fargo Center, the home of the Philadelphia 76ers basketball team. It is now one of the most eagerly awaited dates on the Philadelphia calendar and brings in both local challengers and professional competitive eaters from all over the country to take a shot at winning an impressive $20,000 in prize money.

Jamie was due to arrive in Los Angeles for a few days for another eating event, and we agreed to meet in a restaurant close to my home so he could fill me in on just exactly what the Wing Bowl was all about and what would be expected of me if I joined his entourage. I arrived a little late and peered around the restaurant door, expecting to find a big fat lad with an overfilled plate of food in front of him waiting for me.

As it turned out, Jamie McDonald was not even close to being what I had imagined. He recognized me as I walked in and stood to wave me over to the booth he had claimed. About six feet in height, Jamie had less fat on him than a butcher's apron, and taut muscles in every place that was physically possible to have them without growing extra limbs. As I squeezed my own over-ample frame into the opposite seat, Jamie, who had just turned thirty-seven, told me that as well as eating for a living, he was also a competitive bodybuilder and a former Navy man. He had begun entering competitions when his brother taunted him about his capacity to consume the calories necessary to pump iron. It turned out that he had a talent for the task, had gone on to win twenty-five out of the twenty-eight competitions he had entered in the last eighteen months, and was now ranked as the number one independent eater in the country.

I tucked into a cheeseburger and fries and washed it all down with a cold beer as Jamie poked unhappily at a small undressed salad, sipping on a glass of water. It was, he told me, his regular between-competitions diet. It seemed hard to believe that the man opposite me was, to all intents and purposes, a walking food disposal machine. "I don't really do this for pleasure," he went on. Even though he had proved to be very good at it, for Jamie competitive eating was a means to an end, not an end in itself. "Every penny I make from this goes into my kids' college fund," he explained, "and I can't see myself competing for more than a few years before I am done."

I looked across the table with a new level of respect. Before we met, I have to admit that I had assumed that Jamie would be a man who took part in competitive eating for no other reason than gluttonous pleasure and the admiration and dollars his extraordinary stomach capacity might bring him. Instead, I found a quiet, thoughtful, intelligent man who, like so many Americans, was looking to find any way he could to support his family and to give his children the chance of a great education. There was a price to be paid, however, for the career he had chosen. The night before, he had accepted a challenge from a restaurant in the Valley and had consumed a staggering fifteen pounds of pizza. He was now feeling the consequences. "I am pretty sure I broke a rib," he said with a thin smile, as he lifted a small green leaf gingerly to his lips.

There was, I found out, also a price to be paid for being on his entourage. The Wing Bowl, Jamie explained, was not just an eating competition but a gladiatorial battle, where combatants from all over the country come to Philadelphia and face off against the locals. As a member of Jamie's New England entourage, I would be expected to "represent" by wearing the colors of one of the sporting teams from the area. In my case, he had chosen the Boston Celtics.

On hearing this interesting news, I must have pulled a bit of a sour face. "You don't like the Celtics?" Jamie inquired. I shook my head. Not liking the Celtics wasn't really the issue. In fact, until Jamie explained to me who they were, I could not have even told you which sport it was the Celtics played. No, my genuine horror was the very thought of wearing sporting apparel at all. At the time I was fifty years of age, and I genuinely believe that any person over the age of twenty-five caught wearing replica sports jerseys is, as my dear late mother would have put it, "a little bit suspect." Still, no one can ever accuse me of being unwilling to get into the spirit of things, and I nodded as Jamie suggested I pick up something suitable before meeting up with him in Philadelphia.

True to my word, on the morning of Wing Bowl 2013, I found myself standing outside the Wells Fargo Center at five a.m. wearing a lurid green sweatshirt with a leprechaun on it. Truth be told, I was actually quite pleased to have any sweatshirt, whatever the color. The East Coast had been hit with one of its worst freezes in living memory, and as we waited to enter the arena I was grateful for every layer of clothing I was wearing, even if it did make me look like the world's largest booger.

To make matters worse, I was suffering from quivering indigestion, accompanied by a raging hangover. The day before, I had decided that it would make absolute sense to do a little competitive eating of my own, and fashioned a tour of Philadelphia's legendary sandwich shops. After partaking of the best Jim's, John's Roast Pork, Geno's, Pat's, Tony Luke's, George's, and Paesano's had to offer, I had compounded my stupidity by attending the ceremonial Wing Bowl "weigh-in" at a local pub called Chickie's and Pete's. This turned out to be far less an official occasion for the sanctioning body than a reason to drink as much beer as possible while enjoying the company of

Philadelphia's wide and varied selection of exotic dancers. Quite how I ever made it back to my hotel, I don't remember, and by the time we were finally let into the arena and shown down to the competitors' waiting room, I was beginning to regret ever agreeing to come along, wanting nothing more than a couple of aspirins and a warm bed.

I started to regroup a little as Jamie walked in with his family. He was very much in game mode and I didn't want to distract him, but it was obvious his confidence was high. "It's not a case of if I am going to win, just a case of how easily I'm going to win," he told me before walking off into a corner to psych himself up. This wasn't just a case of empty braggadocio, just a stone-cold certainty that he was better than anyone else in the competition, including local boy Jon "Super" Squib, who had won on three previous occasions and was the hot favorite to win again. It reminded me of the few times I had been in a boxer's dressing room before a big fight.

By six-thirty a.m. I was already hearing loud roars coming from the arena and I left Jamie and the others in the dressing room. As I emerged through a side entrance into the auditorium, I was hit by a wall of sound and an explosion of color. The noise was deafening. The place was already packed to capacity with more than twenty-three thousand people—most of whom looked and sounded as if they had enjoyed as much alcohol as I had over the last twenty-four hours.

On one side of the stadium, a live band was churning out covers of the sort of songs Americans can't seem to live without at sporting occasions, while in front of them a large mechanical rodeo bull on a raised platform was providing exercise for a dozen or so scantily clad and pneumatically chested young women. While proving very enjoyable to watch, their inability to stay in the saddle while the machine bucked made me think that they were probably not raised in the homes of God-fearing cowboy folk.

On the opposite side of the arena was the stage upon which battle would commence in less than thirty minutes. It tiered up over four levels to accommodate all the competitors, comprised of both local amateurs and serious contenders from places like Dallas, Washington, DC, and New York, and, of course, Jamie "the Bear" McDonald from New England.

As I was taking in the assault of sights and sounds (and taking a few pictures with the cavorting strippers, I'm not going to deny it), I felt a tap on my shoulder. It was Jamie's wife, Cheryl, who had changed from her warm winter clothes into a skimpy cheerleader's outfit in New England Patriots colors. "We're ready," she informed me. I followed her backstage to a wide corridor where the competitors were clambering aboard small floats for the pre-competition parade. The locals had obviously spent considerable time and money to prepare their "chariots," and with their entourages they paraded out in a circuit of the stadium to huge cheers of approval from the howling crowd.

The atmosphere became noticeably less welcoming when it came time for the out-of-towners to take their turns. Jamie's float was little more than a rickety trolley with a few balloons attached, and he and Cheryl had to hold on for dear life as we, his entourage, began to pull it over the electric cables on the floor into the arena. The moment we appeared, the boos began, and they increased in volume as our image flashing on the huge overhead TV screens allowed more people to notice that Jamie was wearing a football jersey with number "12" written on the front and the word "Brady" written on the back in large letters.

It also probably didn't help that the louder people shrieked their disapproval, the more Jamie seemed to be enjoying himself. As the crowd screamed at us through the glass partition, he began to smile and flex, showing off his rather impressive biceps in the direction of all those who were making unpleasant hand signals towards us (many just involving a single digit). The more he posed, the more vicious the response became, and the shouting was soon accompanied by missiles of beaded necklaces that had been handed out to the crowd as they entered the stadium and plastic bottles that were filled with what I hoped was water. By the time we had made it less than three-quarters of the way around our intended circuit, everyone in the entourage had been hit at least three or four times. The organizers decided that it would be safer for all concerned if we called it quits and made our way to the rostrum. Jamie and Cheryl fought their way through to the stage while I went to find myself a spot in the crowd from which to get a good view of the proceedings.

For the first of many times on this journey, I heard the national anthem being sung before the event. The crowd in the Wells Fargo Center belted it out with particularly vigorous zeal, despite the early hour and the condition most of them were in. Afterwards, the competition rules were explained by the emcee. Plates holding twenty chicken wings each would be placed in front of each competitor. When they had finished a plate, a referee would give them a point for each wing for which the meat had been fully cleaned from the bone. Then another plate would be delivered for them to continue. The competition would be split into two sections of fourteen minutes and a final "eat-off" of two minutes, the gaps between to allow for advertising breaks on the breakfast sport show that would air the event and to give the competitors time to recuperate before the next wing assault.

Before the battle finally commenced, the competitors were given a firm warning from the master of ceremonies: "You heave, you leave." If anyone threw up, they were not only out of the competition but also had to leave the stadium itself, exiled to the cold winds outside. The admonition was reinforced on every large screen in the arena by the showing of one of Wing Bowl's most famous moments, when a 2001 competitor called "the Sloth" reached the point of no return and projectile-vomited over not only his own food but also the person's in front of him. The multiple showings of this avalanche of puke was almost enough to put me off ever eating chicken wings again, but it did not seem to have any impact on Jamie, who was staring ahead steely-eyed and ready for war.

Once the buzzer sounded, it became obvious which competitors were experienced competitive eaters and which were just hopefuls. Jamie picked each wing up and vacuumed its flesh in one sucking motion before tossing the bone back down on the plate and starting again. As each plate was cleared, Cheryl replaced it with another for him to begin again. All the while, referees moved along, shouting out the running total of scores.

Despite impressive teamwork and his initial confidence, it became obvious that the Bear was not going to have it all his own way. At the end of the first session, Jamie had eaten 130 wings, trailing in third place more than 18 wings off the leader. Cheryl was looking less than happy at the way her husband's plates were being marked and was bellowing her disapproval at the referee. It very much appeared that the chances of Jamie adding to his children's college fund were looking decidedly ropy.

Fortunately, things picked up in the second session. The initial leader faded, Jamie hit his stride, and, as the buzzer sounded with twenty-eight minutes gone in total, he had consumed another 135 wings, putting him at a 265–253 advantage over local boy Jon Squib. Despite a valiant Hail Mary where Squib managed somehow to consume another 29 wings in two minutes, the last count gave the decision to the Bear by the wafer-thin margin of just 5 wings.

Host of the 94WIP *Breakfast Show* Angelo Cataldi begrudgingly announced Jamie as the winner. The crowd booed in unison and then left the stadium almost as quickly as they had filled it. Jon Squib, beaten in front of his hometown fans, was gracious in defeat and, after shaking hands with the victor, left Jamie onstage to receive his crown and an oversized check for $20,000 and to face the flashes of cameras and questions from the local media.

Back in the dressing room, Jamie's family was fizzing over with excitement at his victory. It may only have involved eating more wings than a bunch of other blokes, but they could not have been prouder if he had been the first man on the moon. I was fizzing too, joining in the whoops of celebration and even exchanging a few high fives as Jamie returned from the auditorium sporting a big grin and carrying his check under one arm.

"So, what did you make of Wing Bowl?" he asked, propping the check up against a wall.

"Only in America," I responded without hesitation.

It was true. I'd be hard-pressed to think of any other nation on earth where a competition to watch twenty-three men eat as many chicken wings as they could in thirty minutes would attract twenty-three thousand spectators, including every stripper in the city, at seven a.m.

But it was more than that. In many ways, Jamie McDonald is just the sort of person I was hoping to meet on the Fed, White, and Blue journey, a genuine encapsulation of the great American dream. A man who served his country and then had found something at which he really excelled and had dedicated himself to becoming the best he could be, not just for personal glory but as a way of raising funds to provide for his children's education. The Wing Bowl may well have been a genuinely bonkers event, but the end result was the same as what was happening all over the country, people working hard to support their families. I could not have hoped for a better start to my travels.

A sudden wave of exhaustion hit me as I looked at the clock on the dressing room wall. It was not yet eight-thirty a.m. and the call of returning to a warm bed for some much-needed sleep was becoming too strong to resist. As I gathered my things, I asked Jamie, "So, what's next for the Bear?" expecting him to say that he was now going to take a few days off to let his system recover. Not a bit of it. "I'm off to Chicago," he told me in a matter-of-fact tone. "A restaurant has challenged me to beat their burrito challenge. It's about as long as a man's arm."

"Can you do it?" I asked, already suspecting the answer I would receive. He just gave me another one of those quiet, confident smiles and nodded. Of course he could.

Jamie McDonald can, I suspect, do anything he sets his mind to.

The Bay Rat and the Rebel

have met plenty of interesting people on my travels around the globe. I've hung out with Mongolian yak herdsmen, Indian tea plantation owners, Scottish whisky distillers, Senegalese fishermen, Chinese butchers, and Japanese sushi chefs, to name just a few off the top of my head. However, in all my travels, I have not met too many people quite as interesting as my friend the Rebel Chef Terry French and his fishing captain companion, David "Bay Rat" Kopaz.

I first met Terry in 2012 during the filming of a television show on the Food Network called *Extreme Chef*. It was a quirky little show that, as the title suggests, pitched chefs against each other in extreme circumstances, leaving yours truly to judge the often dubious results that reached the plates. I had a great deal of fun doing the show, and at the end of the second season found myself in Chiang Mai, Thailand, judging the final rounds as the remaining four chefs fought it out for a $50,000 prize. Terry was among them and was having the time of his life.

He went on to win the final battle and the big prize. Once the show wrapped, he leapt into a magnificently rampant celebratory bender to which he invited everybody in the cast and crew, including me. Now that the opportunity for anyone to accuse me of partiality had passed, I accepted the invitation and spent the best part of an evening slowly getting drunk with the *Extreme Chef* champion and his new friends. To say "we" got slowly drunk is not quite true. As I was to find out over the next few hours, the Rebel doesn't do things by half measure. For every beer I finished, Terry would have four or five empty bottles in front of him. By the time I was ready to call it a night and head back to the hotel, Terry was surrounded by empty whiskey glasses and pretty producers, and was obviously just getting warmed up. The last sight I caught of him that night was of his posterior clambering unceremoniously into the back of a tuk-tuk with a bottle of some ungodly local hooch in one hand and a cigarette in the other.

Terry stayed in touch after we all returned to the United States, and over the next few months I would receive regular updates from him as he traveled around the country making the most of his television victory. I found out through our many conversations that he had already led quite the life, long before his casting on *Extreme Chef.*

He had been born and brought up in southern Indiana, where hunting and fishing were a way of life. He had spent more of his early life outdoors than in the classroom, and when he reached seventeen he enlisted in the U.S. Navy. He served for nine years and two world tours, which gave him the opportunity to travel around the globe and visit dozens of different countries, as well as ignite a lifelong passion for the cuisines of Southeast Asia.

On leaving the Navy, Terry found himself in Springfield, Illinois. After a number of short-term jobs, he landed a position with renowned Chinese chef Richard Chen, who became his friend and culinary mentor. Eventually Terry married and moved to New Jersey, where he opened a successful restaurant in Egg Harbor Township. He also started a number of other businesses that, together with the income from his restaurant, provided a comfortable lifestyle for him, his wife, and their two young children.

In 2008, things took a turn for the worse. The economic crash and the death of a business partner took their toll and resulted both in the closure of his restaurant and a decline that saw him hit, in his own words, "rock bottom." He supplemented his income by fishing and sheer dint of hard work, managing to keep his head above water for the next few years until the victory on *Extreme Chef* helped him emerge from the shadows of the previous dark few years and come roaring back to life with a rebel yell.

One day as I was working at my desk, my phone began to buzz. I hesitated to pick it up when I saw Terry's name on the caller ID. Not because I didn't like him, but because I was busy and knew that Terry likes to chat. A lot. Still, I knew that it had been far too long since we'd spoken, so I poked at the answer button.

"Hey, little brother, whatcha doing?" came a familiar drawl through the phone. I had to laugh. Terry has called me "little brother" since we first met, despite the fact (as I have pointed out to him on more than one occasion) that I am actually four years older than he is. When I told him I was busy doing research for more stops on my journey, he added, "We need to get you down to New Jersey."

I paused before replying. In part this was because Terry's accent is an odd hybrid of the Deep South and East Coast, and consequently I often don't understand a bloody word he says, and also because I couldn't think of any reason why I would possibly want to go to New Jersey, unless it was to catch an airplane out of the Newark airport to somewhere better. Terry, however, was in full flow and continued. "Brother, southern Jersey is totally different. Trust me, we'll take you out hunting, we'll go and catch us some perch, some catfish, and some clams, and we'll cook them up right there on the beach."

It already sounded a lot more promising than I could have imagined, and a short twenty minutes later I had decided that it just might be worth a trip. The Rebel was relentless, and over the next few weeks I received regular calls and texts until we finally pinned down a date in the calendar, deciding I would visit after my Wing Bowl experience. "We are going to take real good care of you, little brother," Terry told me once I had committed. "We're going to make you an honorary member of the Bay Rats."

Terry and his wife, Wendi, invited me to come and stay with them, and when I arrived after the short drive from Philly, I found the Rebel skillfully gutting fish in the kitchen. "Catfish, little brother," he cried out as he saw me carrying my bag through the door. "We've got some good eating planned for you tonight." Alongside the half dozen large catfish he was busy cleaning were two sizable bags of clams, a plate of perch fillets, a dish of assorted vegetables, and what looked remarkably like a large slab of venison.

Terry shouted above the sound of Steely Dan's *Aja* pumping out of the stereo system, "Meet Bay Rat." He pointed with the tip of his knife as another guest walked across the kitchen to introduce himself. I have to admit to being ever so slightly intimidated. The man, whose real name was Dave Kopaz, had arms covered in sleeves of multicolored tattoos, which moved as his corded muscles rippled. His smile, which broke through a bristly gray goatee, revealed that his two front teeth were missing. "A fishing accident," he explained with a gravelly chuckle. Although he was stocky and slightly shorter than I was, there was an air about the Rat that made you realize this was a man who would know how to take care of himself if he were ever put in a tight corner.

The Rat, like Terry, had also come to the area almost by accident. "People just seem to end up here and never leave," he said. "There's something about the laid-back lifestyle that just seeps into your blood, and you just stay," he added, explaining how he came to Egg Harbor Township almost twenty years earlier and had stayed, primarily making his living as a fisherman off the coast of New Jersey. He and Terry met when Terry began to captain fishing boats to supplement his income after the failure of his restaurant, and their joint passion for the water and for food had made them firm friends.

"People don't always realize how different southern New Jersey is from the rest of the state," the Rat told me. "Right here, we are just one mile from the Mason-Dixon Line." He went on, "For all intents and purposes, we are in the South, and it feels like it."

Living in Egg Harbor Township has not always been an easy existence. "What with Hurricane Sandy and the slump in the economy," he told me, "this community got hit hard." Terry handed me a beer and joined the conversation: "People lost their homes, their businesses, everything. It's still tough as hell, but we are getting through it." As I drank my first of too many beers that evening and helped with the preparation of the fish and clams, Terry and Dave told me all about how the community had come together to help each other get through the challenges of the last few years.

"We didn't just hunt and fish for a living," Terry told me, "we had to use what we caught to feed our families." Dave added, "We shared what we had left with our friends, and between us, we just about made it." Hearing their stories made me appreciate all the more the meal that we were about to eat, and as he brought the plates to the table, the pride Terry took in serving me and his family food that they had all worked so hard for was obvious. He smiled as he took his seat.

The sea and the land had obviously been kind. The table was laden with ten large serving plates, each piled high with food. As well as fresh clams, there was a tray of clams casino, the shellfish hidden beneath a bubbling layer of garlic, wine, shallots, herbs, and golden bread crumbs. There were the catfish, which Terry had smoked on the grill outside. There was a plate of perch fillets that had been battered and deep-fried, and strips of venison that had been sliced thinly and then flash-fried on a griddle before being drizzled with olive oil. Accompanying these were baskets of hot bread, salads, and half a dozen bottles of wine.

Terry poured me a glass of red. It was dark and rich and tasted delicious as the first sip coated my tongue. "This is great," I said. "What is it?"

"Oh, Rat made it," Terry answered as if it were the most natural thing in the world that the tattooed fishing captain seated to my right might also just happen to be an expert winemaker. As I was to find out over the next couple of days, there was far more to David Kopaz than first meets the eye.

After helping Terry and Dave clear the plates, I made my excuses and went straight to my room. I wanted to check in with Sybil and, after a hefty meal and a little bit too much to drink, I was thinking a comfortable bed and a good night's sleep would be the perfect preparation for what I anticipated would be quite a memorable day out on the water with the Rebel and the Rat.

The sky was clear and blue the next morning as I joined Terry out on the deck of his house, where he was enjoying his first cigarette of the day and a cup of coffee that I strongly suspected had been "fortified" with Kentucky's finest. "It's going to be a great day for fishing, little brother," he growled in his morning voice as he blew smoke out into the crisp air. "We better get going soon. The Rat will be waiting for us at the dock."

As we drove, Terry pointed out some of the destruction that still remained from when Hurricane Sandy tore the waterfront apart. "We've all done our best to help put things back together," he told me, "but some people just left and never came back." I could tell from the derelict state of some of the buildings we passed that it would be a good many years until the area truly recovered.

By the time we pulled up in front of a ramshackle bait-and-tackle shop at Dolphin Dock, Dave was already loading his boat, the *Mudd Shark*, with rods and bait buckets. Terry and Dave jumped on board the twenty-foot California skiff as if they had been doing it all their lives, which they more or less had. I, on the other hand, am very much a lubber-of-the-land variety and had to be helped onto the boat like an elderly Victorian dowager descending from her hansom cab. Dave held my hand to make sure I did not go headfirst into the water.

"Don't worry," he said, laughing, as he grabbed me, "you'll soon get your sea legs once we pull out into the bay."

If Dave had come prepared with everything we needed for fishing, Terry had come prepared with everything we needed to enjoy ourselves. It was barely nine a.m. when I heard the *plop* of a bottle opening as Terry started in on his first beer, and about 9:01 by the time I joined him in a liquid breakfast. "Life on the water isn't just about fishing, this is where we come to play and to hang out. I couldn't imagine being away from the water." He tossed me another beer even though I had barely taken a sip of my first. "We'll fish for a couple of hours or so, go dig up some clams, and then we'll sail on out to the Dredge so we can cook up some lunch on the beach before we head back to the Rat's house."

By now the *Mudd Shark* had pulled well out into the bay. On our left was the outlet into the Atlantic Ocean, and on our right, a few miles into the distance, was the skyline of Atlantic City. Dave pulled the boat to a standstill and tossed out the anchor. "Let's see if we can catch some perch." He handed me a rod.

Around the bay, a score of other boats had done the same. "I'm still considered a newbie here," the Rat told me as we stood on the deck, hoping for a bite. "Some of these captains have been here all their lives. They know the water better than they know the land." I could only hope that they were having more luck fishing than I was. After an hour or so of casting and reeling with progressively less enthusiasm, all I had managed to hook was a perch about three inches in length that Terry and Dave made me toss back into the water after they had taken the requisite embarrassing photographs. Fortunately, they had more success and had filled up a sizable orange plastic bucket with enough fish to at least ensure we would not go hungry for supper that night.

We made two more stops before lunch. The first was on a small strip of beach that remained uncovered at high tide. Dave unearthed a small hand shovel from the front of the boat and leapt into the sea. The water came up to his waist but hardly hindered him as he smoothly pulled the boat up onto the beach until it was resting on the shore. "Clams, little brother!" Terry yelled as he jumped into the water to join Dave in securing the boat. I followed them off the boat rather more gingerly, but the coolness of the water on my skin felt incredibly welcome and I was soon wading with them between the pools on the beach looking for the small sand bubbles that were the telltale signs that clams were hiding just beneath the surface. "At the right time of year, we can catch pounds and pounds of them," Dave told me as he plucked a large specimen from the sand. "They are the juiciest clams you will ever eat. We sometimes just sit here with a beer and eat them live straight from the shell."

As soon as Terry and Dave thought we had enough, we climbed on board the boat and sailed off towards a spot where a local home owner had allowed Dave to anchor a couple of crab cages to the dock at the end of his land. As he pulled up the ropes that secured his traps, I could see that the haul of blue crabs was pretty good. At least thirty clung onto the cages as Dave transferred them to a bucket of water.

I was already planning how I would cook them that evening when Terry disturbed my culinary calculations, calling out, "Enough work already, brothers. It's time to cook up some of this shit." He didn't get much argument from either of us, and we set off to a secluded inlet known as the Dredge. "This is a local place," Dave shouted above the noise of the engine. "Come here at the weekend and it is filled with people from the harbor. But," he added, "I think we'll have it to ourselves right now."

There was not another person in sight as we tied the boat up on the beach. I clambered out and helped Terry carry a cooler to the shore while Dave grabbed a few clams and brought them onto land. Before he left the boat, he turned up his radio full blast. The tinny radio speakers began blaring out the unmistakable southern sounds of "Sweet Home Alabama" by Lynyrd Skynyrd.

"Now we are talking, baby," Terry yelled. He had already begun to start a fire with some dry wood kindling on a metal grill unit that had been cemented in place for anyone who came to the Dredge. In one hand he had a wicked-looking hunting knife, which he used to poke at the wood as the fire took hold, and in the other, a clear bottle of rum into which he had already made a frightening indentation. The Rebel was obviously settling in for the afternoon. I declined his kind offer when he extended the bottle in my direction, reaching instead for another beer from the cooler.

The fresh air and a hard morning's work had given us all an appetite. Dave began shucking clams and handing them to me to wash down with my beer, while Terry cooked more of them on the grill, adding a few drops of rum to the natural juices in each shell to create steam as they cooked. "This is how we roll, little brother," Terry said as he clinked his bottle of rum against my beer.

We stayed on the beach at the Dredge for most of the afternoon—shading ourselves from the sun under some tall trees, drinking beer and rum, eating seafood, and listening to the sounds of southern rock banging out from the radio on board the *Mudd Shark*. It was easy to see why, despite the problems they had faced in the last few years, both Dave and Terry loved their life on the water. As we sat, Terry and Dave told me more about their lives and how they had come by their nicknames.

"Mine was inevitable, little brother," Terry explained. "I am from the South, I was always getting into trouble in the Navy, and I can cook your ass off in any circumstances. What else was I going to be but the Rebel Chef?"

"As for me," Dave chimed in, "the people from around here who earn their living on the water are known as the Bay Rats. I started making T-shirts for everyone, and I guess the name Bay Rat just stuck to me."

I could have stayed there for the rest of the day, but I was shaken awake gently by Dave just as I was falling into a very pleasant clam-induced nap. "We need to make a move before the tide changes, or we'll be stuck here." He added, "And we have people to cook for back at my house." We put out the fire and cleaned up after ourselves before climbing back on board the boat. "Always leave it like you find it," Dave told me. "It's one of the unwritten rules of the Dredge."

Back at Dolphin Dock, we washed down the boat and loaded up our catch onto the back of Dave's truck. I already knew that I loved my chum the Rebel Chef, but after a few hours in his company, I was really beginning to understand why Terry had always spoken such high praise of his friend the Rat. After my first slightly intimidated impression, David Kopaz had proved himself to be a hugely articulate and highly intelligent man whose loyalty to his friends, and particularly to Terry, was unconditional.

He also proved to be far more than just a good friend and an able fisherman. His house and gardens, most of which he had designed and built himself, were not only beautiful but also decorated with artifacts that he had made himself from driftwood and his rather impressive paintings of the seascapes we had enjoyed today. His basement was filled with racks containing bottles of wine, beer, and mead that he had made in the last few years, as well as large glass containers of new brews that were fermenting. The shelves were lined with cans and jars of fruits and vegetables that he had grown, and his kitchen cupboards and fridge contained just about every ingredient any cook could require, including many that you would be hard-pressed to find even in the most well-stocked of professional kitchens.

It all made for a fun evening of cooking, and Dave, Terry, and I carried on from where we had left off at the Dredge, drinking beer, listening to music, and preparing the bounty that the waters of the Atlantic had provided that day, as well as two thick and meaty eels that Dave had caught the day before.

If the feast on my first night in Egg Harbor Township had been memorable, the feast on my last night was even better. Terry pan-fried the eels with olive oil, butter, and lots of garlic and parsley, while I took charge of the crabs, tossing them in a wok with red chili peppers, ginger, and garlic before coating them with a hot-and-sour sauce to make the chili crab dish I have enjoyed so much on visits to Singapore. All the time, David worked tirelessly as our kitchen bitch, prepping and sourcing unlikely ingredients that he, of course, just happened to have in his cupboards.

By the time our guests arrived, we were able to lay before them a meal that I was proud to have shared in both catching and preparing. By the way they cleared every plate of food, I could see that our guests appreciated the effort we had undergone to bring their supper from sea to plate.

Long after everyone else had left the house, the three of us were still collapsed back into the comfortable chairs in Dave's dining room. "I've got something for you," he said, easing himself up from his seat and disappearing into his workshop at the side of the house. He returned carrying a gray sweatshirt. He held it up to reveal a motif, which of course he had designed. Underneath it read "Bay Ratz."

"See, little brother," Terry told me as he reached over to clink glasses one final time, "I told you we'd make you a Bay Rat."

"Wear it with pride." Dave laughed as he tossed it over to me and drained his glass.

I was sure I would. I was also sure that it would not be too long in the future before I headed back to New Jersey to see my new brothers, the Rebel and the Bay Rat.

The Baron and the Bronx

O utside of London, my home for the greater part of twenty-five years before I moved to Los Angeles, I probably know New York better than any other city in the world. Well, I should qualify that. I know Manhattan really very well indeed, as that is where I stay every time I am in town and it is where nearly 100 percent of my business in New York takes place. As for the other four boroughs, my experience has been much more limited, a few fleeting visits for meals or an occasional meet-up with friends, but certainly not enough for me to claim that I have any in-depth knowledge of them or the culinary riches they might offer.

So when I began to think about what I might learn about America from New York City, it was to these boroughs I turned to for inspiration. My time was limited, giving me only one day to allocate for culinary exploration, which left me to choose between Brooklyn, the Bronx, Queens, and Staten Island.

My decision was made for me when I received an e-mail from my friend Justin Fornal, better known in the Bronx as Baron Ambrosia. Justin is an underground filmmaker who created this larger-than-life character, the Baron, in 2006. He bills his mercurial alter ego as a "quaffer of culinary consciousness" and has used his filmed exploits to promote the many different ethnic cuisines available in the Bronx. He has also made a number of feature-length movies involving the

Baron and even created an excellent, if unlikely, series for the Cooking Channel in 2012.

I first met Justin, er, Baron Ambrosia at a food event in 2013, where we bonded over the butchering of Mangalitsa pigs. We hit it off immediately and spent most of our time swapping stories of our travel exploits around the world. We've kept in touch ever since, and I was genuinely thrilled when I received an invitation to join him for a day while I was in New York.

Prior to this day, I had previously only ever set foot in the Bronx on two occasions. The first was in 2006, as I waddled through a sliver of the borough when I was foolish enough to run the New York Marathon. The second was during a visit to the Italian enclave of Arthur Avenue. The Baron wanted to prove to me that there was far more to the Bronx than just Italian American cuisine, an old zoo, and hip-hop, and he gave me instructions to meet him at nine-thirty a.m. outside the Baychester Avenue subway stop a few days later.

He was waiting for me as I emerged from the entrance of the station and climbed from his car to give me a forceful bear hug. He was, as always, dressed immaculately, in a black collared shirt, blue silk tie, pressed black pants, and a dark gray vest. His long hair was pulled back and gathered into a knot on the top of his head. "We'll start at the top of the Bronx and work our way down," he boomed as he ushered me into his car.

Our first stop was just a short drive away and in a few minutes we pulled up in front of a small wire fence with a green gate. Whatever was behind the fence was obscured by a hand-painted sign in the shape of a vitamin bottle that read, "Sundial. Traditional Jamaican Organic and Wood Root Tonic," while underneath was written the Rastafarian phrase "If It's Ital, It's Vital."

"These are my Jamaican herbalists," the Baron said as he opened the gate to reveal a compound far bigger than I had anticipated from its outside appearance. The confidence with which he said it made the notion of anyone having a personal Jamaican herbalist sound like the most natural thing in the word. As soon as we stepped inside, we were greeted by Adoni, the son of the Rastafarian owner of Sundial Herbs. "We've been in the Bronx for nearly forty years now," he told me in a gentle lilting accent as he led the two of us to a small building at the side of the courtyard. "We make and supply herbs and tonics to treat ailments and promote wellness."

His father, Baba Rahsan Abdul Hakim, was waiting for us and immediately began telling me the story of the company. "Herbalism is a long tradition in Jamaica and dates back to our time in Africa," he began. "All of our family has been healers going back more than one hundred years, and I was chosen to carry on the tradition when I was just eight years old. We make everything here, from tonics to teas and cereals that can help anybody feel better, but it all began with this." He held up a brown bottle that bore a label with the same design as the sign that had been on the wire fence outside. "Wood root tonic," he said, dispensing some into a small paper cup.

"It's good for vim and vigor." He gave us a broad grin. "It's made the same way that the Maroons of Jamaica would have made it hundreds of years ago." It was incredibly bitter, and I shuddered violently as I took a tiny sip. Baba Rahsan seemed pleased, so I downed the rest of the shot in one gulp, more out of good manners than because I thought I was in desperate need of any extra vim or, indeed, vigor.

Before we left, Adoni and Baba Rahsan put together a goody bag for me. It included tonics for calming bad nerves, powders for gout, and a large bottle of brown liquid for helping to suppress appetite. I have no idea if any of it will work, but I can tell you that Baba Rahsan Abdul Hakim is obviously an extremely good judge of character.

The Baron seemed pleased. "We are only just getting started," he assured me as he pulled the car back out into the traffic. No one would ever be able to claim that the Bronx is the prettiest of New York's boroughs, but as we headed along the slightly grubby streets towards our next destination, it was obvious, from the loving way he described it, just how much the Baron adored the place.

I could still taste the bitterness of the wood root tonic in my mouth when we arrived at our next stop. The lettering on the slightly tattered purple awning read "Ali's Trinidad Roti Shop." Although the country is still on my bucket list of places to visit, I am a great fan of Trinidadian food and could not have been more pleased that this was our first "proper" eating halt. It was lucky for me that of the more than four hundred thousand people of Trinidadian and Tobagonian descent in the United States, the majority of them live in the five boroughs of New York City. As we climbed from the car, the smell of spices, so familiar to me from my half-Indian upbringing, was escaping through the front door of the building.

This is the Baron's town, and all doors appear to be open to him all the time. Once we entered the small shop, he marched us straight through to the kitchen, where four people were hard at work rolling dough or scooping fresh roti from simmering pans of hot oil.

Everyone seemed delighted to see him and stopped work immediately so they could embrace and catch up with his news. He told them why I was there, and the elderly lady who had been watching over the roti insisted, "Him gotta have buss up shut."

I knew that "buss up shut" was a particular type of roti popular in Trinidad, which takes its name from the fact it's broken up into pieces before being served, giving the effect of a ripped-up shirt. The small pieces are perfect for sopping up juices of accompanying stews and curries. Having taken in the smells of curry goat wafting from a large pot on the stove, I agreed with her immediately.

She rolled out a large circle of dough and flapped it onto the griddle, allowing it to cook for a few minutes on both sides before she attacked it with a dabla—a pair of large wooden spoons that are used to break the roti up into smaller pieces. She scooped it expertly onto a plate and then began to spoon large chunks of goat meat next to it, covering it all with plenty of rich, thick, spicy gravy before handing it us.

"Enjoy now." She smiled as she returned to her work. I did not need telling twice and used a piece of the hot, fresh roti to scoop up a piece of slow-cooked meat from the plate. Both the Baron and I made noises that drew appreciative smiles from everyone in the kitchen, as did the fact that we finished the plate in about five minutes, mopping up any leftover gravy with the last strips of the buss up shut.

I had barely wiped my hands with a napkin before the Baron thrust some money at the woman by way of payment and gave her one more hug by way of thanks. He turned to me, saying, "Time for some Puerto Rican cuchifrito," and made a dash for the door. I scampered behind him while waving good-bye to everyone in the kitchen.

I was just catching my breath by the time we parked outside our next stop, 188 Bakery Cuchifrito's on 188th Street. But, on the way there, the Baron had filled me in on one of his favorite things to eat. The word "cuchifritos" comes from the Spanish and originally referred to small cubes of pork that have been deep-fried. However, it has now come to refer to a whole style of cuisine that the Baron called "Puerto Rican soul food."

The relationship of Puerto Rico with the United States is a fascinating one. Puerto Rico has had trading relations since it was a Spanish colony and, indeed, has been under the sovereignty of the United States for well over a century. It has yet to become a fully fledged state, although Puerto Ricans pay federal taxes and are eligible to vote in presidential elections, providing they are residents in the continental United States.

In 2012, a census showed that there were nearly four million Puerto Ricans living in the continental United States. (To put this into perspective, this is greater than the number who live in Puerto Rico itself.) The biggest community of Puerto Ricans is in New York City, with neighborhoods in East Harlem and the Bronx serving as home to the majority.

As we walked to the restaurant from the Baron's car, it felt like I could easily have been in any street in San Juan. Spanish music was erupting from storefronts, and every wall was covered with posters advertising shows by Puerto Rican bands, most of which laid claim to be "Los Originales de San Juan."

Once inside, we fought our way to the back of the restaurant and claimed the two remaining spare seats at the counter. "We don't want to overdo it," the Baron shouted above the din of the crowd and the music. "We have a big one coming up next." The Baron's idea of not overdoing it and mine are obviously entirely different things, as, minutes after we took our seats, an exceedingly large plate of deep-fried pork was placed in front of us. "Chicharrón," he said, beaming and spearing one of the bigger pieces with his fork. It was a dish that was very familiar to me, much like the versions I have sampled in the Philippines, Mexico, and in countries all over Central America, all of which owe their culinary love of the pig to their histories as colonies of Spain.

I too am a great lover of pork that has been introduced to its own fat in hot liquid form. Even with the warning that there was lots more food to come, I soon began a battle of dueling forks with my aristocratic friend that didn't end until there was little more than a smear of grease on the plate. These chicharrónes were particularly excellent. The outside had the requisite crunch, while the remnants of meat attached to the crisp skin remained juicy thanks to the quick cooking process. The large plate was set off by a topping of sharp pickled red onions and slices of hot peppers, all of which served to cut through the fat of the pork with their heat and acidity.

We had again barely wiped our mouths clean before the Baron was pointing me back to the car for the next stage of the tasting menu. "What do you know about Garifuna food?" he asked as we fought our way through the crowded restaurant towards the street. The truth was not a lot. Although I had heard the name before, I knew almost nothing of the cuisine or the people who prepared it.

The Garifuna—or the Garinagu, as the wider diaspora is known—originated when the native Arawak and Carib tribes of the Caribbean island of Saint Vincent intermarried with black Africans who had survived a slave shipwreck in 1635. They immigrated to parts of Central America, at first under duress when they were exiled to the Roatán Island off the coast of Honduras by the British in the late 1700s. After they petitioned the Spanish to be allowed to work, they moved to the mainland, and their descendants still live in Honduras, Belize, Nicaragua, and Guatemala.

The Garifuna are still a small community of no more than three hundred thousand people worldwide, of which nearly ninety thousand live in the United States, but their culture is a vibrant one, with highly respected musicians, language, and complex religious beliefs. In fact, in 2001, UNESCO declared that its language, threatened by a declining population, was one of the "masterpieces of the oral and intangible heritage of humanity" and sought to protect it by seeking official recognition for it in the homelands of the Garifuna. I was to find that along with this culture also came a rich cuisine that draws both on the native cooking of the Caribbean and on the West African traditions of the original Garifuna.

The Baron had persuaded one of his many friends, Callita Diego, a Honduran Garifuna, to make what constituted our third meal of the day. She was hard at work when we entered her apartment on Fox Street in the South Bronx. "Come in, I'm making machuca." She smiled as she pointed us towards some kitchen chairs. Machuca, as I learned, is a traditional dish from Honduras made with shrimp, fish, and coconut milk, all of which were in plentiful supply to the Garifuna in Central America.

Callita made her own coconut milk by grating the flesh of the coconut, soaking it with the coconut water, and then straining it all through a sieve. She flavored the milk with garlic and onion and set it to simmer away on the stove. It was time-consuming work, but Callita insisted that it was necessary to make the dish authentic. "You can use coconut milk from a can, but it's never going to taste as good."

Callita went on as she poked into another pot of boiling water on the stove to retrieve golden plantains that had been simmering for some time before we arrived. She strained them and placed them in a large wooden mortar on the floor, before taking up a pestle almost half as tall as she was and beginning to beat the plantains with swings that evidenced a lifetime of practice. "You have to totally break them down, so they can soak up the sauce," she instructed us as she gave the plantains a beating from which they would never recover.

By the time she had finished some fifteen minutes later and scraped the contents of the pestle onto a serving dish, they resembled a mound of yellow mashed potatoes. Now it was time to cook the fish and seafood. Callita dropped large pieces of kingfish into the gently simmering pot of coconut milk to cook for just a few moments. "You mustn't overcook them," she warned.

As she moved around the kitchen, Callita stopped to pass the Baron a glass bottle that had obviously once contained rum. Now it was filled with a brown liquid that reminded me of the bitter wood root tonic I had sampled earlier in the day. "It's called guifiti," the Baron told me as he poured a small amount into each of two shot glasses. The Baron explained that each Garifuna family has their own recipe, but the drink is basically a selection of herbs and roots that have been soaked in rum. I have no idea exactly what roots were in the bottle, but the moment I had downed the first shot my head started swimming and I had to lean against the chair back to steady myself. "It's good stuff," said the Baron as he downed a second one, "but you have to be careful with it."

I declined a second shot and was more than happy when I saw that Callita had begun to plate up our meal. She had filled two soup bowls with the coconut broth and placed in each the tails of the kingfish along with two pink shrimp. "We like to eat with our fingers," she instructed as she sat with us.

I pushed aside my fork and spoon and began lifting meaty pieces of fish with my fingers. Alongside the bowls were two plates containing the mashed plantain and, as Callita demonstrated, I formed a small ball and used it to sop up the broth. Although the Baron and I had both already eaten a great deal that day, the clean tastes of the fish, broth, and plantains were so subtle and so delicious that it was not long before we had both drained our bowls, leaving nothing but fish bones as evidence. Thinking back, it was easily one of the most memorable tastes of the whole Fed, White, and Blue tour and I am sure that it was even more so because we had been invited into Callita's home to experience it.

I could easily have stayed and eaten another bowl while I listened to Callita tell me more stories of Garifuna culture, but the Baron gave me a nod, which I, by now, knew meant we were moving on. At Callita's suggestion, I took one last shot of guifiti. "To help with digestion," she insisted as she gave me a warm hug and waved us off to continue on our culinary adventures.

"Now," the Baron ordered, "let's finish in Puebla, Mexico. I think they've killed a goat for us."

Just in case anyone is wondering, this was not actually the first time someone had killed a goat in my honor. In 2012, my Filipino in-laws decided that slaughtering a fatted goat was the perfect way to welcome me to the family home and insisted I stand in the back garden to observe as the butcher dispatched a young kid with a swift cut across the jugular. It may have looked like a scene from *Scarface*, but I still enjoyed the meal that followed.

There was thankfully no bloodbath to be seen on this occasion, which was just as well, given how much I had already eaten. What there was, as we walked into the small, charming dining room of

Xochimilco Family Restaurant on Melrose Avenue, were warm greetings from the owners and an incredible array of wonderful smells emanating from the kitchen. As soon as we had taken our seats, the owner placed steaming bowls of bright red menudo soup in front of us. It tasted as hot and fiery as it looked and was flecked with large chunks of honeycomb beef tripe, which is the slow-cooked lining of a cow's stomach. Although it seemed impossible that I could still be hungry by this point in the day, this wondrous soup proved to be the perfect palate awakener, and a few spoonfuls were enough to perk up my appetite.

Next up was the goat's head, presented whole on a platter, its eyes popping out and skull cracked to show the brain beneath. Neither the Baron nor I were particularly fazed by the appearance of a platter that looked like it had come from the set of a horror movie, but some customers, seated at tables adjacent to ours, looked a little less sanguine about its arrival. Such meals are definitely not for the faint of heart, particularly in the United States, where I have seen diners grow pale if a whole fish with eyes is served to them on a plate. However, they do serve to remind us that in most parts of the world, "nose-to-tail" eating is not a gimmick or a trend, but a necessity for people who must put the whole of the animals they kill to good use.

They can also be delicious. I followed the Baron's lead and reached for a piping-hot tortilla to wrap around chunks of the brain I had plucked from the skull. I doused it with plenty of fresh lime juice and a spoonful of chunky salsa before taking a huge bite. It was another culinary surprise, the softness of the tortilla and the brain combining beautifully with the crunch of the salsa and the acidity of the lime juice. It was not long before the Baron and I were in full free-for-all, tearing off chunks of juicy cheek meat from the skull and gleefully taking an eye from each side of the face to pop in our mouths like meat candy.

We had almost picked the skull clean to the bone when the final dish of the day arrived in the form of a giant blood pudding, which was about the size of a basketball and wrapped in the goat's stomach. It reminded me more of Scottish haggis than of anything else I had seen on my travels around the globe. I took a tentative bite. It was fantastic, but I was completely done by this point and made my apologies to the disappointed restaurant owner. He seemed happy enough, particularly when he smiled and said, "Don't worry, anything that's left, I'll be taking home for dinner."

The Baron seemed happy enough as well, now that he knew I was completely and utterly defeated. In one marvelous day of eating he had taken me from Jamaica to Trinidad, from Puerto Rico to Honduras, and finally to Mexico, on an adventure that had proved beyond all doubt that the Bronx was ready for its culinary day in the sun.

On the basis of this escapade alone, I have to say that the borough definitely deserves it. I also have to say that no place in the United States could have a prouder or more fervent ambassador than Baron Ambrosia. I suspect, very soon, the borough will have to give him a promotion, because in my mind he is King of the Bronx.

A Pilgrim's Progress

I n September 2012, I found myself filming a one-off television show called *Back in Time for Thanksgiving* for the Cooking Channel. It turned out to be quite an odd program, with me acting as the besuited straight-faced host offering historical information about the origins of the Thanksgiving meal, while two very talented but slightly nonplussed comedians dressed as Pilgrims improvised skits in the background.

The end result certainly provides one of the more unusual additions to my television résumé. It was also bloody hard work, as the whole show had to be shot in three long days and required me to memorize more pages of lines than I had since the age of eighteen, when I gave a sidesplitting (my words, not the reviewers') rendition of Old Gobbo during a college production of *The Merchant of Venice.*

One upside of the whole experience was that we filmed the show on location at Plimoth Plantation, the open-air living museum in Plymouth, Massachusetts, where hordes of American schoolchildren have been flocking since 1947 to learn about the origins of their country. It's a genuinely remarkable place, and during the inevitable long periods of "hurry up and wait" that are a part of the making of any show, I had plenty of time to explore the plantation and to interact with the dozens of people who work in character as "interpreters" to explain the lives of the first settlers to the thousands of people who come to visit every year from all over the world.

I was also fortunate enough to spend a great deal of time with the people who worked behind the scenes at Plimoth Plantation, supporting the interpreters and researching the lives of the original Pilgrims. When they heard of my plans to tour around the United States, they were all quick to suggest that I should plan a revisit to Plimoth Plantation. "If you want to find out about the United States," Deputy Director Richard Pickering insisted, "it makes sense to start at the beginning."

There was an obvious logic to his argument and in the following couple of months I swapped e-mails with their media relations person, Sarah Macdonald, to create a short itinerary that would allow me to spend time both with those who research the food and customs of the Pilgrim settlers and those who represent the original native community, the Wampanoag.

There was a lot to cram into a short span of time, so the day after my arrival from New York, I met Sarah early in the morning to go through my schedule. "Today will be all about the Wampanoag," Sarah told me as we sat in a small meeting room. "And tomorrow we'll show you how to prepare some of the dishes that the original settlers would have eaten."

As I was scribbling down some notes, we were joined in the meeting room by Carol Wynne. Carol had recently retired from the Wampanoag Indigenous Program at Plimoth Plantation and had agreed to tell me more about the original native people of the region and the food they typically ate long before the first settlers arrived.

The name "Wampanoag" literally means "People of the First Light." In the early part of the seventeenth century, there were nearly forty thousand tribe members living up and down the East Coast as far as Martha's Vineyard and Nantucket. Their numbers were decimated in the second decade of the century by an outbreak of what is believed to be yellow fever, and by the time the settlers arrived, there were only about twelve thousand natives left. Many historians now believe this is part of the reason the colonialists were able to establish a firm foothold in the new territory.

"Now there are around five thousand of us," Carol continued, "and we are working to preserve our culture. The language was almost destroyed by the settlers, but we have been rediscovering it again in the last twenty years and teaching it to the new generation." She sighed a little. "It's a beautiful language. We are a people who lived and thrived by the ocean in summer, even our language is reminiscent of the sounds of water, and, of course, so much of our diet comes from it."

The staples of the original Wampanoag diet, she told me, were the "three sisters" of maize, beans, and squash. These were supplemented by fish, clams, and lobster, and fruits that were harvested from the surrounding land. "This afternoon I'll show you how to make some of the dishes we prepare with the maize and beans, and before you leave we're going to show you how to prepare a traditional lobster-and-clam bake." While I finished working through my itinerary with Sarah, Carol disappeared to change into traditional native attire.

By the time we walked over to the small enclosed piece of land that was the education site for the Wampanoag Indigenous Program, Carol was waiting for us, wearing a beige dress with long tassels that reached down almost as far as her calf-length moccasin boots. She had already begun to build a fire in an outside pit. "We're going to make boiled bread and a traditional quahog sobaheg," she said as she began to sort her ingredients into a large shallow wooden dish.

The boiled bread was a staple of the Wampanoag diet and would be eaten at almost every meal. It was an incredibly simple dish to prepare, and Carol handed me a hand-carved wooden bowl and spoon so that I could help mix the ingredients, which consisted of a combination of cornmeal, corn flour, and regular flour with nuts, seeds, and dried fruit such as blueberries and cranberries. I added enough water to create a sticky dough and broke it into small patties, which I then dropped into a pot of barely simmering water that Carol had already placed on the fire. The patties sank to the base of the pot, only rising to float on the surface of the hot water once they were cooked.

As they rose, Carol scooped one from the pot with a spoon and passed it to me. I tossed it around in my hands to let it cool and then tore off a chunk. The texture of the bread itself was slightly grainy, but not unpleasantly so, and the nuts and seeds added extra crunch to the softness of the cornmeal, while the berries added sweetness. It was, however, very bland, so I could understand when Carol told me that it was usually served with other dishes rather than eaten on its own.

On this occasion that other dish was a sobaheg. I had heard of it before. In fact I had actually demonstrated how to make a version of one while filming the television show, as many historians believe that it was a dish that would have been served at the first Thanksgiving meal. However, the ingredients that Carol had prepared looked very different from the ones I recalled using.

"The word 'sobaheg' means 'stew' in our language," she told me. "It is something that we make all the year 'round with different seasonal ingredients, so the one they would have served at Thanksgiving would have been quite different from the ones they would have made in spring or summer. We are going to make this one using quahog clams."

Carol had placed another pot of water on the fire, and as soon as it began to simmer she added fresh green onions and plenty of dried garlic and herbs. In another wooden bowl she had a bunch of fiddlehead ferns and nearly thirty clams of the size and sort that you would normally use if making clam chowder. "These clams can be a little tough, so they work best when they are cooked in a sobaheg," she told me as she pushed them from the wooden bowl into the metal pot over the fire. She gave the pot a stir with the wooden spoon and said, "We save the clamshells to make jewelry," then pointed at a set of stunning earrings and at an equally beautiful necklace she was wearing to accompany her tribal outfit.

The pot was soon bubbling away and the clams began to open, releasing their briny juices into the broth. After about twenty-five minutes, Carol decreed that the dish was ready. She handed me a small wooden bowl and told me to help myself.

I used my spoon to scoop half a dozen clams into the bowl along with plenty of the cooking liquid. Like the boiled bread, it was a very simple dish, but it was filled with flavor. The barely cooked fiddlehead ferns added a fresh green crunch, while the clams themselves were meaty but not chewy. The broth was highly aromatic and had been seasoned well by the liquid of the clams. After I had finished the seafood, I tilted my head back and sipped the broth directly from the bowl. I dipped my bowl into the pot one more time, filling it almost to the brim.

Carol seemed pleased. She told me that the men of the tribe would often be very hungry on return from a hunting expedition and the broth of the clam sobaheg would be what they craved most as soon as they came back to the village, believing that it would restore their energy. I may not have just returned from a hunting expedition, but I could definitely testify to the restorative powers of quahog sobaheg.

If Carol Wynne had shown me that the Wampanoag natives had eaten simply but well with the ingredients they harvested from the land and the water, Kathleen Wall, the colonial culinary expert at Plimoth Plantation, would show me that the first settlers from England were to find things much harder.

Kathleen's job was to research the diet and recipes of the first arrivals and to make sure that the way they were portrayed by the interpreters was completely accurate. On my previous visit, we had spent a great deal of time together as she shadowed the film crew, making sure we got things just right. We discovered a shared a passion for food history, and I was delighted to have the opportunity to pick her brain during the long periods of downtime between scenes. On this occasion, she invited me to spend time with her in the kitchens so she could show me some of the dishes that the Pilgrims would have eaten on their arrival and during their first years in the new world.

I agreed to meet with her early the next morning, and I spent the night wandering around the small but pleasant town of Plymouth before returning to my hotel. After my day spent at the museum, my modern room, with its comfortable bed and hot shower, stood in even more stark contrast to the conditions that would have been faced by the Pilgrims, and it made me appreciate even more just how hard they would have had to work to survive in those very early days.

Kathleen's initial plan was for us to cook in one of the re-created Pilgrim cottages that the museum used for education purposes. Unfortunately, when I arrived the next morning, the weather had taken a decided turn for the worse and it was impossible to get a fire started in the damp confines of the wooden structure. Unlike the poor Pilgrims, who would have found the inconsistent weather of their new home a constant challenge, we were able to make alternative arrangements and decamped to one of the museum's indoor kitchens. This new space may not have had quite the 1620s ambience I was hoping for, but it was at least warm and dry and would suit our purposes as Kathleen began to explain more to me about the diet of the first arrivals.

The first colonists arrived on the *Mayflower* in November 1620, and, after a miserable winter stuck on board the ship, they were finally all able to move to land in March 1621. They brought with them their culinary tastes from the English motherland. Although the land they found in the New World was rich and fertile, the first settlers were merchants rather than farmers and they depended more on the provisions that they and subsequent ships brought with them than on what they were able to grow and harvest. The fact that there were no restrictions on hunting, as there had been in England, also meant that they were able to supplement their diet with a plentiful supply of meat and fish. Despite this (and because of their lack of skill in farming), the colony still came perilously close to being lost to starvation on more than one occasion in its first few years of existence.

Gradually, and with considerable help from the Wampanoag, the Pilgrims began to farm the land and adapt the dishes that they knew and loved in England to the plentiful ingredients of their new home. Chief among these was, of course, corn, an ingredient that is still (for better or for worse) a huge part of the American diet. The multicolored corn that the Pilgrims began to grow was very different from what was grown in England—and very different from the yellow sweet corn that we know today. They referred to it as "Indian" corn. The Wampanoag showed them how to fertilize the soil by burying herring in the ground before planting the seeds on top of them. At first the Pilgrims had to laboriously grind the harvested corn by hand, but it soon became such an important staple for them that within a decade they had built their first water-powered mill by a brook in the settlement. The museum has recently opened a working re-creation of this mill, and it was corn grist or "grits" from here that Kathleen used to make our first dish, hasty pudding.

The term appears in an early version of the famous song "Yankee Doodle Dandy":

Father and I went down to camp
Along with Captain Gooding
And there we saw the men and boys
As thick as hasty pudding

But most Americans who know it will associate it with the name of the legendary social club at Harvard University that counts at least five presidents among its alumni.

However, hasty pudding is, in fact, an English dish that has its roots in the pottages, or porridges, of medieval times. As the name suggests, it can be made quickly to serve anyone in need of cheap and immediate sustenance after a hard day's work. Traditionally, it is made with wheat, oats, or even leftover bread. It certainly would have been very familiar to the Pilgrims, who soon began to make hasty pudding in Plymouth using their most available ingredient, corn.

There was little more to making the dish than adding handfuls of the coarse grits from the mill to boiling water with a little salt and then stirring them continuously until they formed a thick porridge. It reminded me much of the grits I have been served on my many travels through the southern states. "The Pilgrims would have topped it with a little milk and maybe added berries or a little molasses," Kathleen explained as she spooned the rather unattractive brown slurry into a bowl. It was, much like the Wampanoag boiled bread that I had sampled the day before, a dish to provide fuel rather than pleasure.

The second dish, however, did actually involve some real cooking and used another ingredient that would have been a regular on the tables of the first arrivals: quail. Quail were abundant in Plymouth, and there are a number of recipes that the Pilgrims would have known from England. One of the earliest mentions of cooking quail is in Thomas Dawson's *The Good Huswifes Jewell* from 1596, which contains the recipe "to boyle quailes":

> *Firste, put them into a Pot with sweete broth, and set them on the fire, then take a Carret roote, and cut him in peeces, and put into the potte, then take perselye with sweete hearbes, and chop them a little, and put them into the potte, then take Synamon, Ginger, Nutmegges, and Pepper, and put in a little Vergice, and so season it with salt, serue them vpon soppes, and garnish them with fruit.*

The recipe shows us two things. The first was that the food the English of that time cooked was far more sophisticated than many people today would ever imagine, containing many herbs and spices that would have been brought into England by trade. The second is that it tells us the way Pilgrims prepared their food was surprisingly similar to the way we might prepare the same ingredients today.

"The way they ate it would have been very different, however," Kathleen corrected me when I pointed out how much like a modern pot roast dish this recipe was. She explained that there were no courses in those days. Everything would have been brought to the table at the same time, sweet and savory. Interestingly, the dishes would not have been passed around—the Pilgrims ate the food that was placed in front of them, the best dishes being set in front of the people who were highest up the social ladder.

"We'll roast our quail today," Kathleen told me as she took six plump little birds from the fridge. "I did want to show you how the Pilgrims would have done this over an open fire, but this will have to do." She switched on the oven to come up to temperature and placed the birds on a baking tray. "I think the sauce is just as interesting as the birds themselves," Kathleen said once we had put the quail in the oven. "The Pilgrims would melt butter and then add wine or vinegar, some sage leaves, a little of the drippings from the quail, and then they would add pieces of bread to that. These were the sops."

The quail only took about twelve minutes to cook, and Kathleen was soon serving them up at the kitchen table on a big silver platter with a small dish of the sauce beside it. "There were no forks at this point," Kathleen reminded me. "They would have cut the meat with their knives and used their fingers for eating." Ever one to do as the Romans do, I quickly began dismembering the small quail that Kathleen had placed on my plate, dipping meat from the breast into the buttery sauce. It was very good indeed, with the sharpness of the vinegar and the taste of the sage working well against the meat of the quail.

Early on my last morning, I left my modern hotel room one last time, packed my bags into the back of my car, and drove back to the plantation. This visit had been even more enjoyable than my first time. I had really sensed the dedication of all of the people who worked there and the huge importance that they all placed on educating the next generation about the origins of the United States. I was definitely sad to be moving on. But my final adventure at Plimoth Plantation was also the one that I had been looking forward to most—the lobster bake.

Before I could feast, I had been told that I actually had to do some hard work, collecting seaweed. I arranged to meet Wampanoag native Darius Coombs in the parking lot of the museum and we drove down to the waterfront, where he was soon showing me how to pluck seaweed from the shoreline until we had enough to fill three large plastic trash containers.

Back at the plantation, we made our way back to the same open space that I had been in with Carol Wynne, to find two other members of the Wampanoag Indigenous Program, Timothy and Brian, who were waiting for our arrival to finish off preparing the ground for the lobster bake. They had already dug a pit and started a fire, over which they had laid rocks to heat up in the flames. We soon leveled off the rocks, which were now white-hot, and then I helped the three men cover it all with a thick layer of seaweed. The moment we placed the first mound of wet seaweed over the rocks, it let out an enormous cloud of steam—perfect lobster-cooking conditions.

Darius pointed towards twenty or so beautiful live specimens whose claws had been taped and that were being kept in a bucket near the fire. We laid the lobsters out at even intervals on top of the seaweed and then filled in the gaps with small net bags filled with clams and ears of fresh corn. We covered it all with another layer of seaweed and then with a thick plastic tarpaulin, which we weighted down with heavy logs. "Hardly traditional," Brian said with a laugh, "but it keeps the steam in."

While we waited for the food to cook, my new friends insisted on taking me on a tour of the area of the plantation where Wampanoag dwellings had been re-created and native members of the Wampanoag Indigenous Program demonstrate craft and culinary techniques for visitors. We soon ran into their colleague James Moreis, and I began to realize that my new buddies had far more planned for me than just a pleasant amble among the tourists.

James was well over six feet tall and about as wide as a small truck. He was instructing a group of eager schoolchildren in the arts of Wampanoag football, a game of legendary ferocity where teams often comprised more than one hundred men on either side and goals could be miles apart. I had read about the game when I was research-ing Pilgrim history and was not particularly comforted by the know-ledge that it had been a regular occurrence for men to be killed during the matches.

When he saw us approaching, James's eyes lit up with the same look of glee that my wife usually takes on when she discovers a choc-olate bar at the back of the fridge. It was obviously not the first time this ruse had been employed and, as Timothy pushed me forward, James turned to the children, saying, "Why don't we ask this guy if he wants to play?" The kids, of course, had no mercy and started cheer-ing. I am pretty sure I even heard one of them say, "Kill him!"

I had no way out, so I nodded in agreement, hoping that James would at least realize that this was all a bit of fun and take it easy on me. No such luck. As soon as Timothy launched the leather-bound ball into the air, I found myself being knocked into the middle of next week by three hundred pounds of Wampanoag fury. This particular native tribe, it would appear, has no notion of "all a bit of fun," and I found myself on the end of a beating equivalent to that I might receive if I decided to have a good old grope of Mike Tyson's mother. Thankfully, after ten minutes of humiliation in front of America's future, James took pity, lifted me up off the floor like a used rag, and pushed me back towards the supporting arms of Timothy, who was grinning like the Cheshire cat. I staggered from the arena to the sounds of James being cheered and adored by his new legion of young fans.

I was relieved to hear Brian say, "We should get back, the food should be ready." And even more delighted to see that by the time we returned to the education site, the tarpaulin had been removed from the top of the pit and the pile of seaweed scraped back to reveal the cooked seafood beneath. The lobsters had turned bright orange, and the clams had opened in the steam inside their net casings. A dining table had been set out for us and we had been joined by about a dozen other people from the Wampanoag tribe to enjoy the feast.

I was invited to serve myself and I wasted no time in plucking a choice lobster from the pile, along with a net full of clams and corn. Once we were all seated, I took a nod from my quail-eating experience and cracked the lobster open with my hands to reveal the white meat inside. The flesh had taken on a smoky saltiness from the steam, while the clams had cooked to perfection. The corn too, although supposedly a side dish, seemed to be a favorite, and as I finished cleaning the sweet and juicy kernels from a second ear, I could certainly understand why it had become such an important staple for both the Wampanoag and the Pilgrims.

It was the perfect way to end my time at Plimoth, but I still had a long way to go on my journey, and eating that sensational lobster reminded me that my next task was to go in search of the perfect lobster roll.

Next stop, Maine.

On a Roll in Maine

Not long before I headed to the East Coast, I found myself in one of Las Vegas's legendary steakhouses. The liveried server had just placed the first of several powerful, bathtub-sized martinis on the table and was reciting a lengthy list of specials to me and my three hungry companions.

"We have a bone-in rib eye at sixty-five dollars. That's our most flavorful cut, and it comes with garlic mashed potatoes and bacon-wrapped asparagus." I winced a little at the use of the word "flavorful." It's not a word that is in common use in British English and it still sounds very grating when I hear it in conversation.

He went on, "And we also have a five-pound Australian lobster that will be served with drawn butter."

"That sounds good," one of my companions said as he unfolded a crisp white napkin across his lap. "How much is that?"

The server barely batted an eyelid as he responded, "A hundred and twenty."

This time we all winced a little. We were seasoned diners and most of the conversation during our drinking session before dinner had been about restaurants we had just visited or that were on our upcoming itinerary. However, even with a group of people who all admitted spending far more on food than on clothes, the thought of a

$120 lobster was certainly enough to take the wind out of our culinary discussions.

But that's lobster for you. It has become part of the lexicon of luxury, along with other such culinary delights as truffles, foie gras, caviar, and Kobe beef, and, as with them, the extravagant cost of eating it is made more tolerable by the fact that it usually repays the price in deliciousness.

Quite how lobster reached this elevated status from its original lowly roots is a story that has always fascinated me, and I decided that I should head up to Maine from Plymouth to find out a little bit more about how the best lobsters in the world are caught and served.

I had already been in touch with my good friend Chef Michele Ragussis, who has worked in Maine for much of her professional life. She was going to be out of town on the days that I planned to visit but put me in touch with Davina Thomasula, her sous chef at the excellent Pearl Restaurant in Rockland, leaving me with the promise, "They'll look after you. We'll get you out on a lobster boat, bring the lobsters back to the restaurant, and then make you the best f**kin' lobster roll of your entire life."

How could I turn down an offer like that?

Native tribes on the east coast of the continent had been harvesting what is now known as the American or Maine lobster for generations before the arrival of the first settlers. The shellfish was so plentiful that hunters would simply wade into the water to collect them or pick them up from the windrows that had been washed ashore with the tide. Amazingly, they were not really considered food. The flesh was used primarily for baiting fishing traps, and the shells, which were full of calcium, were used to fertilize fields before the planting of crops.

The first reference to lobster fishing almost as we know it today is found in 1605 in the writings of one James Rosier, who accompanied Captain George Weymouth on his explorative voyages around the Virginia coast. He published a journal about his adventures called *A True Relation of Captain George Weymouth. His Voyage, Made This Present Yeere 1605; In The Discouerie of The North Part of Virginia.*

He recounts:

> *And towards night we drew with a small net of twenty fathoms very nigh the shore; we got about thirty very good and great lobsters ... which I omit not to report, because it sheweth how great a profit fishing would be ...*

Even though at this point, however, lobster was being eaten by the new arrivals, it was still thought of more as fertilizer than food and its human consumption was consigned to the poor, orphaned children, incarcerated prisoners, and the indentured servants who had signed on for a term of service in America in return for a payment to support their families or for an excusal from debt.

I have read many articles suggesting that these downtrodden folk became so fed up with eating lobster so often that prisoners rioted and many indentured servants had it written into their contracts that they would not be fed lobster on more than three occasions every week. Although I have yet to find any hard evidence that this was ever the case, what is certain is that for nearly two centuries lobster was primarily a food for the poor and not considered right and proper for the table of a gentleman.

By the beginning of the 1700s, lobster fishing had already become established in the New World. But it was not until the 1800s when it really began to take off with the development of the canning industry. The first lobster cannery in Maine opened in 1842, and alongside this new development grew a fleet of "smackmen," or lobster fishermen, who sailed small boats known as well smacks. These vessels had holes drilled in the sides of the hull that allowed water to flow in, which helped fishermen keep their catch alive until they returned to shore.

This new industry had two major consequences. The first was that the size of the lobsters caught was reduced. Until then, any lobster under two pounds was tossed back into the water, deemed too small to be worthwhile. In fact, it was not unusual for lobsters to weigh in at four pounds or more, with a whopper of around twelve pounds being the highest ever recorded. However, these lobsters were too large for the machinery used by the efficient canning industry, and so fishermen were urged to catch ones even as small as half a pound. The inevitable impact of this new demand was that fewer lobsters made it to maturity and their numbers began to decline.

This did not happen immediately, however, and for some years there was a massive increase in demand for lobster, as canning made it more readily available and the creation of new systems of railroads made it easier to transport cans and live lobsters around the country. This increased demand for lobsters in general—and smaller lobsters in particular—did finally begin to take its toll by the end of the 1800s, and in 1874 the first legal limitations were imposed in Maine which banned "catching, preserving, selling or exposing for sale lobsters of less than 10 ½" (head to tail) prohibited 15th October to 1st April."

Limited supplies coupled with the fact that Americans had developed a taste for live lobster, now available across the country, meant that prices began to rise and the shellfish that was once considered almost worthless had become a delicacy.

While other food supply industries such as beef, pork, or wheat can be controlled to a degree by government intervention, lobster fishing and fishing in general is much more difficult to manage. Despite a great deal of regulations, the amount of lobsters caught can vary a good deal. This is reflected in the prices that lobster meat fetches, both when sold by fishermen to markets and restaurants and, as we found in Las Vegas, when it reaches the diner's table.

More recently, after a period of decline, lobsters have become abundant once more, and in 2011, more than 103 million pounds were caught off the coast of Maine—a haul that was worth over $300 million to the fishing industry of its ports.

If you put the words "New England" and "lobster" together in the same sentence, the chances are very high that the word "roll" is also going to be included in there somewhere. While lobster has, as I mentioned earlier, been eaten for centuries in New England, the lobster roll as we know it is very definitely a creation of the twentieth century, made possible by the start of commercial production of hot dog and hamburger buns in 1912.

There is no single recipe for lobster rolls that dominates. In fact, during my research prior to arriving in Maine, I found over thirty different variations in as many minutes. In Long Island, they use cold chunks of lobster with a light covering of mayonnaise, finely sliced celery, and a toasted flat hot dog bun that has been dredged on the outside with butter. In Connecticut, the lobster is served warm, tossed in butter, and on grilled rolls or even just sliced bread. Maine seems to adhere more to the Long Island style. I couldn't wait to see what Davina and her team did at the Pearl.

I arrived in Rockland after a pleasant drive from Plymouth through some of the most breathtaking scenery in the country. As I pulled into the lot of my motel, the weather changed suddenly for the worse. The skies filled with dark clouds, and a heavy persistent rain began lashing against the windshield of my rental car.

It brought back all-too-unpleasant memories of a distressing experience I had on a fishing boat in 2009, when I spent time with a crabbing crew on a small trawler five miles off the east coast of England. After five hours of abject misery, which involved plenty of hefty projectile vomiting over the side of the boat, I swore an oath to myself on all sorts of internal bibles that I would never put myself in that situation again.

As I stared out of my car wondering if I could make it to reception without getting drenched to the skin, I began to regret changing my mind. If the skies didn't clear, there was a chance that we would not even go out on the boat the next day, but just in case, I began a concerted regimen of travel sickness pills and hard liquor that conspired to send me into a very deep sleep almost before I had managed to get undressed.

I woke up the next morning with the thick head and dry mouth that my overindulgences of the night before had earned me and was happy to see a sliver of light coming in through the heavy curtains of my motel room. Pulling them back, I was even more pleased to see that the dark forbidding gray of the previous night had given way to bright, clear blue skies. I showered quickly and walked the short distance past the small town center to the front of a seafood market called Jess's Market, where Davina had instructed me to wait for her. I was delighted to notice as I walked that, although there was very definitely a crisp breeze in the air, the water was mirror-flat. It was looking as if it might be an altogether more pleasant day than my previous experience some years earlier.

The others were already inside. Davina came over to meet me as soon as I walked through the doors and quickly introduced me to Jamie Johnson, the owner of the market. He was a former lobsterman himself and was taking the opportunity to step away from his store for a few hours to join us back out on the water.

"We need to get moving," Davina said, explaining that we would be meeting the captain of our lobster boat a few miles down the coast.

Captain Eric was indeed ready and waiting as our truck pulled up to the jetty. He quickly guided the five of us into a dinghy that transferred us to one of the small lobster boats bobbing gently in the waters of the harbor. As soon as we were all aboard, he revved up the motor and pointed our boat towards the general direction of the Atlantic Ocean. The waters were, thankfully, still very smooth, and, as my stomach seemed to be behaving well enough, I accepted the beer Captain Eric tossed in my direction from the cabin.

"Every boat sets their lobster cages and marks them with a different-color buoy," Eric explained. "It's very serious business," he added, "you never stray into someone else's territory or mess with anyone else's buoys or things can get very, very messy." It's serious enough, in fact, that Eric told us Maine has never actually repealed an old law making it legal for a lobsterman to kill someone who tampers with his lobster traps. I was not entirely sure he was joking when he added, "I haven't had to kill anyone in ages."

After fifteen minutes or so of smooth sailing through the harbor, we hit the slightly choppier waters of the open sea.

"This is where the cages are set," Eric said pointing at one of the brightly colored buoys that marked his patch. "We need to pull them up and see if we have caught anything. Then we need to measure any lobsters that have been trapped."

There are very strict rules for which lobsters can be kept and which have to be returned to the ocean, Jamie explained as he helped Eric pull up the first of the traps from the water. Each lobster caught would be measured using a special double-pronged gauge to make sure that the distance from its eye socket to the beginning of the tail was no less than three and a quarter inches and no more than five inches in length. In addition, any lobster that was bearing eggs would immediately be released after the lobstermen had cut a small V into its tail shell to mark it out as a breeder in case it was trapped again.

"There are big penalties if you break the regulations," Jamie told us. "You can be fined up to five hundred dollars for every illegal lobster you bring in." He went on, "It's not just the fines, though. Most fishermen stick to the rules. We realize that this is our living, so it is in our best interest to protect the stocks of lobster."

Even though it was obvious that the regulations are certainly in everyone's best interest, it still served to make the whole experience of lobster fishing a slightly frustrating one. There were three lobsters in the first trap, but only one was a "keeper." "That's a breeder"—Jamie showed us the V mark in the tail of the largest as he placed it back in the water. "That one's too small." He put a second one back into the ocean. Only the final lobster passed all the tests, and Jamie put it into a tank of water to keep it alive until we got back to shore. He rebaited the trap with herring and had me toss it back into the waves as Eric pointed the boat in the direction of the next buoy. We checked about twenty traps in total over the next few hours, and at the end of our rounds we had just five lobsters to show for all our efforts. Although I had thoroughly enjoyed my time with Eric and Jamie (and they assured me that they had much more successful days than this), I was aware that this was a very meager reward for so much work, and it made me begin to appreciate just why lobsters are not always a cheap restaurant option.

The five lobsters we had caught, however, were absolute beauties. As soon as we hit land, we headed straight back to the Pearl with only one mission on our minds: to make the perfect lobster roll. As soon as we were in the kitchen, Davina took charge. The lobsters soon found their way into a pot of boiling water and were cooked for ten minutes until their shells had turned from the mottled black of live lobsters to a bright orange.

"Making a lobster roll is, in theory, very simple," Davina told me as she rolled food-safe latex gloves onto her hands, "but it's also very easy to mess one up." We let the lobsters cool for a few moments before she began cracking the shell of the largest one. "You need just the right balance of meat from the tail, the claw, and the knuckle of the lobster." She went on as she built a small pile of lobster meat on a kitchen scale, "Each one has a different texture and a slightly different taste."

Once she had measured out the right amount of lobster, she placed it in a bowl and added just enough mayonnaise to give it a light coating. She then added a handful of diced celery, a pinch of salt, a twist of pepper, and a tiny squeeze of lemon juice. That was it. I was surprised, but Davina insisted, "Maine lobster is one of the greatest ingredients in the world. Adding too many other flavors would be a crime."

While she had been preparing the lobster, a New England hot dog bun had been warming up on the kitchen grill. The outside had been brushed with butter. "We want it to have some crunch on the outside, but we want the inside of the bun to steam and remain soft," she told me as she filled the roll before placing it on a large white plate alongside a dish of fresh coleslaw.

It was a deceptively simple affair, but having just experienced all the effort that went into getting those few ounces of lobster from the ocean to my mouth made me appreciate it all the more as I took my first bite. The slight crisp bite of the outside of the bun gave way to the soft fluffy inside, which then gave way to the tangy, creamy coating of the mayonnaise and the crunch of the celery before the main attraction took its rightful place on center stage. The meat managed to be both sweet and to taste of the salty ocean in which the lobster had been crawling only a few hours before. As Davina had promised, the meat from the claw, tail, and knuckle each gave a different texture, and the small hint of acidity from the lemon juice lifted all the flavors to another level. I polished it off to the last crumb and the kitchen staff looked approvingly as I licked my fingers clean of the last remnants of mayonnaise.

I may not have eaten enough lobster rolls to know if this is "the best in the "f**kin' world" as Michele had promised, but what I can say is that if there is a better one, I want to try it. I also know that my appreciation was not only because of how perfectly it was prepared by Davina, but also because I had seen all the efforts and frustrations that go into bringing seafood to our tables.

I left the restaurant pledging to myself that I would not look quite so aghast next time a steakhouse server told me the price of their lobster special.

Trust me, I can testify that America's fishermen deserve every bloody cent they get.

Minnesota, Nice

One morning while I was sitting at my desk finding lots of interesting ways not to do any writing, I received an e-mail from my talented and very patient editor, Christina, requesting an outline of the adventures I had confirmed for the book. I suspect she was slightly worried by a response I had given to a Twitter follower who asked what my motivation was for writing, and to whom I had replied, "I have already spent the advance money."

Alarmed or not, Christina seemed placated by the list I sent her, but suggested one addition. "You don't have anything about July Fourth," she chided me gently. She was absolutely correct. In fact, the thought of adding a specific trip about one of America's favorite and most important holidays had never crossed my mind. That might seem a bit silly, but is perhaps understandable if you take into account my British heritage and the fact that until that point it had never been an important date on my calendar.

I had no idea where to start, so I posted a request on my social media accounts asking, "Where should I go for a real 4th of July experience?" The ideas began to flow in almost immediately (along with a sizable number of insults that suggested I should go back to England. Don't you just love the Internet?). Some suggested that I visit the cities where the treasonous rebellion, er, I mean the birth of liberty actually began, places like Philadelphia and Boston. They are, of course, terrific cities that I love to visit whenever I can, but they didn't quite seem to hit the mark of what I was looking for from this trip. I wanted an opportunity to see small-town America celebrating the Fourth of July—the sort of celebration that I had seen in movies or had been described to me by friends who were brought up in the more rural parts of America.

Just when I had resigned myself to the fact that I was not going to receive the kind of invitations I was hoping for, I was contacted by a gentleman called Tim Klabunde, who recommended that I spend my Fourth of July in the town of Brainerd and the surrounding lake area in Central Minnesota. He wrote to me, "I have been fortunate to travel extensively for my work and while I've enjoyed most every destination, I can say without reservation that the Brainerd Lakes area is my favorite place in the world." It was quite a claim, particularly as, until I received his e-mail, I didn't even know that there *was* a Brainerd, Minnesota. However, when he went on to tell me that Brainerd and its neighboring towns celebrated the Fourth of July with parades, firework displays, barbecues, and a host of other small-town pleasures, I decided that it just might be the perfect place for me.

Tim was kind enough to put me in touch with two of his contacts, Frank Soukup, the director of marketing for Grand View Lodge on Gull Lake, and Kathi Nagorski from the Brainerd Chamber of Commerce. By the time I picked my rental car up from Minneapolis–Saint Paul International Airport to begin the two-hour journey to Brainerd, I had not only somewhere to stay but also the promise of a packed itinerary showing me the best small-town America had to offer.

Grand View Lodge is one of the oldest resorts in Central Minnesota and has been providing a retreat for the people of the state for nearly a century. Construction of the resort was begun in 1916 by its owner, M. V. Baker, and by 1919 business was so brisk that he decided to build the large Norwegian pine lodge that still remains today. That building is now a protected landmark and retains much of its original charm, as it can only be restored and repaired using materials from the period in which it was built. It is surrounded by a full resort and conference center, which attracts hundreds of families every summer and winter to enjoy its golf courses, hiking, and, of course, the attractions of the lakes.

After checking in at the lodge, I met with Kathi in the warm and welcoming reception area. "We have quite a full day planned," she told me after I introduced myself. "But, first of all, you are probably hungry. Do you like pie?" It was a slightly redundant question, as one glimpse at me would be enough to confirm to any person that not only do I like pie a great deal, I actually like other people's pie a great deal as well.

However, I did have to pause for a minute to remind myself that when Americans say the word "pie" they are not talking about the pies I grew up with in the United Kingdom. Not savory pies, such as the ones my lovely late Welsh grandmother used to make for me— filled with thick chunks of chicken in a rich and creamy béchamel sauce or, even better, steak pies, where the short crust pastry case cracked to reveal cubes of beef soaked in a dark, rich, meaty gravy. No, indeed. When you American folk talk of pie, you mean sweet pies: apple pies, pecan pies, pumpkin pies. All very delicious in their own way, but should you ever meet me and happen to use the word "pie," please do be patient if you see a slight longing in my eyes as I have a Proustian memory of steak and kidney.

I reassured Kathi that yes, I did like pie very much indeed, and she seemed pleased. "Good." She beamed at me. "We are going to go and meet a lady who makes the very best apple pie you will ever try." I was thrilled. There are few things quite as American as apple pie, so to eat one that was claimed to be among the best would be the perfect way to start my July Fourth adventures.

We found the sprightly seventy-two-year-old Mary Etta Durham, who in fact reminded me a great deal of my Welsh grandmother, along with her equally lovely sister, Elsie Van Horne, presiding over the hectic scene in a store called Schaeffer's Foods in nearby Nisswa. Both of them were hard at work when we arrived, but stopped their floury endeavors as soon as I appeared so they could show me around the bakery and, even more important, top my pie table up to its safe levels.

Mary Etta's pies are legendary in the area. Kathi told me that people even drive up from the Twin Cities just to buy them. Mary Etta had run her own pie-making business for nearly ten years and had recently been in semiretirement until she was persuaded to come on board at Schaeffer's. Now she and her sister were making more than two hundred pies a week, with demand even higher now that the holiday was upon us.

I didn't want to disturb them on one of their busiest days, but both Mary Etta and Elsie insisted that I stay in the kitchen observing as they worked in the sort of steady rhythm that can only come from years of practice. Rolling the pastry dough, lining the pie plates, filling the casings with their apple mixture, and placing the pies in the bakery oven to cook until their crusts were golden brown and the contents bubbled beneath the surface, blowing hot apple-scented steam through the vents they had gently poked in the center. When the pies were removed from the oven, they were generously topped with sugar, which melted immediately to form a fine shiny coating on the surface of the pastry.

The two expert bakers performed this process with such good humor and such loving precision that I had to give them as much respect as any of the pastry chefs I have met on my visits to some of the finest restaurants in the world. My admiration grew once I had tasted the pies. They were every bit as good as Kathi's buildup had led me to believe. The short-crust pastry was beautifully buttery and broke on the first bite to reveal the filling of apples that had both been pureed and cut into a small dice, giving the contents wonderful texture.

However, the thing I liked most of all about Mary Etta and Elsie's apple pie was that it wasn't too sweet, with a slight tartness that was very appealing. I soon found myself brushing the crumby remnants of the first slice from my sweater and reaching for another.

They seemed pleased and insisted that I sample their complete range for good measure. It would have been rude to refuse, and my mother certainly didn't raise no fool, so I spent the next half an hour or so happily shoving juicy slices of various flavors of pie into my mouth until even I had to wave the white flag and inform them that I was "totally pied out." They both gave me that slightly disappointed look that only women of a certain age who love feeding people can give you, conceding to let me go only when I agreed to take an apple pie with me "just in case." My grandmother would have been very proud.

The surfeit of pie combined with my red-eye flight began to take its toll and I suggested to Kathi that I might need to return to the lodge for a few hours of shut-eye. She was, however, having none of it and responded by suggesting that what I really needed was some exercise to work off all that food, adding that she had just the perfect activity in mind.

Pequot Lakes was about half an hour's drive from the lodge and, as we drove, Kathi explained to me that every year they held a "Stars and Stripes" celebration for the Fourth of July. Although I would be spending the day itself at Grand View Lodge, at Pequot Lakes they began the activities on the third and there was one in particular that she seemed worryingly keen for me to be part of.

The event was to be held in a small park, and as we pulled into the parking lot I could see that the organizers were already raising stalls for vendors and performers for later in the day. An enclosed track had been set up in the center of the space. "That's for the pig races," Kathi told me as she gave me a tour of the grounds. "There will be a parade on Main Street tomorrow, and fireworks in the evening," she went on, "but there will be lots of events today too."

"This is the Bed Push Race," she announced as she led me to a stretch of path at the side of the grounds that had already been cordoned off to create a short racetrack. "You are going to be a guest on one of the teams." She smiled again as she pointed towards a gaggle of teenage girls who were walking towards us from a distance away. They were all aged around fifteen and were sporting lurid bright yellow T-shirts emblazoned with the name of their team, "Lightning Hockey," in large letters.

Ice hockey is almost entirely unknown in Britain, so when Kathi mentioned the sport, I had assumed that she meant field hockey, that relatively genteel game that I recalled from my own school days back in England. She soon put me right, and as the girls got closer I realized that they were a good deal more sporty than I had anticipated, high-fiving each other in a way that only people who exercise on a regular basis are allowed to do.

If I was perturbed at being asked to assist them in their sporting endeavors, the young women seemed even less enthusiastic when informed that I would be joining the squad. One of them tossed me a yellow T-shirt and said, "You can change in the bathroom," pointing towards a small building a few yards away. I readily agreed, knowing that the sight of my chubby torso might traumatize these poor young women for life, and soon after emerged to find the girls in a huddle around the frame of an old bed set on wheels that had been fitted with pieces of blue metal piping at each end so that it could be pushed.

Begrudgingly, the girls let me join their prerace team talk, and it was then that I began to realize why they were taking the whole affair much more seriously than I was. "We're racing against our moms," one of them informed me, pointing off to where a group of older women were gathered, all decked out in matching white shirts and whooping enthusiastically as they prepared for the mother-daughter battle ahead. Although my teammates seemed confident that we would win easily against the "old people," it was slightly disheartening to notice that their moms were not only considerably younger than me, but all in much better shape.

The race rules were explained to us by a lady carrying a clipboard. Each team was instructed to choose a member to ride on the bed and carry out challenges as the rest of the team pushed them along the course. Showing wisdom beyond their years, my team chose not to place me in this key role, and once we were ready and in position the race was begun at the piercing blow of a whistle by the same person who had invested in the clipboard. I don't remember many of the details of the race, apart from the fact that the young women's assumption that their moms were easy meat was very misplaced and that my team had its backside handed to it on a plate by our opponents.

It appeared that my presence was singled out as the primary cause of this embarrassment, which I thought to be rather unfair, given that I had managed to complete the ten minutes of moderate exercise involved without keeling over or requiring additional oxygen. However, the young folks seemed to lay all the blame at my door and disappeared with undue haste, grunting their displeasure and leaving me standing alone on the racetrack in my bright yellow T-shirt looking like nothing more than a despondent Meyer lemon.

I changed back into my normal attire quickly and spent the rest of my time with Kathi wandering around the event meeting people and watching families enjoy the food and activities that were on offer. It was everything I could have hoped to see when I began thinking about a Fourth of July experience, and I could have happily spent the rest of the day there if the killer combination of pie, red-eye, and bed push racing had not driven me to the brink. Kathi understood and, after I joined her for an enjoyable supper and a few too many glasses of wine at one of the lodge's restaurants, she left me to have an early night.

Before I crashed, I called Sybil. As with so many of my journeys, this particular trip had begun with me leaving the apartment at four a.m., trying desperately not to wake my wife as I showered, dressed, and headed out to the awaiting taxi. She had become used to waking up alone in the morning, and I liked to speak to her each night, just to make sure she did not forget who I was.

We chatted about our days and about how she would spend the Fourth of July with her family. Although I knew I had a lot of fun activities waiting for me the next day, I was sorry not to be able to share the holiday with her. After we'd talked for about half an hour, she told me, "Honey, you sound exhausted. You aren't making any sense." I hoped that she understood that the two things were connected and, saying good-bye, I was asleep almost before I had put down the phone. It was just what I needed and I was only woken, twelve hours later, when the morning sun broke through the gap in the blinds of my room and began to warm my face.

Frank Soukup had invited me to join his family and friends for their Fourth of July celebrations, and we had agreed to start with lunch in the company of Tim Klabunde, who had made the initial introduction. By the time I had showered and left my room, the grounds of the lodge were beginning to crowd up with families who had come to take advantage of Grand View's facilities. Flat-bottom pontoon boats were lining up alongside jetties that protruded into the lake, and families were staking claims to prime spots on the lawn or on the beachfront for the day ahead.

The lake and the land surrounding the lodge were astonishingly beautiful, and my enjoyment of my morning's amble was only hampered by the rather voracious Minnesota mosquitoes that seemed to be attracted to any spot of flesh that I had left exposed, even though I had doused myself in insect repellent before I left my room. By the time lunchtime swung into view, I had already been bitten well over a dozen times and I made a tactical decision to retreat to the lodge's welcoming pub, where I knew I could escape the bugs (and have a pint or two of beer) while I waited to meet up with Frank, Tim, and their respective families.

It was during lunch that I was given my first introduction to one of Minnesota's culinary specialties, the hot dish. When the lodge's executive chef, Michael Manders, heard that I was visiting, he wanted to make sure that I had the opportunity to try this culinary "delight." As described to me by my lunchtime companions, the hot dish didn't sound terrifically enticing. It is basically a one-pot casserole made out of canned soup, tater tots, frozen vegetables, and ground beef, and originated, they told me, as a "use-up" dish created by the farming community to take to reunions and Lutheran church potluck suppers. To be perfectly honest, it sounded more like the kind of dish I made during the more desperate moments of my student days when money levels were low enough that I had no choice but to raid the back of the food cupboard to see what other students had left behind. However, I am always game to try something new and have to admit Michael's skills lifted this otherwise humble culinary dish up to levels where I found myself reaching across the table for an extra helping on more than one occasion.

Tim and his family left us after lunch to continue with their own celebrations, while Frank, his wife, Julie, and their two sons invited me to join them on their pontoon to enjoy the Fourth of July activities. They had plans to attend a beachside celebration on the far side of Gull Lake, and after an hour or so of touring around the lake Frank pulled the pontoon up alongside the jetty of a small cabin situated close to the water's edge.

It was owned by a family called the Chaneys, who host an annual party for members of the family and their friends. When Frank had mentioned to them that I was visiting Grand View Lodge, they had generously agreed that I should join them. It was yet another example of the sort of hospitality that I found so common on my journey, and once again I was deeply grateful that these people would allow a complete stranger to join a family gathering.

"You're also going to eat something I am certain that you haven't tried before," Frank told me as he helped me climb unsteadily from the pontoon. "Army ribs."

I was intrigued. "What makes them Army ribs?" I inquired once my feet were planted on terra firma.

"Come with me and I'll show you," Frank replied, walking off to a small space at the side of the cabin from where I could already see a ribbon of smoke snaking into the air.

When I caught up to him, he introduced me to Tom Chaney, the patriarch of the family, who was seated in a camping chair keeping a watchful eye on the contraption that had given the ribs their unusual name. Tom's son Jay had set up an old cot acquired from an Army barracks and had encased its sides with squares of sheet metal to form a rudimentary BBQ pit. On the ground beneath the wire springs of the bed, he had built a fire using charcoal and wood, which had already burned down, leaving hot gray coals that were pushing heat upwards towards twenty slabs of pork ribs. The meat had already taken on a rich mahogany color from the slow cooking process, and the smell of roasting pork wafted into my nostrils.

"They'll be ready soon," Tom told me as he rose from his chair to tend to his porky charges. He explained that this unique cooking method was something he had acquired during his time in the Army and he had been cooking his ribs this way ever since. He had even catered weddings and other events over the years where, he told me, "the ribs are always the center of attention." They definitely had my attention, and even though I had already enjoyed a sizable lunch I was impatient to try them.

The Army ribs were not the only thing on the menu. More people had arrived by now and each arrival brought with them a dish to add to the celebration. Frank had wandered inside the cabin while I was talking to Jay and waved through a small screened window for me to come and see the spread that was being laid out on the dining table. Looking back, I have no idea how the table managed to stay intact under the weight of food it was being asked to bear. There were at least half a dozen assorted salads, a large platter of deviled eggs, pasta dishes, trays of sweet yellow corncobs, bowls of steaming Boston baked beans, and plates piled high with warm dinner rolls. And, of course, to top it all off there were those ribs, which were given prime place when Jay removed them from the Army cot. Each slab had been broken down into individual ribs and eager hands reached out to claim them the moment we were told to help ourselves.

Frank told me not to be shy and I soon emerged from the fray of eager diners triumphant and carrying a plate laden down with a Kilimanjaro-shaped mountain of food, topped off with the best part of an entire slab of ribs. I grabbed a cold beer from an ice-filled cooler and stepped out of the cabin onto the shorefront, so I could enjoy my Fourth of July meal with a view of Gull Lake as a backdrop.

I made repeated visits to the dining table to replenish my plate and after far too many Army ribs, I switched from savory to sweet, finishing off my meal with an unfeasibly gooey chocolate brownie. I pushed aside my plate and sank into a comfortable deck chair with the good intentions of chatting with my new friends. However, the combination of fresh air, all those ribs, and a couple of cold beers conspired to make me doze off and I was woken an hour or so later by a nudge from Frank informing me that it was time to head back to the lodge. I apologized profusely to my hosts for falling asleep in the middle of their biggest party of the year, but they did not seem too put out, having clearly gotten on with the task in hand of devouring all the food, as most of the platters on the dining table were now completely empty.

Frank pointed the pontoon back across Gull Lake, giving me the opportunity to take in the scenery one last time before I had to leave the next day. The United States really does have some of the most stunning scenery on the planet, but if I were asked to create a ranking of the most beautiful parts of America, the lakes of Central Minnesota would definitely make the playoffs.

Frank and his family had another celebration to attend and said good-bye to me once we had docked the pontoon at the jetties of Grand View Lodge. I thought that was fair enough. They had already let me take up far too much of their time on such an important holiday.

Later that evening I returned to the shores of the lake. It was getting dark and the bugs were still out in full force. Frank had told me that many of the families in the houses around the lake would be setting off fireworks, and I wanted to catch the free display. I stood near many groups who were also enjoying the spectacle. The children, happy at being allowed to stay up past their normal bedtimes, squealed with excitement each time a rocket exploded in the air, showering colorful streams across the sky. For just a brief moment, I felt slightly lonely as I stood apart, but the alone time gave me a chance to dwell some more on just how generous people had been to me on this particular portion of the trip.

I had heard the term "Minnesota nice" used a number of times before and during my visit, and many of the locals I had met said that it referred as much to the reserved politeness of the people of the state as it did to their kindness. I don't know its true origins, but over the last few days, the welcoming warmth of the people had been just as impressive as the scenery, and I knew for certain that every time I heard the phrase used in the future it would remind me of my time at Grand View Lodge.

Freezing with the
BBQ Brethren

People are often a little surprised by my love of BBQ. I think they are misled by my slightly villainous British accent into thinking that I am irredeemably highbrow and only ever eat at places where tables are covered in crisp napery and servers have to spend six months in the gym before they are strong enough to carry the wine list.

Nothing could be further from the truth. Don't get me wrong. I love fine dining and have been fortunate enough to experience some of the very best examples at restaurants all over the world. However, you are just as likely to see me standing at the counter of my favorite Los Angeles burger joint (the Apple Pan, for the record) or taco stand enjoying a bite as you are to find me enjoying the multicourse menu at Thomas Keller's legendary restaurant the French Laundry. And, more often than any of the above, you will find me eating BBQ whenever and wherever I can, peeling the meat from a rack of baby backs, cutting into a slice of fatty brisket, or slathering a sharp vinegary sauce over shreds of smoky pulled pork.

My passion for BBQ was born nearly fifteen years ago, after a road trip through Texas with my older brother, Robin. Our journey took us to Lockhart, Texas, the "Capital of 'Q," and we spent the day waddling from one legendary BBQ joint to the next, discovering the simple joy that is smoked meat. I was immediately hooked and have spent many of my subsequent vacations to the United States traveling in search of the best examples.

If you were to look at my calendar at the beginning of every year, you would see that four sacred days are blacked out in October, those that I spend on the "Burn Rate" team at the American Royal in Kansas City, the world's biggest BBQ competition. And, while we may be more enthusiastic than successful in our yearly BBQ activities, I am rarely happier than during the time I spend pulling membranes off slabs of ribs or applying our secret rub to pork shoulders or beef brisket, and I am pleased to say that, over the last eight years or so, many of the people on Burn Rate have become my very dear friends.

It was at the American Royal that I first met my good friends Matthew and Jackie Burt, who own and operate Phat Jack's Restaurant in Lincoln, Nebraska. In 2009, I stopped by their small booth to admire a rather beautiful self-built smoker and, BBQ people being what BBQ people are, it was approximately five seconds before they had offered to put a beer in one of my hands and a freshly sliced rib in the other. To this day, that rib remains the single best piece of BBQ I have ever eaten. The meat was cooked to perfection, coming away from the bone only in the place where I took a bite, rather than falling from it completely, and the balance of smoke from the cooking and sweet heat from the glaze Matt had just applied lingered on the taste buds for about five minutes after I had tossed the cleaned bone into the trash.

I made a note to find out more about Phat Jack's and was not in the least bit surprised to find that they were already one of the most highly ranked teams in the country and had actually placed at the Royal on previous occasions. We stayed in touch after that and at subsequent Royals I would time my tour of the event to make sure I wandered past the Phat Jack's stand just when I knew the good stuff would be coming off the smoker.

When they heard about the Fed, White, and Blue journey, Matt contacted me to suggest that I might like to join them on one of their competition weekends so I could see what went on behind the scenes. "This competition is going to be in Kearney, Nebraska. It's our first of the year," Matt explained. "So we'll be a bit rusty, but we'd love it if you came along."

It was a no-brainer to accept immediately. Even if I had no clue where Kearney was (and I didn't), I was certain that I would learn as much about BBQ by spending a weekend with Matt as I had in the last ten years with my enthusiastic but amateur Burn Rate team. But it was far more than that. For me, one of the greatest appeals of BBQ is not just all the incredible food I get to eat, but the community it brings together. I really hoped that by spending time with the Phat Jack's team at a smaller regional event I might have even more opportunity to interact with this very special group of people.

Matt explained that, compared to some teams, the Phat Jack's effort is very much a family affair. Matt and Jackie are often joined at the competitions by their two young children and their parents. They close their restaurant for the weekend, attach a trailer and smoker to the back of Matt's truck, and head off across Nebraska or into neighboring states like Kansas, South Dakota, or Missouri to compete in smaller competitions that award prize money and also points towards an overall championship.

I joined Matt at the restaurant the day before we set off so I could help him prepare the meat he had selected for the competition. I flew into Nebraska after yet another of my brutally early-morning starts from LAX and, excited as I was to be spending time with one of the best pit masters in the business, I was slightly less thrilled when I landed in Omaha to find a three-inch-thick white blanket of snow covering the ground and more falling heavily. Not the best welcome when one knows that one has a night in an unheated camper to look forward to.

However, such matters (while rather nerve-wracking for someone now based in SoCal) are everyday affairs for hardy Nebraska folk, and when I pulled into a space in front of Phat Jack's just before midday, there was already a line of regulars at the door waiting patiently for their turn to be served. I could smell why, as a hit of top-notch BBQ blasted me full in the face the moment I walked through the door. I could also see why, as every wall and counter in the restaurant was covered with the medals, pennants, and certificates that Phat Jack's had been awarded since they'd opened their doors in 2006.

Jackie was at the counter, fashioning sandwiches for the long line of hungry people, while Matt was in the back, knife in hand, working on the meat we would be preparing. After a brief greeting, he pointed towards a box of disposable rubber gloves and indicated that I should come and help him.

Matt is a Lincoln boy, born and bred, and by his own admission had led a fairly checkered past since leaving high school. I am not sure you could say that BBQ and Jackie saved him, but both certainly contributed to turning him into the proud family man and business owner he is today. It's his father, a former butcher, whom he thanks for his interest in BBQ. The combination of that knowledge and his own skills helped Phat Jack's become successful enough that six years after opening, it had to relocate into this larger space in a shopping center on the edge of downtown.

Matt demonstrated how the slabs of spare ribs he had selected for us would be trimmed to make the "Saint Louis" cut, an almost perfect rectangle that allows them to brown evenly. "That's part of what they will be looking for when they judge," he explained as he deftly removed any excess meat and tossed it into a tray alongside other remnants of the morning's trimming, which would all be turned into ground meat.

Matt passed me a knife and asked me to help. My own attempts were nowhere close to being as proficient, but he nodded and placed the ribs I had trimmed on the "approved" pile. "I have trimmed thousands of these," he added, "so if I can't get it right by now, I might as well quit."

Matt wheeled out a large trolley and added the ribs to the pile of meat he thought had potential for championship cooking. He pointed out exactly what he was looking for in each piece of meat as we gave it one final look-over. "There are four main categories," he explained, "ribs, pork, brisket, and chicken."

We trimmed the briskets he had selected until they had a perfect quarter inch of fat to help them keep moist during cooking, and then we chose a dozen of the most uniform chicken thighs that would make a perfect presentation when we turned them in for judging. When it was time to select the pork butts, Matt declared, "We need to find the ones with the perfect money muscle."

He explained that the championship BBQ teams would turn in not only pulled pork but also medallions of meat cut from this particular muscle that connected the shoulder to the neck. "The first people to do this kept on winning all the top prizes," Matt went on as he began to trim the excess fat from one of the larger pork butts. "That's why it became known as the money muscle." He showed me where the muscle sat behind the bone of the butt and then how to trim it back to reveal the well-marbled cut. According to the rules, it could not be removed from the pork butt, but trimming it in this way would allow smoke to enter the meat evenly. It seemed like a lot of effort to get such a tiny proportion of meat to use, particularly given that Matt was going to cook four whole butts just to get six small pieces, but he reassured me, "Nothing goes to waste. Everything we cook will be used in the restaurant."

I agreed to meet Matt and Jackie early the next morning for the drive to Kearney. "It's not that far away, but with this weather and the fact that we are pulling the trailer, I want to give it a little more time," Matt suggested as he walked me out to my car.

The snow was even thicker the next morning and, as we loaded up the truck with all of our provisions outside Matt's house, both he and Jackie expressed doubts that the competition would actually take place. Jackie must have seen me looking crestfallen, because she added quickly, "But we'll head out there anyway, just in case."

Fortunately, when we arrived at the Buffalo County Fairgrounds in Kearney, location of the Heating Up the Bricks BBQ competition, we found that forty other teams had also decided to turn up "just in case" and we had a sufficient number for it to be an official Kansas City Barbecue Society (KCBS) competition. We may have had enough people, but it was still going to be a challenge, as the snow had been falling steadily all the way along the freeway and was now coating the parking lot into which Matt was trying to reverse the trailer and smoker.

A freezing blast hit me the moment I emerged from the truck and I shivered, thinking of Matt's warning that we would have an early start the next morning to fire up the smoker. A three a.m. wake-up call was daunting enough, but I was comforted by the fact that at least we had somewhere sheltered in which to spend the night protected from the snow. Others were not quite as fortunate. As I guided Matt back into our allocated space, I saw that stationed to the side of us was a team with nothing more than a slightly ratty tailgate canopy to their name. Rummaging around inside the tent was a stocky man who had the sort of ruddy face one might get if one had to push a tank up a steep hill every day for a living. He seemed oblivious to the cold and was busy unloading bags of charcoal and bundles of wood from the back of his truck and placing them next to a small indirect-heat smoker.

"That's Parrothead," Matt said when he saw me staring. "His real name is John and he's a one-man team. He's from South Dakota and drives all over the country to compete. He travels lightly, but don't let that fool you. John is number one in the country right now."

I watched as Parrothead began to cover the sides of his tailgate canopy with tarpaulin so that the inside of the tent was hidden. "He is very secretive about what goes on in there," Matt went on. "He even has to hide his trash. He wins so many competitions that people will rummage through it to see what he uses. He'll just sleep on top of his bags of charcoal tonight, using the heat from his smoker to keep warm."

I love BBQ, but I knew that I could never be as dedicated to it as Parrothead. He gave us a friendly wave when he saw Matt emerge from the front of his truck and then slipped behind the covers of his makeshift tent to carry on with his nefarious BBQ doings.

We returned to unpacking our own fuel supply and then took the cuts of meat from their coolers so we could add the finishing touches before they were cooked. The brisket and pork butts were massaged with the Phat Jack's rub and then injected with stock, using a large and slightly frightening syringe. "Not everyone does this," Jackie explained as Matt pierced the brisket in half a dozen locations, "but we think it adds extra flavor that the judges notice." I had seen that process before, but what Phat Jack's did to their chicken next was a little bit more unusual.

"Do you know what this is?" Matt held up a blue plastic container that looked like a detergent bottle. "It's Parkay," he added as if that might help, before finally clarifying, "fake butter." He sprayed a little on my hand. It tasted every bit as grim as one might imagine and I had to wipe my mouth out with a cloth. "It's one of those little trade secrets of the top BBQ teams. It helps give the chicken a fantastic color." Personally, I would have rather drunk the detergent, but just as I was about to get all food critic on him, Jackie reminded us that it was time to go and hear the rules of the competition read out in the main hall of the fairgrounds.

Although most in attendance probably knew these regulations better than the KCBS supervisors, they welcomed the opportunity to spend time in a heated room. There were a few newcomers among the teams, but many were people whom Matt and Jackie knew well from the circuit.

We spent the next few hours wandering around the fairground, shuddering in the freezing temperatures in front of the few smokers that had already been fired up, sharing stories, and sipping on the drinks and snacks that were offered everywhere we stopped. For all the great food I was hoping to eat and the tips on making great BBQ I was hoping to collect, this unique camaraderie was what I had really been looking for when I accepted Matt's offer. The warm welcome I received from everybody made me feel like I was definitely part of a great and truly American BBQ family.

I stayed up until past midnight, which was not the smartest decision I have ever made, given that we had to be up a few hours later. Less than half of the trailer had been turned over to sleeping quarters, with the rest being set out into a well-appointed kitchen space that had everything Matt needed to turn out perfect 'Q. Matt and Jackie were already asleep on a loft bed above the seating area, and I claimed one of the sofa seats below, curling up to keep warm under a thick blanket they had laid out for me.

I managed to get a couple of hours' sleep, but it only seemed like a scant few seconds before Matt was shaking me awake. "We need to start the smoker," he whispered, not wanting to disturb Jackie. Much as I wanted to turn around, cover my head, and go back to sleep, helping Matt was the main reason I was here. I dragged myself from below the covers, threw on my thick coat, and emerged into the blisteringly cold night air. Matt was fumbling around for wood by the back of the trailer and I could see that other teams were beginning to stir too, not that their activity made me feel any warmer.

Matt had a carefully planned schedule. "Great BBQ is as much about perfect timing as it is about good meat." He raised his voice above the noise of the wind. "Everything needs to be put in the smoker at the right time or the meat will be ruined." He poked the wood he had placed in the smoker's burner until it began to glow bright red from the flames. "Now we have to wait until the temperature gets up to two hundred twenty-five degrees Fahrenheit and we'll be ready."

I was impressed with the dedication of everyone at the competition. I knew that very few BBQ teams make a living from any prize money they may win at competitions. In fact, Matt and Jackie often close their restaurant early if they have to travel a distance to compete, but they do it for their love of BBQ and the opportunity it gives them to meet with their friends on the circuit.

Matt lovingly placed each piece of meat in the smoker, knowing which part would provide just the right amount of heat. "Smokers can be temperamental," he told me as he nudged pork butts around so he could fit everything in. "Even if you have cooked on them a hundred times before, they can surprise you."

Once everything was in place, he told me to go grab more sleep. But I was wide-awake by now, so I slipped out of the trailer and walked around the quiet lot, watching the other teams working away. Some were obviously full-scale professional operations, with lavish motor homes and state-of-the-art smokers the size of small European sports cars. Others were more down-to-earth affairs but still obviously took their 'Q seriously. Others yet were very homespun and belonged to teams that were just getting started or were there just for the heck of it.

Matt takes his BBQ very seriously indeed, and every thirty minutes or so I would see him emerge from the rear of the trailer to check on the temperature of the smoker, add more wood if necessary, and move the meat around if he thought it was cooking too fast or too slowly. By the time the sun rose, doing its best to break through the thick sheet of snow-laden clouds over the fairground, all the teams were hives of activity.

Turn-in, the delivery of the different categories to the judging table, was very much a team effort for Phat Jack's. While Matt watched over the smoker, Jackie lined the presentation boxes with a bed of bright green curly parsley. As soon as each category of meat was ready, they would look it over together to see which portions looked the best, and then Jackie would taste to see if the flavor matched the appearance. "I never taste it," Matt said, and shrugged as Jackie handed me a spare thigh of chicken to try. "Jackie is the one with the palate, and we've won enough prizes that I trust her judgment."

I didn't argue when they insisted that I help with the tasting, and my first bite of a meaty spare rib reminded me of why I had been so keen to come along on the trip. The chicken was just as good, and despite my qualms the Parkay had given the skin a lustrous golden sheen that made the thighs glisten against the bed of parsley.

Best of all, however, was the pork. Matt removed the money muscle from each of the pork butts, examining them to see which had the best color before slicing a small amount of each for us to taste. The marbling had kept the meat moist, and the smoking had given it a color that made it look like it had spent a few happy days in the Caribbean. Once the meat had been chosen, Matt finished the presentation by dusting it with a fine coating of their rub and brushing it with glaze to give it a final shine. I had put presentation boxes together before, but the ones that Matt prepared were at a different level altogether. I made notes to take back to my own team for the American Royal.

Despite the early start, turn-in time came around quickly, prompting a last-minute mad rush as teams carried their boxes gingerly through the snow to the judging table. All of our presentation boxes were delivered on time, and I helped Matt and Jackie clean up in preparation for our departure. "The weather is closing in," Matt announced, looking at the sky. "We'll need to make a quick getaway." Parrothead had obviously had the same thought, as his canopy was already dismantled and loaded onto the back of his truck and his smoker was cleaned up and attached to the rear. He looked in pretty good shape for a man who had slept the night with such little protection from subzero temperatures, and he seemed happy but noncommittal when I questioned him about the BBQ he had turned in.

"Don't be fooled," Matt reminded me again. "Anyone who beats him today will probably win." He seemed less certain about his own chances. "I'll be happy if we win a category, given it's our first event of the year. But this is a new event and with a lot of inexperienced judges, so it could be a total crap shoot."

That turned out to be a very accurate assessment of the results. Despite all our efforts, Phat Jack's returns were disappointing, with a top-ten placing in the chicken category being the best we received. We placed eighth overall out of the forty teams taking part, and Matt gave me a "What can you do?" kind of shrug as the winners came to the front to collect their awards and prize money.

Matt was also right about the overall winner. Despite his low-fi approach, Parrothead managed to place highly in every category and win the competition outright. There were a few audible groans as he came up to collect his prize, primarily from the bigger teams whose investment in their equipment was probably twenty times that of this one-man band. "It goes to prove that you can spend all the money you like on equipment, but you still have to know how to cook great BBQ to win," Matt whispered to me as he gave his friend a generous round of applause.

I was disappointed for Matt and Jackie that we had not done better in the competition, but they seemed much more sanguine about it. "Of course we want to win," Jackie said as we pulled out of the lot and onto the freeway back towards Lincoln. "But BBQ is about a lot more than that. It's a chance to spend time with our family and a chance to connect with friends in the community."

"And," Matt added, snapping me out of my reflections for a moment as he pointed at a familiar truck toting a small smoker as it passed us on the freeway, "where else would we get to see Parrothead piss off so many of the big teams?"

I joined in their laughter, and, not for the first or last time on the trip, I felt tremendous gratitude that people had let me join in their lives, if only for a brief moment. I made a note to myself that, once the Fed, White, and Blue journey was done, I should seriously consider starting my own BBQ team. I wanted even more than ever to be part of this American community. But I knew that I would have to remain true to my British roots when I came to choose a name.

So, if you ever see a truck pulling a trailer that says "Please Form an Orderly 'Q" on the sides, that'll probably be me.

From Pasture to Plate

I knew that there was no way I could write this book without some reference to the amount of beef Americans eat and how it is produced. It would be like writing a book about the food of Italy and skipping over pasta. Quite where I should go to find out more was not so obvious. There are many regions in the United States that are famous for their beef. Texas, Kansas, Iowa, and others—all would be able to give me a great story and are all parts of the country I love visiting.

My inspiration to head to Nebraska came, ironically, not from anyone in the United States but from a flying visit to London. I had agreed to meet a good friend for lunch at Goodman Restaurant in Mayfair. I was particularly enjoying my journey through sixteen ounces of bone-in rib eye when the GM, David Strauss, appeared at my shoulder to check that everything was up to scratch. He seemed pleased with my effusive response to the steak and walked away with a smile on his face, leaving me with the words, "It's from Nebraska."

So taken was I, that the same evening, I began to do some research into the Nebraska beef industry and found that not only does it rank number two among the beef producers of the United States, it's also home to nearly two million head of beef cattle. I had a few free days in my schedule after my time with Phat Jack's, so it made sense to try and combine the journey.

Before I left L.A., I read up some more. In early 2013, the imperial empire of the American beef industry was under attack across all its borders. The U.S. government bowed to public pressure and asked the industry to monitor even more carefully the use of antibiotics in cattle, acknowledging they were necessary for the health of the animals but cautioning their use as a means to promote unnatural growth. While this was a call for self-regulation, the writing was very clearly on the wall. If the house could not be put in order internally, there would soon be demands for legislation bringing regulations closer to those in Europe, where antibiotics were strongly prohibited for anything other than health reasons.

Then there were environmental issues. These challenged not only the short- and long-term impact of mass meat production on the land but also looked at the impact climate changes were having on meat production itself. The chronic droughts of 2011, 2012, and 2013 have had a devastating effect on grazing lands, leading to a decline in the nation's numbers of cattle (which has led the prices of wholesale beef to rise to record highs).

Finally, there has been increasing pressure from the consumer, creating not only a demand for more "healthy" sources of protein but also reflecting the changing demographics of the country. (An increase in the numbers of Asians and Latin Americans living in the United States has coincided with an increase in the demand for pork and chicken. In fact, according to the website Priceonomics.com, chicken outstripped beef as the primary meat of choice for America's dining table in 2012.)

If all this seems to paint a rather bleak picture, it is worth noting that the American beef industry is down, but it is definitely not out. The average American still consumes nearly sixty-five pounds of beef every year, and the cattle industry still produces nearly a quarter of the world's beef annually, contributing more than $36 billion a year directly to the U.S. economy. Add this to the "ripple" effect it has on other industries, and it would be rather foolish to underestimate the importance of beef and the cattle industry to the American story.

And what a story it has been so far, particularly when one considers that until the founding of the Jamestown colony in 1611, the only domesticated animals in America were the small herds of berrenda cattle brought over by Spanish settlers. Even then, the English cattle the first Pilgrims brought with them were considered sources of milk, hide, and tallow rather than of meat, as the colonists took advantage of the plentiful supplies of wild game to fill their larders and bellies.

It wasn't until after the Revolutionary War and the inevitable move west fueled by the spirit of manifest destiny that cattle numbers grew to fill the new lands both purchased and conquered. That momentum gained speed after the Civil War and cattle raising became de rigueur on lands on which it proved more of a struggle to cultivate crops. Beef eventually became an integral part of the American diet. Along with this growth came the origination of breeding systems, many of which are still familiar to farmers today—the "cow/calf" breeding operations, the use of feedlots to fatten steers, and the efficient dispatching and processing of those cattle in packing plants once they were ready for slaughter.

The industrial revolution of the United States in the second half of the nineteenth century also played its part. Advances in railroads meant that cattle could be transported more speedily and in greater numbers than had been possible in the glory days of the cowboy, and this led to the creation of vast stockyards in cities such as Chicago and Kansas City (and consequently the cities' long association with great beef) and to the development of highly efficient systems, allowing beef to become an everyday source of food across America.

Such efficiency, while helping to promote the sales of beef, also had its share of problems, as ranchers were dealing with living creatures, not inanimate objects. This mass movement and cramped storage of animals led to inevitable health problems for the cattle. But demand was so high at this point, towards the end of the nineteenth century, that downsizing was not an option. Instead, advances in medical science saw the development of antibiotics to combat these diseases. While these antibiotics certainly improved animal health, they also had other benefits for the farmers, as they promoted additional growth in the steers. The size of a steer today, at around sixteen hundred pounds, is almost double that of a similar animal at the beginning of the twentieth century, one of the many reasons the beef industry is now under such close scrutiny.

All of this development has led to the creation of a highly systematized business that is both immensely efficient and profitable as well as the employer of nearly one million people across the United States. However, this success has created a problem in the form of consumers who now demand that beef be both readily available and affordable. This in turn delivers new pressures on the industry and all those who depend on it, be they the cattle farmers themselves, the corn farmers who supply the majority of their feed, and even the predominantly immigrant communities who work at the packing plants cutting meat on the line.

Increased availability of information is also beginning to play its part, as we are demanding to know more about all the food we put into our bodies, including beef. Words like "organic," "traceable," and "grass fed," which may have been of little importance two decades ago, are now on the tips of everybody's tongues, and consequently the industry is in one of the most interesting and challenging times of its whole existence.

I contacted David at Goodman and asked him where exactly he had sourced that superb beef I had eaten back in London. He put me in touch with Stan Garbacz, the international trade representative for the Nebraska Department of Agriculture, and we swapped e-mails for the next few weeks before I flew out to Omaha.

I told Stan that, ideally, I'd like to follow the trail of beef production from the breeding of the cattle to the point where I might be able to sample some of Nebraska's finest as it sizzled on my plate fresh from a hot grill. It was a lot to ask but didn't seem to faze Stan, and by the time I met up with him in Lincoln the day after my BBQ exploits, he had my itinerary all planned.

"Farm-to-plate, Simon." He smiled as he picked me up from outside my hotel. "The one thing about Nebraska is that you can follow the cattle every step of the way, from the day the calf is born to the day it appears on someone's table." It was just what I wanted to hear, and I strapped into the passenger seat of Stan's small car for what he said would be a long drive to our first stop out in the Sandhills of Nebraska.

Shovel Dot Ranch, which takes its name from the design that has been branded into its cattle since the ranch was founded in the 1880s by Benjamin Franklin Buell, is owned by Homer Buell and his brother, Larry. They are fourth-generation calf breeders and run their operation on thirty thousand acres of land. As he drove, Stan explained that in 2012, Homer had been inducted into the Nebraska Cattlemen's Hall of Fame, primarily for the conservation work he has undertaken to protect wildlife on the land. "They see themselves very much as caretakers, looking after it for the next generation. They need to make a profit, of course, but this land is their life as well as their livelihood." It was pleasing to hear about the real people behind what could otherwise be seen as just another anonymous industrial complex.

Homer's charming wife, Darla, had prepared lunch for us, and as soon as we arrived we were ushered to the farmhouse kitchen table while she filled it with enough delicious homemade food to feed a dozen people. As we ate, Homer explained how their operation works. "We keep a permanent herd of Angus and Hereford cows here throughout the year, and we calf them in April. Those calves are weaned and grazed out on the pastures and then we background some of them over the winter and keep the others as stockers."

"Backgrounding" is a method of adding weight to calves by bringing them to feedlots over the winter before they are sold, while "stocker" calves remain on the grazing land until the grass gets too short for them to forage, at which point they are sold. It was quite a complex-sounding operation, and Stan added, "It really is a balance of what will be best for the herd and what will bring in the most profit. It also depends on weather conditions."

The droughts of the last few years had obviously had a severe impact, and after lunch Homer drove us out onto one of the pastures so we could see the effect the lack of rain had had on the land. What should by this time of the year have been green was yellow and dry. "It means that we might have to send the cattle to the feedlots earlier because there simply isn't enough grass here to keep them going." This would obviously impact his profits, as he had to pay for the upkeep of his cattle at the lots rather than feed them on his own land.

Although it clearly provided a good living, this was obviously far more than just a business for Homer Buell. It was where his family had farmed for generations and where he was determined they would do the same for generations to come. His pride as he pointed towards where his predecessors had built the original farmstead and tiny schoolhouse was apparent, as it was when he introduced us to his son, who was already carrying on the farming tradition. "This land is in our blood," he told me as he walked us back to our car. It struck home a point I was to experience again and again during my time in Nebraska, that while beef is certainly a big and often controversial business, it is, for the most part, a business run by people for whom it is a way of life and who really do care about their animals and their land.

Perhaps one of the most controversial aspects of the beef industry is the feedlot operation. Like many others, I have been disturbed by the sight of huge cattle feedlots on my travels around the country. Pens seemingly overfilled with animals, fighting for food from troughs, all for the purpose of being fattened up for our enjoyment. I have even heard them described as "beef concentration camps," and while I think this might be taking the analogy too far, the image of feedlots as cruel fattening stations is a hard one to shake from one's head.

Stan wanted at least to show me the other side of the coin, and so our next stop was at Darr Feedlots in Cozad, Nebraska. This forty-thousand-acre facility is owned by Craig Uden, another fourth-generation cattleman. As he gave us a tour, he was keen to explain to me the rationale of the feedlot system.

"Once cattle have been purchased by the feedyard or are brought to us by the rancher, they will come to us to be fed until it is ready for slaughter. They usually come in here when they reach around six hundred and fifty pounds and they stay with us for three to six months until they are sent off for slaughter." He went on to explain that cows are fed a grain-based mixture that allows them to put on up to four pounds in weight every day. He drove us to one of the lots that held the feed, a towering yellow mountain that he explained is primarily comprised of corn by-products along with barley, alfalfa, and a number of micronutrients and vitamin supplements.

Craig was obviously keen to show the upside of the feedlot method of cattle raising and gave us a tour of the pens that house from sixty-five to two hundred animals at any given time. "We use very scientific methods," he explained as he pointed to the electronic terminals that attached to posts by each pen. "We know exactly what feed is being given to each steer on any given day, their weight, and their state of health." That raised a good point, and when I questioned Craig about the well-being of the animals when being held in close concentration he pointed towards the ear of one of the steers, which was studded with more tags than a punk diva. "Everything is heavily regulated," he insisted, "we have to note every time we give an animal antibiotics and they are tested to make sure they are clear of any residual traces before we can move them on." He also added that any animal showing signs of sickness is entirely removed from the herd and that, because of these precautions, feedlots actually have a very low rate of cattle loss.

It certainly was a highly scientific process, as it would need to be when dealing with such numbers of animals, and Craig was determined to show how closely they monitored everything internally and how strict USDA regulations are for all aspects of the process, including stocking density. However, it would be wrong for me to say that I was entirely won over, and I later told Stan that this highly mechanized system of fattening cattle up for slaughter was one that still left me feeling more than a little uncomfortable, particularly given the latest questions being asked by the federal government.

His answer was an honest one. "It is a balance, between giving the market what it wants and finding the most efficient and safest way to do that." He was right, of course. It is one thing for the consumer to demand that any particular food be readily available at an affordable price, but quite another to, at the same time, complain about the systems that have to be put in place to achieve that. Feedlots are not a particularly pleasant aspect of the U.S. beef industry, but they have become somewhat of a necessary evil, given the combination of delivering profit for their owners and consumer demand, which simply can't be met by a more ethical grass feeding system. While the feedlot system is a reality for the foreseeable future, the task in hand is to make it as safe for the cattle and the consumers as possible.

If feedlots make the average person slightly uncomfortable, the fact that the cattle then leave them for slaughterhouses is even worse. Even if it doesn't make them want to give up eating meat altogether, most people don't want to be reminded of the fact that something with eyes and a face has to get snuffed for them to have their supper.

Admittedly, I don't have any great concerns on this matter. I am a carnivore by nature and am well aware that for me to be that way something has die. My only demand is that the animals have a healthy life beforehand and are killed in an efficient way that does not create any undue stress (and I choose my meat suppliers accordingly).

Over the years I have visited a number of slaughterhouses, large and small, in different parts of the globe and have actually dispatched a few animals myself. I say this not as some primeval "I am a man" boast, but more to show that it takes quite a lot to shock me when it comes to the commercial killing of animals.

However, even with that experience, I was not ready for the scale of the operation I was to see at our next stop, Greater Omaha Packing Company, a packing plant that has been running in Nebraska's largest city since the 1920s and currently provides employment for almost one thousand workers. "This plant has the capacity to process nearly three-quarters of a million steers a year," Stan told me as we were being ushered into the company's boardroom to meet with their executive vice president, Angelo Fili, and Jerry Wiggs, an export sales representative. It was a staggering number, and even harder to conceive when Stan pointed out that there were plants with even bigger capacity here in Nebraska.

Angelo and Jerry led me to a changing room so that I could put on protective clothing for my tour of the processing floor. "Cleanliness is everything," Angelo added as I donned a pair of rubber boots, a white coat, and pulled a slightly redundant hairnet over my head. I could see what they meant as we stepped onto the viewing deck of the plant. For a room that was dedicated to the butchering of animals, the first thing that struck me was how scrubbed everything looked. The second was the smell, which wasn't bad, but like a mild distillation of every butcher's shop you have ever walked into. The third thing was the noise. The sound screamed out from buzz saws being used by those manning the production lines as they removed their specific cuts of meat from the carcasses of the steers passing by on chains overhead.

The speed at which the animal progressed from the point at which it was killed with a stun bolt to where it was boxed into separate cuts of meat ready for dispatch was genuinely remarkable, and I remarked to Angelo that I found the extreme efficiency both highly impressive and slightly frightening. I don't think it was the first time he had heard such a comment, and it served to remind me that, with few small exceptions, meat production in the United States is indeed an industry that depends on the same efficiencies as any other production-line-based industry. It is a long way removed from the "one-man-and-his-cow" farming of previous generations, which simply could not cope with the demands made upon food production by a population of three hundred million people.

I commented to Stan once we had left the plant that every one of the thousands of carcasses I had seen at Greater Omaha Packing was being butchered to exactly the same specifications. "Box cutting," he replied. "Again it is to do with efficiency. People used to have to buy the whole animal or at least a side when what they really wanted were specific parts. Eventually, after the Second World War, the processing plants began to break the animals down into eight parts, or 'primals,' so that butchers could buy a box of the part they wanted. Then they started to cut these primals down into smaller parts and that is what you will find being supplied to restaurants and supermarkets." This explained why I've often found it so hard to find some of the more unusual cuts of beef that I like to cook with in the United States without a visit to boutique butcher stores.

I wanted to find out more and was delighted when Stan told me, "Tomorrow we are going to visit the University of Nebraska Meat Science program. They have a whole side of beef they have put aside for you to break down so you can see all the different cuts." I am not going to deny that I may well have gone to sleep that night having slightly unsavory thoughts about cuts of beef.

The University of Nebraska Meat Science program in Lincoln is one of the most respected in the whole of the worldwide beef industry. An extension of the university's Animal Science Department, it specializes in courses on fresh and processed meat production. My butchery guru for the day was Dr. Dennis Burson. He had selected the steer for us to break down and, after dressing me in as much protective armor as an extra from *Game of Thrones*, led me through to the large walk-in cooler adjacent to our classroom.

Until you get up close and personal to one, you forget just how big a fully grown steer can be. It appeared to be about one and a half times in length as I am tall as it hung from the ceiling. Its hide had been removed, and it had been split in two pieces from neck to tail, revealing the bone structure within. "This one was about fifteen hundred pounds," Dr. Burson said as he called me over to help push the steer on its supporting chain through to the cutting tables. Even though the chain and pulley were doing most of the work, it still took a huge amount of effort to move the beast to a point where we could flop it down on to the table.

"A good-looking choice grade." Dr. Burson pointed towards the ribs of the steer. Beef in the United States is separated into twelve grades ranging from "Standard" at the lowest end up to "Prime +" at the highest end. The grades are awarded based primarily on the maturity of the animal and the amount of marbling that can be found in the meat. The average consumer will encounter "Select" found on supermarket shelves, "Choice" at higher-end supermarkets and in most restaurants, and "Prime" as the expensive cuts one might find being touted by servers at famous steakhouses.

Dr. Burson soon had me hard at work breaking down the side of beef first into primal and then subprimal cuts with a series of lethal-looking saws and sharp knives. Even though it was dead, the steer put up plenty of resistance and I broke into a running sweat underneath all my heavy protective clothing as I peeled away layers of hard fat to reveal the deep-colored flesh of the animal.

It was worth all the effort, however. After two hours of hard work, we had reduced the animal to a glorious array of cuts. Thick T-bone and porterhouse steaks ready for the grill, complete rib roasts, a well-trimmed tenderloin, blocks of short ribs ideal for braising, shoulder cuts ready to be ground, and meaty shanks that would be great in a stew. The combination of all that hard work and the sight of so much appetizing meat made me appreciate all the more the hard work that went into getting beef onto our tables and into my belly. I suddenly realized just how hungry I was and I wondered if there was any way I might be able to slip a porterhouse or two into my coat without anyone noticing.

Before I had a chance to act on this rather foolish fantasy, Stan reappeared carrying two portions of the short loin from the other half of the beast we had broken down. One half was wrapped in plastic and had been wet-aging, while the other had been dry-aged and had taken on the color of chocolate. "Cut these up into steaks," he said with a smile, "and we can take them to the Nebraska Club and cook them up for supper." It was the best offer I had received all day and seemed like the perfect way to finish off what had been both a hugely enjoyable and equally informative few days finding out about the Nebraska beef industry.

Chef Eric Leyden at the Nebraska Club cooked the steaks to perfection over a grill of hot coals. The outside took on a slight char, while the inside remained rare and juicy. I would have enjoyed them under any circumstances, but eating those steaks after my few days of travel around Nebraska with my genial host Stan Garbacz took on a whole new dimension. Not least because I had, as he had promised, followed the beef from farm to plate.

While there were still many aspects of this highly systematized business that I did and do find discomfiting, during my visit I did at least have the opportunity to meet some of the real people behind the scenes at what sometimes seems like a faceless and unstoppable industrial machine. By doing so, I found that even though most of them operate on an enormous scale, they care a great deal about their land, their animals, and the product they supply to our tables. It is far from being a perfect system, but if we want to change it, we are going to have to think about the way we buy and eat beef—eating less and paying more.

The process is beginning. Head to your nearest grocery store and look at the range of beef cuts. You can already see plenty of labels that read "organic" or "antibiotic-free." Given America's two-hundred-year love affair with the cow, it may be a slow process, but it is going to happen. One thing is certain: the next few decades are going to be very interesting for the American beef industry.

Pressing the Shabbat Reset Button

O f the many invitations I received during the Fed, White, and Blue journey, perhaps the most intriguing was from a gentleman in Overland Park, Kansas, named Yosef Silver. I had been put in touch with Yosef as someone who could give me more details about the sizable Jewish community in the United States as well as, perhaps, even allowing me to visit with him and his family so that I could share a Shabbat celebration.

His immediate response was very positive, and he told me that I would be more than welcome to join him, his wife, Daniella, and their two children at their weekly holy meal. He also pointed me in the direction of his excellent blog *This American Bite*, which catalogues his attempts to put a gourmet spin on traditional Jewish cuisine.

It was, however, the second paragraph of his e-mail reply that really caught my attention. He added that, as well as being invited to join his family on Shabbat, I might also like to help judge a kosher BBQ competition that was due to take place on the same weekend that I had marked down to visit the Midwest.

Given that Overland Park is in Kansas, no mention of BBQ— however unusual the context—should ever come as a surprise. So, even though I had only recently frozen my bits off during the Phat Jack's adventure, the offer of judging a kosher BBQ festival was one I was keen to explore.

Yosef put me in touch with Rabbi Mendel Segal, the organizer of the competition. He self-styles himself as "the BBQ Rabbi," and told me during our initial phone call that this one would be the first-ever kosher BBQ competition sanctioned by the BBQ world's primary ruling body, the Kansas City Barbecue Society. For obvious reasons, Mendel added, categories like "pulled pork" and "pork ribs" would be replaced in the competition, but otherwise the event would be run and judged strictly by KCBS rules.

I also agreed to help promote the competition by appearing with Mendel on a couple of local morning news shows, and the day after I arrived in Kansas City he pulled up in a large SUV outside my accommodation so that we could travel together.

Mendel and I had lots of time to get to know each other before we were summoned on set to do our thing, and I was able to find out more about his background. He had been ordained as a rabbi in Westwood, California, back in 2003, before moving to Chicago and then to Overland Park in 2009. He had been through a number of careers before his love for food and hospitality had seen him first take charge of the kosher department of a well-known local grocery store and then, in 2011, accept an offer to become the executive director of the Vaad HaKashruth of Kansas City, where his job was to help maintain the kosher standards of businesses in the city.

To people from outside the Jewish culture, such as myself, the notion of keeping kosher is perhaps one of the most challenging to understand, and I thoroughly enjoyed the chance to discuss its origins and its ongoing relevance with someone who not only lives by its rules every day, but who had also studied its meaning at a high academic level.

The word "kosher" refers to a series of Jewish dietary restrictions that have their roots in a body of Jewish law known as "Kashrut." This word is derived from the Hebrew word meaning "proper" or "correct" and the laws deal with all aspects of diet, including what animals may be eaten and how they must be slaughtered, what agricultural products may be eaten and how they should be grown, how utensils should be used in the preparation of food, and finally, what products should be avoided because of their cultural impact.

When the laws of Kashrut were first laid down in the Torah, adhering to them was easier. However, the growing prevalence of highly processed foods, as well as the increase in the variety of ingredients available thanks to trade and immigration, has made keeping kosher a much more complex affair in modern times. Those who wish to live in accordance to these dietary rules are often in need of considerable guidance.

This is where rabbis like Mendel, who are experts in the details of kosher law, come into play, working with restaurants and manufacturers making sure that the ingredients they use and the preparation are suitable. This is a crucial step to receiving the kosher certification that they can display on their packaging or menus.

As an outsider, it might be easy to dismiss these challenging dietary requirements as an anachronism dating back to when restrictions might have been needed for both health and cultural reasons at a time when Jews lived among pagans. However, talking to Mendel, I could see that, for him, kosher rules were not proscriptive but a way of displaying his own self-discipline and obedience to God.

"I keep kosher because the Torah tells me to," he told me, and his genuine sincerity convinced me that this was probably the only reason he would ever need.

By the time we had finished our promotional duties, it was time for Mendel to return home to prepare for his own Shabbat celebration. He dropped me off at my accommodation and roared his SUV up the street with one last wave from the window. Even in this very short space of time, I had grown to like Mendel a great deal, and his tireless enthusiasm made me realize that the next couple of days were going to be a lot of fun. But first it was time for me to share Shabbat with Yosef Silver and his family.

A Jewish friend in London once described his Shabbat meal to me as his "spiritual reset button." It was, he said, a cocoon into which he climbed every week to be closer to God and his family, and where, for a brief time, the cares of the world outside were of no concern. This was a notion that I really understood, even if I was not of the same faith. I was very much looking forward to finding out if my hosts for the evening felt similarly about Shabbat and also how the Jewish community in the United States differs from the one I knew from back home in England.

The Jewish American community in all its many forms now numbers a little shy of seven million people and dates back to the arrival of twenty-three Sephardic Jews from Brazil in 1654. Its culture now, however, is primarily the result of waves of immigration of Ashkenazi Jews from Germany and Eastern Europe fleeing persecution in the nineteenth century.

It's a community that continues to face a number of challenges. While Jewish identity is held on to with a great deal of pride, younger people often see themselves as Jewish by culture rather than by religion, and only 21 percent of Jews live according to kosher rules.

Yosef Silver and his family are part of that 21 percent. All of the recipes on his blog strictly follow kosher guidelines. Yet, Yosef does not see these rules as a hindrance to his enjoyment of food but rather as a chance to display his culinary creativity to take the traditional Sephardic and Ashkenazi cuisine of Jewish heritage to a higher level. I also discovered that he is excellent company and as food-obsessed as any person I met on the entire journey.

When I arrived at the Silvers' home in Overland Park, preparations were already well under way. One of Yosef's other guests, Chris, handed me the first of several very powerful gin and tonics, and I was invited to sit down at their kitchen table. Yosef's wife, Daniella, was hard at work, methodically rolling grape leaves tightly around a filling of ground lamb and layering the resulting little green cylinders in a baking tray.

"Lamb aplakes," Yosef told me, adding, "Daniella is very particular about how they are rolled, so I usually leave her to it." As we sipped our drinks, Yosef began to reel off the menu for their Shabbat meal.

"We'll begin with the aplakes, then we have olives, figs stuffed with garlic, hummus made with red peppers, bread, and a Moroccan carrot salad."

That sounded plenty enough for the number of people they were planning to feed, but I realized as Yosef drew a breath that he was only just warming up.

"Then we we'll bring out the main courses. A rib roast, some asparagus, and plenty of garlic potatoes."

And finally, as if he thought I might actually dare to question if there was going to be enough, he added with a final flourish, "There'll be plenty of kosher wine and then Daniella has made a few desserts to finish us off." It was obvious to me a huge amount of thought had gone into deciding what to serve and into making sure that it would be prepared within observance of the Sabbath laws on cooking, which can be almost as complex as the laws of Kashrut.

The early evening passed quickly in a haze of strong booze and excellent food-related conversation, and Yosef told me more about his family background and why his faith in general—and Shabbat in particular—means so much to him.

Like me, Yosef was born in England. He moved to Israel in 2005, which was where he met his wife. Their move to the United States happened a few years later, after a period of volunteer work with Habitat for Humanity in Overland Park. The Midwest plays home to only about 10 percent of the Jewish population of the United States, but it is a section of the community that has a well-deserved reputation for being welcoming and for its philanthropic nature. Yosef found this very attractive, and he and Daniella settled there in 2012.

I found that Yosef's views of Shabbat reflected those of my friend in the UK. It was not uncommon for them to fill their house with family and friends for this weekly meal, and they both obviously took considerable pride in how welcome they made their guests feel. I began to feel even more grateful that they had chosen to include me among their number on this occasion.

When it was time to move to the dining room, Yosef explained that the table had been set in the traditional way, with a tablecloth and four candles. Daniella lit the candles, the first two to represent their marriage and one for each of their children. Two loaves of challah bread covered with a white towel were placed in the center of the table. They represented the double amount of manna God had provided for the Jews for Shabbat during their time in the desert.

As Yosef started the meal by reciting the "Shalom Aleichem," a prayer to welcome the Sabbath, I thought about how this ritual would be taking place all over the world, as observant Jews connected with their family and God.

After further blessings were sung to the women of the house and the children, Yosef stood to offer a blessing for the wine, lifting a small cup and reciting the Kiddush.

Blessed are You God, King of the Universe, who made us holy with His commandments and favored us, and gave us His holy Shabbat, in love and favor, to be our heritage, as a reminder of the Creation. It is the foremost day of the holy festivals marking the Exodus from Egypt. For out of all the nations You chose us and made us holy, and You gave us your holy Shabbat, in love and favor, as our heritage. Blessed are You, God, Who sanctifies Shabbat.

After everyone had replied, "Amen," we all took part in the ritual washing of hands. I noticed that a genuine sense of peace had come over everyone at the table and that even for a brief moment, my own stresses seemed very far away.

Later, over dinner, Yosef told me, "There's a real moment of serenity when I say the Kiddush prayer over the wine each week. No matter how tired or stressed I am, in that moment I feel relaxed and recharged as though there's a magical sense of bliss that I can share with my wife, kids, and guests."

That sense of peace rapidly dispersed, however, the moment food appeared, as the Silvers became like any other family with a good appetite sharing a meal. Even as a stranger in their house, I was made to feel immediately at home, and on more occasions than I think has ever happened in my life I was chided for not topping up my plate on regular enough occasions. The food Yosef and Daniella had prepared was really very good indeed, whatever restrictions it had to be prepared under. I am also not going to deny that I may have held on to the plate of garlic potatoes for long enough to make one of their small children slightly teary.

I had just enjoyed a hefty second slice of Daniella's excellent chocolate torte when Yosef began the "bentch," or blessing, at the end of the meal to thank God for all that he had provided. We retired to their living room and I chatted with them until my return taxi arrived.

I left the Silver family to enjoy the rest of their Shabbat celebrations in peace, thanking them once more for their incredible hospitality and promising to catch up with them at the BBQ competition the next day. I also knew that the next time I tired of lonely solo meals on my travels, I would think fondly about the time I broke bread with my new Jewish American family.

The BBQ competition began the next day at the B'nai Jehudah Temple in Overland Park. The teams had arrived after Shabbat had ended at sunset. As I pulled into the parking lot at around ten p.m., I could see that booths had been erected for the twenty teams taking part. Although the setup looked just like the BBQ competition I had recently attended in Kearney, Nebraska, the fact that this was a kosher competition meant that there would be some necessary alterations to typical KCBS procedures.

All of the ingredients used at the event had to be certified kosher. This included the meat, spices, and anything that could be used to make sauces. This presented a number of challenges to the teams, including the fact that one of the side effects of the koshering process is that it makes meat considerably more salty.

The teams were not allowed to use their own smokers, so that the organizers could be certain that they had never been used to cook nonkosher ingredients. And finally, before they could get started, each team had to have their smokers lit by a rabbi. "To maintain the kosher status of the food, a Jew must be a part of the cooking process," Mendel explained as he worked his way around the teams. This was a practice established by the sages at a time when Judaism was really at risk of disappearing through intermarriage.

One thing that did seem to be exactly the same as every other BBQ competition I had ever attended was the regular *pop* of beer cans being opened the moment the teams had settled down to keep a close watch on their smokers. I knew from experience that things could get rowdy pretty fast once that sound began to hit the air, so I made my excuses and left them to it until the next day.

When I arrived the next morning I could see that Mendel had obviously done a terrific job promoting the event. A large awning had been erected and most of the tables and chairs that had been set up were already occupied by families enjoying music from a band that was belting out country songs from the stage. To the side of the lot, long tables had been set up and a group of volunteers was organizing a station to feed visitors with the food that was being prepared in the smokers behind them.

Mendel, the BBQ Rabbi, was in full effect, running everywhere, making sure that everything was going smoothly and dealing with issues when they arose. He always spared a moment for anyone who approached him with a question, and when he saw me he bellowed from across the lot, "I've been smoking meat since the end of Shabbat." His cell phone stuck to his ear, he gave me a huge grin as he whizzed past me, disappearing back into the crowd to firefight another problem.

His cooking efforts had certainly not been in vain, and I began to help the volunteers carry slabs of BBQ brisket and trays of chicken thighs and ribs from the smokers, placing them on the tables alongside foil trays of bread rolls, beans, and coleslaw to be served to the hungry crowd that was already beginning to congregate in the dining area.

I was enjoying myself so much that I almost forgot that I was there for a reason. Although I have cooked at many events, this would be the very first time I crossed the table and acted as a judge.

I rushed back to the judging chamber, where one of the KCBS supervisors asked me if I would read out the Judges' Oath. I was honored and joined the others as we stood and raised our right hands to pledge:

I do solemnly swear to objectively and subjectively evaluate each Barbeque meat that is presented to my eyes, my nose, my hands, and my palate. I accept my duty to be an Official KCBS Kosher BBQ Certified Judge, so that truth, justice, excellence in Barbeque and the American Way of Life may be strengthened and preserved forever.

If we had been asked to say such a pledge back home in the UK, I suspect there might have been quite a bit of snickering around the room. But, as I have learned over the last few years, Americans do love their pledges, and I rather liked the fact that everybody here was totally straight-faced.

Once the judging was over, I was at liberty to mingle with the teams and went to find Yosef and his partner, who had called their team "the Epicurean Bite." We sat for a while, drinking beer and talking about what they thought of their first kosher BBQ cook-off.

When the results were announced, I was disappointed that they had only placed in the turkey category. Yosef and Chris, on the other hand, took it on the chin and applauded the winners generously as they went up to collect their trophies from Mendel. "It was our first time and a learning experience." Yosef shrugged. "We'll be back next year."

Mendel was nowhere to be found as I readied to leave—no doubt he was good-humoredly solving more problems as the cleanup operation got under way. As I walked to my rental car, I peeked into the small goodie bag that had been given to each of the judges as we left the chamber. I pulled out a small brown bottle. It bore a label that read "Mendel's Kansas City BBQ Sauce" and had a very familiar bearded face printed on it. I twisted off the top and stuck my pinkie in to coat it with the sauce and licked it off. This wasn't just good kosher BBQ sauce, it was good BBQ sauce that happened to be kosher. I smiled. I suspect that the world is going to be hearing a lot more about the BBQ Rabbi.

Whey Out in Wisconsin

This may well come as a bit of a shock to some of you, but when it comes to food, I have always been quite an opinionated man. My father recently reminded me of a time when I was four, when, after tasting a bowl of my mother's normally delicious red lentil dahl, I inquired, "Was the shop that sold the good lentils closed today?" Which goes to prove both that I was a thoroughly odious little brat and that I probably ended up in the right job.

For years, such opinions were only shared with a relatively small group of lucky individuals until, in 1999, I discovered Internet food discussion boards like Chowhound and eGullet. These were the first places where like-minded food-obsessed individuals could come together to swap recipes, share stories, and express opinions on restaurants, ingredients, chefs, and food-related television programs. Some fifteen years later, in the world of Twitter and Facebook, it is hard to understand the impact early sites like this had, particularly on those like me, who believed until that point that such an obsession was an unhealthy aberration limited to me and members of my family.

It was good to discover that I was not alone, and I soon found myself becoming a regular on these sites, with posts that often ruffled a few feathers and stirred up debate. *Plus ça change.*

One particular post of mine garnered a large number of responses. It was entitled "America, Where Good Cheese Goes to Die," and had been prompted by sampling a number of desultory cheese-tasting boards during otherwise enjoyable meals on a recent business trip to New York City. While most of the responders might have expressed their opinion that I was an impudent British twerp, it was very hard for them to disagree with my main point that the state of the U.S. cheese scene just after the millennium, certainly by comparison to its European counterparts, was a sorry one.

It wasn't always that way, of course. America has a long tradition of cheese making, dating back to the arrival of the first group of Pilgrims, and has extended both in scale and variety with the arrival of new groups of immigrants from different parts of Europe, all of whom brought with them skills at making the popular cheeses of their homelands. By the mid-nineteenth century, Cheddars from Britain, Goudas from the Netherlands, and Limburger from Germany and Belgium were all being made in the United States, mainly in small farmstead operations and more often than not by the wives of farmers.

As the country's population began to grow rapidly during the 1800s, so too did the urgency in finding ways to feed it. Small homesteads simply couldn't produce enough food to meet demand, and so the need for larger-scale, mechanized means of food production became ever more pressing, including cheese making.

In 1851, the first U.S. cheese factory was opened by Jesse Williams in Oneida County, New York, and thus began the decline of farmstead American cheese. It came to the point where, by the middle of the twentieth century, the majority of Americans associated the word "cheese" with grim block Cheddar or those individually wrapped fluorescent squares of plastic that have no other culinary purpose than to be placed on top of a hamburger.

While there remained some small-scale cheese-making operations during this time, these were relatively few in number and the cheese they produced was mainly for the consumption of the cheese makers themselves. It was not until the late 1970s and early 1980s, when pioneering women like Laura Chenel in California began to sell fresh goat's milk cheese, that things began to change and the numbers of artisanal cheese makers began to rise once again.

The American Cheese Society was founded in 1983 to support both this new breed of cheese makers and retailers whose knowledge did not, at that time, match their enthusiasm for the product. However, it was still a tough struggle to persuade the average American that even a small proportion of the thirty pounds of cheese they ate every year should not come from a company whose name rhymes with draft.

Add to this the fact that the artisanal cheeses that were being offered even into the new century were of decidedly varying quality. Cheeses imported from Europe struggled to survive the torments of transport to America in any decent condition, while the quality of domestic cheeses could be up and down like a whore's drawers. To make matters even more difficult, regulations set down by the FDA also meant that all milk used in cheese making had to be pasteurized or that the cheeses had to be aged for sixty days, meaning that the various cheeses were, invariably, dramatically different from and nearly always inferior to their counterparts from Europe.

Move on to the present day, however, and the situation has changed. The advances made in both the quality and consistency of American artisanal cheese has made it one of the fastest-growing sectors of the craft food movement. This is thanks, in no small part, to the work of the American Cheese Society, whose membership now comprises nearly fifteen hundred members, made up of cheese makers, retailers, and enthusiasts—all of whom have worked tirelessly to raise the standards of American cheese making through the use of cooperation, education, and internships with European cheese makers.

Sales of artisanal cheese may still only represent a tiny percentage of the eight billion pounds sold in the United States every year, but if I were to write now a sniffy little post like the one I posted on that a food board well over a decade ago, I would quite rightly be laughed out of the room.

The American Cheese Society launched its annual conference in 1985 and it is held in a different city each year. In 2013, I discovered, it was to be held in the city of Madison, Wisconsin, so I cleared a week in my calendar and booked myself into a bed-and-breakfast within walking distance of the convention center.

Although I had planned to attend no matter the conference location, I was particularly delighted when I found out that it was going to be in Madison. I had only passed through the city once very briefly, but in the short time I was there, I was rather taken with it and its residents and really looked forward to having more opportunity to explore. Added to which, my visit also gave me the opportunity to spend time in Wisconsin, without argument the dairy capital of the United States.

My first invitation was for a cheese maker's party being held on the evening I arrived at the Uplands Cheese Company farm in Dodgeville, Wisconsin. The farm is about an hour's drive from the city and famous among members of the cheese-making community for producing Pleasant Ridge Reserve, a multi-award-winning alpine-style cheese. After depositing my bags at the bed-and-breakfast, I walked to the convention center and joined a long line of excited conference attendees who were being shepherded onto tour buses by volunteers. They were all keen to catch up with one another and paid little attention to me as our bus emerged from the suburbs of Madison into the rural landscape of Wisconsin.

Staring out of the window of the bus, it really wasn't very hard for me to understand why Wisconsin has become America's go-to place for dairy and cheese. The sun was just dipping in the summer sky, its light throwing a golden hue over the miles and miles of lush green fields that were to be seen from either side of the bus. In each one I saw clustered dots where cows huddled together to feed on the rich pasture. It was easy to imagine that I would have seen similar scenes back in the mid-1800s when the Wisconsin cheese-making industry first began, when a woman called Anne Pickett began selling cheeses that she made with excess milk from her neighbor's cows in Lake Mills. The regional industry grew rapidly from that point.

I took the disinterest of others on the bus to chat with me as chance to do some research on my smartphone. What I found told me that Wisconsin now has a population of about 1.3 million cows, approximately one cow for every five people in the state, which are now kept on over eleven thousand farms and provide enough milk (over 3.2 billion gallons, to be exact) to support a dairy industry that includes more than 125 cheese-making plants.

The party at the Uplands farm was lively and fun, and there was, inevitably, lots and lots of really good cheese to eat. But, after less than an hour, the combination of the fresh air and a couple of strong beers began to take its toll and I claimed a spot on the first bus that was heading back to the city. Before I made my excuses, I took the chance to corner Andy Hatch, the tall, wiry cheese maker at the Uplands farm, and persuaded him to allow me to come back after the conference to help him make a batch of some of his revered cheese.

The next morning, after a very welcome night's sleep, I headed to the convention center early so that I could collect my credentials and make sure that I snagged spots on all the talks, lectures, and classes that appealed. There were plenty of options available, including rather specific-sounding sessions such as "Common Cheese Defects and How to Avoid Them," "The Art & Science of Smear Ripened Cheese," "Striving for a Successful FDA Inspection," and my particular favorite, "Sensory Evaluation of Mexican Cheese." I signed up for enough events to make sure that the next few days would be particularly hectic.

Afterwards, I joined a crowd of people who were waiting in the ballroom for the keynote address at the opening breakfast. The rather rambling speech containing plaintive calls for a return to small-scale agriculture were very well received by the converted to whom the speaker was preaching. However, much as I admire craft food, I tend to have a more pragmatic approach to food production and often find such well-meaning speeches almost as irritating as they are inspiring. All too often they fail to recognize the fact that we now live in a world of over seven billion people. America does not exist in a vacuum and must play its part. Telling people that we need to return to a mythical era of local and seasonal eating is Pollyanna-ish at best and down-right irresponsible at worst. It serves to disenfranchise those who don't have the time, opportunity, or income to do so, wherever they may be in the world.

It was at the point when the speaker uttered the words, "Local is a distance best measured in our hearts," that I decided it might be wise for all concerned if I headed to my first session before the urge to shout out, "Blessed are the self-righteous!" overcame me. I made my way to the back of the room and escaped into the lobby.

After that uncertain start, I am delighted to say that things at the conference improved markedly over the next few days, as I attended half a dozen or so very informative sessions that taught me more about the cheese industry than I will probably ever need to know. This included an excellent "Cheese Making 101" course given by a teacher from Wisconsin's Center for Dairy Research that I hoped would stand me in excellent stead for my visit to the Uplands farm.

In between sessions, I also finally had a chance to connect with some of the other attendees. If I ever had doubts about the desire of American cheese makers and retailers to raise the standards of their craft, they were quickly dispelled as we chatted during the coffee breaks. The people I talked with, almost every person, acknowledged that American-made cheeses still have some way to go to match the consistent excellence of their European counterparts, but there was a fierce determination to do so, as well as a genuine pride in what had been achieved so far, particularly in such a relatively short space of time. This is still a movement that, in its current form, has only been in existence for a little over thirty years, and so, while cheese makers should always be supported in their urge to improve, they should also be given enormous credit for now producing many cheeses that are not just good American cheese, but very much capable of holding their own on a world stage.

If I needed any more confirmation of the variety and quality of the cheese being produced in America, it came on the final day of the conference. I had already circled the words "Festival of Cheese" in the conference guidebook as something that I should not miss. When I found out that the event gave attendees the opportunity to sample all of the two thousand cheeses that had been entered in the American Cheese Society's competition for 2013, I knew that I had been correct to do so.

I had been fortunate enough to receive a media pass for the conference, which meant that, along with other members of the cheese-related media (that's a thing, honest to God), I was able to enter the hall nearly half an hour before the general population. As the doors opened to the vast conference room, our noses were assaulted by a huge waft of assorted cheese aromas.

In front of us were well over thirty long white-linen-covered tables, and displayed on each were towering mounds of different cheeses covering every category imaginable. Placed next to every display were bowls of crackers and slices of bread to use as delivery systems from plate to mouth, and around the perimeter of the room were tables where liveried servers offered glasses of wine and beer to accompany the feast. In the center, elevated from its counterparts like Excalibur rising from the lake, was the cheese which had won the coveted prize as Best in Show.

Winnimere, made by Jasper Hill Farm in Greensboro, Vermont,

is a raw-milk, spruce-bark-wrapped cheese that is similar to many Vacherin-style cheeses I have tried on my travels and, like them, it was soft and runny enough to be eaten directly from its bark casing using a spoon. Traditionally a winter cheese, it takes advantage of the high fat content of the milk the farm's cows produce at that time of year. Although it was not in season, the cheese maker, Mateo Kehler, had been persuaded to make a batch just to be entered in the competition. His efforts had been repaid, and he stood next to his winning cheese like a proud father next to his firstborn child.

I nudged my way through the small crowd of media folk that had already begun to assemble around Mateo and picked up a tiny plastic spoon to scoop a taste from the winning cheese. One small sample was all I needed to confirm that this was a very fine example of the cheese maker's art indeed. There was a slightly sour funkiness to the initial taste, which came both from the spruce bark wrapping but also from the fact that the cheese is washed in a sour lambic beer before being allowed to age in a cellar. The taste lingered pleasingly in my mouth and it was at least ten minutes before my thoughts turned to sampling any more of the other 1,999 cheeses on offer. By now the doors had been opened to the general attendees and the ballroom was flooded with eager caseophiles, who were swarming around the table like mutants from *The Omega Man*.

I fought my way to a few other tables and sampled about thirty other cheeses. Some were good, some not so much, but none quite lived up to the Winnemere. I decided that, as I had a very early start the next morning at the Uplands farm, I would say my farewells to the American Cheese Society Conference and return to my bed-and-breakfast for an early night.

The Uplands farm was started in 1994, when two neighboring farming families joined together to produce cheeses inspired by the alpine regions of France and Switzerland. Their efforts had been a huge success, and one particular cheese, Pleasant Ridge Reserve, styled after the Beaufort cheese of the Savoie region of France (and named after the land on which the farm sits), had itself won Best in Show at the ACS festival on three occasions. It was a cheese I had sampled on numerous occasions and was one of the first to really begin to earn recognition for American cheeses on the international stage.

I arrived at the farm at eight-thirty a.m. as requested, and found Andy Hatch and his team already hard at work preparing the freshly collected milk for the day's cheese production. They only use milk from their own herd of 150 cows and the cheese is only made in the summer when the pasture of the farm is at its most lush.

It was not the first time I had seen cheese being made, nor indeed was it the first time I had actually helped make some, but I still found Andy's explanation of what we were going to be doing for the next few hours fascinating.

Despite the almost infinite variety of cheeses that are available, most are made in much the same way, with milk being curdled and coagulated with bacteria and rennet to form curds that are then formed and pressed. Small variations to the process are what lead to differences in the appearance, texture, and, of course, taste of the various cheeses.

It usually takes about ten pounds of milk to make one pound of Pleasant Ridge Reserve, and before any actual cheese making began, Andy tested what we would be using to be certain that it did not contain any harmful substances, like blood. Then he added a starter culture, which is used to eat the lactose in the milk. This releases lactic acid, reducing the acidity of the liquid and beginning the coagulation process of the milk. Although the dairy has meticulous records, a lot still depends on the skill of the cheese maker, and as soon as Andy thought that the time was right he took the milk to the next stage with the addition of rennet.

Although there are vegetarian and even synthetic varieties, most rennet is made from the lining of the fourth stomach of the cow, which contains enzymes that force the proteins in the milk to clump together in batches (the beginning of cheese curds). No one is quite sure how this process was discovered, but many historians believe that, as some of the earliest containers for liquid were made from animal stomachs, there is a good chance that the first cheeses were created when the bag's contents of milk accidentally became heated in the sun.

After adding the rennet, Andy and I left the cheese to set, which he told me could take a matter of hours. What he was looking for, he informed me, was a "clean break" in the milk, where an inserted finger would leave a clean incision in the solidifying milk that would be filled immediately by the whey that had been produced during coagulation.

Once the milk reached that stage, it was time to cut the curds, using tools that look like larger versions of those I have seen restaurants use to cut potatoes into fries. The purpose of cutting the curds is to increase their surface area, allowing more liquid and whey to escape. The smaller the curds, the more surface area each curd cube has and the more liquid they release. This allows for a denser, harder cheese. For a cheese such as Pleasant Ridge Reserve, Andy told me he tries to cut the curds into tiny pea-sized cubes, resulting in the unmistakable firm texture of the Beaufort cheese on which it's based. We salted the curds to prevent spoilage during curing and then heated them again for a short while to help promote the expulsion of even more liquid before the whey was drained. The cheese was placed into molds to create the traditional wheeled shape.

Although I had seen the process many times before, it was a genuine pleasure to spend time with a cheese maker like Andy, who took such pride in what he did and in every cheese he produced. While it was all pretty straightforward, it was at this point that things went, as we say in England, "tits up." The next step was to drain the whey from the vat holding the curds. It was a simple enough task, consisting of the whey flowing down a large pipe to a tank outside, where it was collected to be sold as a valuable by-product to the farm feed and vitamin industries. Unfortunately, as we worked, the pipe came loose, flipped over, and began spraying floods of hot whey over much of the cheese-making room floor and, primarily, over me.

The white coat and hat that Andy had given me to wear for sanitary reasons when I first arrived protected me from some of the deluge, but they were ultimately no match for the whey, which soaked me pretty much to the skin. I winced as hot liquid began to dribble through my T-shirt and down the small of my back.

Andy stood motionless, with a horrified look on his face, for a brief moment before he quickly came to his senses and rushed to reconnect the pipe and collect some clean towels so that I could dry myself off. I decided, in an all too rare moment of maturity, that running off in a hissy fit was probably not the best thing to do, so I made lots of "Oh, it's okay, really I only got a little bit wet" noises and insisted that Andy carry on with the next stage of cutting the curds that remained in the vat into the traditional round molds.

I helped as best I could, easing blocks of cheese into the molds and then placing them on a rack where they would be gently pressed overnight to remove even more moisture, but the whey I was covered in had already begun to dry out in the heat of the room and my clothes began to stiffen uncomfortably as I moved around. I also noticed that I had begun to reek of an unpleasant mixture of sweat and dried cheese, the combination of which was actually beginning to make me feel slightly nauseous. I could only imagine how Andy felt.

After we had finished placing the day's batch onto the presses, Andy took me through to the aging rooms, where the cheeses would be turned and washed several times a week in brine to protect them from microbes, and then left to age for up to eighteen months. We spent the next hour or so tasting. Andy dug into a range of cheeses of varying ages to show me how they developed over time. The difference between the young and old cheeses was truly remarkable. The young cheeses were simple, light, softer, and had an almost fruity aroma and taste that reflected the pasture on which the cows had fed before giving their milk. The older cheeses were far more complex, with a slightly earthy flavor and a more crystalline texture.

Andy carved one more chunk out of his busy day to walk me around the fields surrounding the farm. His pride, as he showed me the rolling green fields of pasture and the cows that were grazing them, was obvious, and with the taste of Pleasant Ridge Reserve lingering on my tongue (and the smell of it lingering on my body) I said my good-byes, made my way to the car, and headed back to Madison. It may have taken a decade or more for me to change my mind, but my brief time at the American Cheese Society Conference and my even briefer time making this remarkable cheese convinced me that my damnation of America as being a country where "good cheese goes to die" was definitely one that I needed to seriously rethink. These cheeses may have had their origins in Europe, but with cheese makers like Andy Hatch they are becoming very much America's own.

Oh, and just in case you're wondering, it took me two showers and three cycles in the washing machine, respectively, for me and my clothes to stop smelling of cheese whey.

K-Town Rocks

There are some cities with which you have an immediate affinity. Cities with which you connect deeply the first time you arrive, and that continue to excite you every time you pay them a visit after that. London is obviously one of them for me; it created an affection so strong that I remained in the city for more than twenty-five years after coming down from the north of England to study the unlikely subject of theology at King's College in 1982.

Then there are cities that leave you cold. If I never have to go to Paris again in my lifetime, I won't shed a tear, and despite three visits, I have yet to discover quite why the rest of the world loves Sydney so much.

My current home, Los Angeles, falls somewhere in the middle of these two extremes. It was not always like this. In fact, when I first started coming here on a regular basis to visit Sybil, I positively loathed the place. The excitement I felt at seeing her again as my plane came in to land at LAX—officially the most depressing airport in the developed world—was dissipated by the thought of having to spend time in a place that to my eyes offered little in the way of beauty or culture. While I suspect I shall never develop any deep affection for Los Angeles, over the last four or five years I've discovered a few of its charms and the City of Angels and I have somehow come to an agreement to tolerate each other.

There is, however, one aspect of being in Los Angeles that has always impressed me, and that is its food scene. I do need to qualify that. I'm not talking about its plethora of middle- to high-end restaurants that garner so much attention and which, with a few exceptions, always leave me feeling underwhelmed. In fact, back in 2011, when asked by the *Chicago Tribune* to describe the dining scene in Los Angeles, I replied to my interviewer, ". . . much of [it] seems to be driven by what I call 'the hype and the herd.' The food on the whole rarely lives up to the Twitter-driven hyperbole."

Things have certainly improved a lot since then, and if I were to be asked the same question today, I think I'd be a little kinder. However, it is not this aspect of eating out in Los Angeles that really marks it as a great food city, nor, given the market to which most of these restaurants are playing, is it ever likely to be. Where Los Angeles really excels is in the multiplicity of ethnic cuisines on offer in its many neighborhoods, and the astonishing authenticity and quality of food that they are able to deliver on a regular basis.

Los Angeles lays claim to being one of the most ethnically diverse cities in the world. Driving around any one of its 272 neighborhoods, it is easy to see that this is no idle boast. Just about every nation on earth is represented to some degree, and so too are their cuisines. It was the restaurants in these areas that Sybil was keen to show off on my initial visits to the city, and they are the restaurants that we still turn to most often when we want a meal that we know will satisfy body and soul.

On those first trips, much of our time was spent eating in these neighborhoods, so many of them named for the country or cities from where these immigrants to Los Angeles came: Thai Town, Little Tokyo, Historic Filipinotown, Little Saigon, and Little Armenia, to name but a few. We would often join Sybil's coterie of girlfriends, keen to give me the once-over as a potential long-term partner for one of their dearest friends, for meals which still remain memorable to this day. We slurped the meaty juices from Shanghai soup dumplings in Arcadia; we mopped up doro wot, a thick chicken stew, in Little Ethiopia; we battled over chunks of smoked pork hock hidden in a soup of black bean feijoada in the Brazilian restaurants near Sybil's home in Culver City; and we insisted on extra pork fat in our bowls of ramen in Little Tokyo. In the midst of all of this great food, there were two cuisines, in particular, that I really fell for on my first visits to Los Angeles and that have remained my favorites ever since: Korean and Mexican. It was these cuisines and the communities that produced them that I wanted to find out more about on the Fed, White, and Blue journey.

To help me learn about the Korean community and its food, I turned to my good friends Ted and Yong Kim and Chris Oh, who may be more readily known to readers as the three faces behind the Seoul Sausage Company, winners of season three of the Food Network's *The Great Food Truck Race*. I first met them when they were selling their spicy wares at a food festival in Long Beach. It was one of their first events since starting the company and they were struggling to entice many people to come to their small stall. I was immediately impressed both with them and their sausages and made a point to watch out for them in the future.

Well, it is fair to say that their progress since then has been stratospheric. Since those humble beginnings, they have not only opened their own brick-and-mortar restaurants but have also become television personalities and recognized faces of the Korean American community.

The trio insisted that I spend a night with them and "hit K-Town hard," as Yong put it. Delighted as I was at the idea of hanging out with them, I was also more than a little nervous. I knew from following their antics on social media that "hard" was something of an understatement to describe what the Seoul Sausage boys got up to when they decided they needed to let their well-coiffed hair down.

However, as Yong told me, "You've seen us at work, now you need to see us play." This seemed only fair, so, despite my trepidations, I agreed to meet them for what they promised would be a memorable night.

The United States plays host to well over one million people of Korean heritage. With a population of more than a hundred and twenty thousand, Los Angeles is by far the home to the biggest proportion. While they, of course, live all over the Los Angeles metro area, the biggest enclave of Korean Americans is to be found in the area of the city that circles around Eighth Street and Western Avenue— Koreatown, or "K-Town," as it is known locally. This area of the city really began to develop in the 1970s as its original occupants of European immigrants began to gravitate towards the city's suburbs and were replaced by new arrivals from Asia. It offers up street after street of shops, churches, schools, and, of course, restaurants that primarily cater to the local Korean community but since the 1990s have been become a magnet for other Angelinos in search of a great evening and great food at a good value.

On my first visits to K-Town, I was astonished by the food that was presented to me, a million miles ahead in variety and quality from the handful of Korean restaurants I had visited over the years in London. It soon became my favorite dining destination in the city and prompted my decision to include South Korea at the top of my bucket list of places to visit, which I was able to place a satisfied tick next to in late 2011.

Being back in Los Angeles did at least mean that I didn't have far to travel for this adventure. The fact that I was home, if only for a few short days, was a genuine blessing, not least because it meant that I could spend some quality time with Sybil. She had been patient beyond belief as I toured the country, and, although we had spoken almost every night I had been away, I knew that she was pleased that I was home for more than just a day or two. So was I. Since we'd met,

Sybil has not only become my wife but also my closest friend, and one of the toughest things on my journey was the amount of time that we were separated.

Being home also meant that I could catch up on my research. I find it hard to work on the road, and during the day, while Sybil was at her office, I took the opportunity to organize my notes, catch up with my writing, and send apologetic responses to people who had been waiting for replies to phone calls, texts, and e-mails. By this time in my journey around the country, I was shattered. I had already clocked up dozens of hours of flying time, and it was all beginning to take its toll, leaving me with that twitchy-eye syndrome that only someone else who is perennially exhausted could possibly understand. I spent the day "working from bed" and rose just in time for a hasty shower before a taxi arrived to take me down to Toe Bang, a classic old-school Korean bar on Sixth Street. As I walked into the mostly empty room, I could see that Chris had already arrived and was nursing a beer at a wooden table at the back, with a black baseball cap pulled down halfway over his face. He smiled when he saw me and rose to shake my hand.

"This is going to be fun," he said, just in case I needed any reassurance. He looked almost as tired as I was and I suspected that he was still recovering from a heavy session the night before. Chris is the oldest of the Seoul Sausage boys and graduated from the University of Arizona in 2002 with a degree in economics, compiling an impressive résumé at various businesses in San Francisco before the urge to become a cook became too strong to resist. He moved down to Los Angeles to work in some of the hippest restaurants in town before reconnecting with Ted and Yong and founding the Seoul Sausage Company. Unsurprisingly, his Korean parents were not thrilled that the son who they had hoped would become a doctor or a lawyer had decided to make sausage for a living.

"I am not sure they thought it was a real job until we appeared on *The Great Food Truck Race*," he told me as he stopped a passing server to order me a beer. By the time it had arrived, so too had Ted and Yong. Like Chris, the two brothers both had had successful careers in their past lives, this time in advertising and, like Chris, both had experienced the disapproval of their Korean parents at the outset. In fact, as Ted told me, "We didn't even tell them we had quit our jobs until we signed the lease on the shop and got selected for the TV show."

It was a story that I knew would be familiar to many first-generation Americans, whose parents had arrived in America with the single goal of enhancing their family's future prospects and then became frustrated when their children were tempted by the many other opportunities America had to offer.

Because I came from an Indian family, their story was also one that was very familiar to me. Although my father has always been outwardly supportive of whatever odd choices I've made in life, I suspect that he never thought this latest transformation into food critic/traveler was a legitimate career until he saw me propping up the judging desk on *Iron Chef America*, and even then, his support was qualified with the words, "And they pay you to do this?"

Now that our foursome was assembled, we could get on with our evening.

"This is where we always begin our nights," Ted told me as he summoned back the young server so that he could supplement our beers with food and, more important, a bottle of soju. "No Korean evening can pass without drinking soju," he announced to nods of agreement from Chris and Yong.

Soju is a slightly frightening clear spirit from South Korea that is usually made with rice. It is, my research tells me, the single most popular spirit in the world, and its popularity among Korean men means that they have, per head, the highest rate of alcohol consumption of any country in the world. The Seoul Sausage boys were keen to prove this and the first bottle was emptied into shot glasses and downed with a shout of, "Gun bae!" seconds after the server placed it on the table.

Thankfully, food arrived before the second bottle was delivered. Plates of ddukbokki (spicy rice cakes) and deep-fried chicken gizzards were laid out in front of us and everybody tucked in, keen to line their stomachs for the night ahead. I had tried both of these dishes before and knew exactly what to expect, particularly from the ddukbokki, which, with its thick coating of spicy sauce, was a favorite street food dish on my trip to South Korea. The third dish that arrived, however, was a bit more of a surprise. If I am being perfectly honest, it looked like it was something someone had thrown up after a long evening on the soju rather than something they might eat before drinking it.

"It's corn cheese," Ted told me. "It's just what it sounds like, corn cooked with cheese. Koreans are slightly obsessed with it and it is great when you have been drinking." I prodded at it uncertainly with my fork, but with everyone watching, I felt like I should give it a try. It wasn't bad. A great combination of crunchy corn, sweetness from sugar and mayonnaise, and saltiness from the cheese. It should never have worked, but it did, and I found myself scooping up so many stringy forkfuls of it that Chris was forced to order a second helping. It was just as well, because by the time we came to leave Toe Bang, the table was littered with empty bottles and shot glasses and I had already given up any hope that the Seoul Sausage boys might tone things down for me in respect for my advanced years.

Fortunately, our next stop was only a staggering distance away. Kang Hodong's Baekjeong is situated across a small courtyard from the bar. "It's owned by a famous Korean comedian," Yong said as he pointed to two large cutouts of a man who looked like a chubbier version of Korean pop superstar Psy stationed outside the entrance. There was already a vociferous crowd milling around, and Chris explained that it had become one of the hottest BBQ restaurants in K-Town since opening in 2013.

"People wait for hours," he shouted above the noise, "but I put our names down before I got to the bar and we have a table." He cleared a space through a throng of people and guided us into a cavernous dining room that was laid out with large round wooden dining tables.

We were led through the restaurant by a server clad in a black T-shirt bearing a cartoon outline of a pig, weaving around the packed tables until we reached our own at the far side of the room. At the center of the table was a circular metal grill, fueled by large charcoal logs already lit and with flames licking up onto the grate. The grill was encircled by a shallow metal trench, like a castle moat that had been split into four compartments. Chris took charge of ordering, and two minutes after we took our seats yet another bottle of soju was placed before us and food began to arrive.

Traditionally, a Korean meal begins with banchan, a series of side dishes and appetizers that can include, as they did here, varieties of kimchi, bean sprout salads doused with gochujang, Korean chili sauce, dishes of noodles, and daikon radishes in cold broth. Although these were delicious and welcome, given the amount we had been drinking, they were merely distractions while we made our minds up about whether we wanted our grilling experience to be centered on beef or pork. Once we had decided—quite correctly—that we should have a combination of the two, a server appeared and began filling the compartments surrounding the grill.

In one he placed more kimchi, in another a mixture of red onions, garlic, and green peppers, and I was delighted to see him fill the third with corn and mozzarella. As the meal progressed, the heat of the grill would melt the cheese to create more of that unlikely star dish of the evening, corn cheese. In the final compartment, the server poured a stream of beaten eggs and milk. "These will steam from the heat of the grill," Ted yelled at me over the noise of the room.

At this point the meat arrived, along with a second bottle of soju that Chris had ordered "just in case." Our server began carefully placing slivers of pork belly, thick cuts of beef spare ribs, and marbled slices of brisket on the grill, which began sizzling as soon as they hit the heat. A waft of meaty steam rose up immediately and was greeted by appreciative noises from everyone at the table as we clinked glasses and began to load our plates.

Despite the fact that Ted, Yong, and Chris are as hipster as they come, and dress as if they are auditioning for a Korean rap band (I wonder if they call Korean rap K-Rap?) they are, at heart, well-raised Asian boys who are obviously terrified that their Tiger parents would beat the living K-Rap out of them if they did not show an honored elder (that'd be me, in case you are wondering) due respect. So they made sure that my plate and glass were constantly filled and that the prime piece of meat, already starting to char nicely, was pushed to the side of the grill closest to me. I was not too shy or polite to hold back and began filling my plate with grilled meats, steamed eggs, and, of course, more corn cheese.

It wasn't long before we had laid waste to the contents of the table, and I pushed my seat back to admire our work. I glanced at my phone and saw that it was about ten p.m. As a middle-aged man, this would normally be about the time when my wife and I retire to bed with a cup of tea to catch up on reruns of a show starring Jennifer Love Hewitt. It was clear, however, that my younger companions were only just getting started, and after we paid the bill they told me that we would need to get a taxi to our next destination.

As soon as I stood up, I discovered a Korean secret. Soju has the rare ability to get a person drunk from the feet up. While you are knocking back shots of it, everything seems just fine and dandy.

Unfortunately, when it comes time for you to stand, you realize with horror that your legs are now more or less useless. I wobbled ungracefully towards the door and had to be supported most of the way by two-thirds of my companions until we got out into the cold night air. I managed to regain my balance by leaning against one of the pseudo-Psy cutouts.

Our next stop was a bar called OB Bear on Seventh Street. "This place is all about tong dak—fried chicken," Ted told me as we stumbled out of the cab. Even though I was already stuffed to the gills from the amount of BBQ I had just consumed and was beginning to long for my bed, my ears perked up at the mention of fried chicken. I would be hard-pressed to think of a better iteration of poultry-frying than the one that takes place in Korean kitchens, and I know in that opinion I am not alone. In the couple of years before writing this book, mainly thanks to the self-publicity prowess of David Chang, Korean fried chicken has become extraordinarily hip and begun to appear on menus all over the world.

OB Bear was obviously a regular haunt of the Seoul Sausage Company. We were shown to a booth in the small upper level of the wood-paneled pub and Chris placed our food order without even looking at the menu. It arrived soon afterwards, along with a pitcher of Korean beer and—I noticed with a little shudder—the inevitable bottle of soju. The chicken at OB Bear came in two forms. On one plate was a whole chicken that had been deep-fried to a golden brown and then segmented into four pieces of wings and breast, and legs and thighs. It came with a slightly unlikely side order of shredded cabbage that had been doused with a large glob of bright pink Thousand Island dressing. The second plate contained about twenty or so chicken wings that had been floured, fried, tossed in a coating of gochujang sauce, and then sprinkled with a handful of white sesame seeds.

As I know from my own attempts to re-create the dish, the key to making really great Korean fried chicken wings is to double-fry them, which makes them even crisper. The ones at OB Bear were spot-on, and the skin crunched beneath our teeth as we dismantled the plate until all that was left was a pile of bones. The whole chicken, however, was even better. Even though it wasn't battered, the skin was incredibly crisp and the interior leaked juices as I tore the meat from the bones. While there was no way that I should have been able to eat any more food, the smell of that chicken had given me a second wind and I managed to polish off at least a quarter of our order.

It was now well past midnight, I had drunk more soju in one evening than I had previously done in my lifetime, and I had already eaten the equivalent of four suppers. That alone is not, however, how the Seoul Sausage Company rolls, and despite an amount of embarrassing pleading on my part, the trio insisted that I join them at one last place before they would allow me to seek the safe haven of a taxi home.

Dwit Gol Mok, or DGM, as everybody knows it, is hidden away just off Wilshire Boulevard. It was another Korean BBQ joint, but BBQ was not the reason we were here, my friends informed me, as I stared at them through increasingly blurry eyes.

Ted, Yong, and Chris led me into a slightly shabby dining room. The walls were covered with graffiti and every table was filled almost entirely with young Korean Americans, who, like my companions, looked like they were only getting started for the night.

I wondered aloud why, apart from me, there did not appear to be any non-Koreans in the bar. Ted explained that, while some restaurants had a "come one, come all" approach to customers, others were more insular, some even printing menus only in Korean. This was beginning to change, however. He explained, "With blogs, Yelp, and other social media, people outside are beginning to discover these places and, in turn, they are realizing that they need to reach outside the community if they want to keep ahead of the game." It was a sentiment that reminded me very much of my conversation with Filipino Chef AJ of Salo-Salo at the beginning of my journey.

"We want you to try one more dish before we let you go," they told me as we sat down on either side of a wooden bench table. Once again, our order was placed without the need for a menu, and within five minutes we had our food in front of us. This final dish of the evening was also one of the most interesting, even if I didn't have room for more than just a few mouthfuls. "Budae jjigae" translates literally as "army base stew" and is a dish that originated after the Korean War of the 1950s, when U.S. Army rations were often all that was available to make a meal. Its ingredients vary but can include canned beans, ramen noodles, and sliced hot dog sausages, all of which are boiled together with kimchi, chili paste, and onions to form a spicy hot stew that Chris told me is "the ultimate hangover food."

I had drunk so much soju and beer by this time that I thought some prophylactic measure might be a wise course of action. The soup was, to be perfectly frank, not lovely to look at, but its broth certainly delivered a kick, and rivulets of chili sweat began trickling down my bald head as I scooped up the contents of the bowl to my mouth.

Fine dining it wasn't, but it woke me up sufficiently enough that I was able to stamp my feet and insist that the Seoul Sausage boys finally let me go home. They begrudgingly agreed and helped me to one of several waiting taxis at the rear entrance to the bar. The driver was Korean and Ted negotiated a price for him to take me back to my apartment in West Los Angeles. I was completely done in and drifted off almost as soon as the car door was closed. My last view of Ted, Yong, and Chris was of them turning back to the restaurant to continue a night that I am pretty sure was not yet half over for them.

I don't recall getting home, but my ever-patient wife tells me that I flopped into the bedroom a little after three a.m. and spent the rest of the night emitting loud burps that were a winning combination of soju, garlic, and chili sauce.

It took the best part of three days being nursed back to health by Sybil until I began to feel even vaguely human again. Our marriage thankfully survived, although I am not sure I would survive another night out with the Seoul Sausage boys.

North of South of the Border

I n March 2013, the Latino population of California reached the point where it was in the majority for the first time since the state's inception in 1850. This was a demographic watershed moment that caused quite a stir and also provided an interesting signpost to the future of the United States, as it follows a path that may well lead to a point where Hispanics and Latinos form the majority of the overall population.

There will, I am certain, be continued heated debates about the political, economic, and social consequences of such a change. What-ever their politics, no one can deny that Latin Americans, and par-ticularly Mexicans, have played a huge part in the history of California and Los Angeles since the city was founded in 1781 by the first forty-four pobladores.

In 1848, when vast parts of their territory were ceded to the United States after the Mexican war, nearly thirty thousand Mexican settlers became full citizens of the United States, and their descen-dants have continued to contribute to both state and country ever since. This contribution initially came in the form of laboring and farm work; Mexican immigrants were often the recipients of severe exploitation, which prompted the formation of the National Farm Workers Association by Cesar Chavez in 1962. While farming and hard physical graft is still a key area of employment for modern-day

Mexican immigrants, they have also had significant impact in every aspect of American life, from politics to sport and from culture to food. If you ever doubt the contribution of Mexicans to the food scene of the United States, ask any restaurant chef if their business could function without the technically skilled and hardworking Mexican line cooks who staff just about every kitchen in the country.

From a personal and very shallow "I want my dinner" kind of perspective, what this development also means is that the variety and quality of Mexican food on the West Coast of the United States is usually of an exceptionally high level—particularly in Los Angeles, which is home to well over one million people of Mexican heritage.

I have to admit that until I first started to visit the United States for business in the mid-1990s, Mexican food was very, very low down on my list of favorites. This was nothing to do with any failings of the cuisine itself, but more to do with the fact that there was nothing even closely resembling an authentic Mexican restaurant in Britain at the time. (I'd probably argue that the same is true today.) The only inkling I had of what might be involved came from visits to dreadful Tex-Mex restaurants, where the waiters wore studded waistcoats and sombreros and my meals resembled an episode of *Chopped* where the only ingredients in the basket were roadkill.

However, the moment I discovered, to my delight, that Mexican cuisine was not comprised of rice and brown slurry, I began to develop an addiction that saw me add at least one Mexican meal to my dining itinerary on every trip I made to the United States. This addiction was reinforced by an extended stay in Mexico itself during the travels for my book *Eat My Globe*, and was given the final seal of approval when I began to spend more time in Los Angeles visiting Sybil from 2008 onwards.

At least once a week during my visits, we would walk the short distance from her apartment to Venice Boulevard, where a number of Mexican food trucks, or loncheras, would be parked. By the time we arrived, there would already be lines of workers from nearby construction sites waiting for their food and sheltering from the blazing heat of the midday sun under awnings attached to the side of the trucks. Sybil and I would place our order and join the crowd, listening to the jangly music blaring from the speakers inside the trucks, most of which appeared to involve a corazón that was beyond repair.

We would return to the apartment laden down with quesadilla, tacos stuffed with carnitas or barbacoa, burritos filled with rice and beans, small plastic cartons filled with fresh salads of cilantro and onion, fiery dips of red and green chili, and bottles of Mexican Coca-Cola. It was fresh, it was cheap, and it was delicious. And more often than not, it was followed by an afternoon nap as the carb overload took its toll.

These loncheras were the precursors of the modern street food trucks that have created such a buzz throughout the United States in the last few years. Young vendors from every ethnic persuasion have been turning to four wheels rather than bricks and mortar. They can be found everywhere now, but back in 2008 the craze was just getting under way. On those rare occasions when Mexican food wasn't what we wanted at lunchtime, Sybil would use the Internet to find which one of the latest crop of hipster food trucks was going to be nearest to her apartment. A good deal of their appeal seemed to come not from any great quality in what they served but in the fact that being in the know appeared to bestow upon the diner some level of status among their peers. All it bestowed upon me was desire to go back to the original loncheras, who, without the fuss or the attention given to the new wave of food trucks, went about their business of fueling the Mexican engine room of Los Angeles.

In the evening too, we would often head to East or South L.A. in search of one of the Mexican restaurants with big reputations. Not knowing the city, I turned to Los Angeles' blogging community for help. When it came to seeking out the best Latin American food in the area, I found myself constantly returning to the pages of a website called Street Gourmet LA, which provided detailed descriptions of every mom-and-pop place to be found in L.A.'s assorted neighborhoods.

I became intrigued by its creator, a man named Bill Esparza—who, as far as I could tell, was a professional musician of Mexican origin, whose travels for work had taken him around the countries of Latin America and made him (by his own description) an "accidental expert" on their cuisines. Accidental or not, his recommendations were always spot-on, and when I decided that I wanted to find out more about Mexican food in Los Angeles, he was the obvious person to turn to. Bill was only too keen to show off his favorite neighborhoods and invited me to join him for two expeditions. The first to South Central Los Angeles, and the second to the east of downtown Los Angeles in an area known as Boyle Heights.

South Central Los Angeles, now more commonly called South Los Angeles, is a neighborhood whose population has historically been dominated by African Americans but within the last decade has primarily become home to a sizable Latin American community from El Salvador and Mexico. It is probably best known to people outside of Los Angeles for being the center of the bloody 1992 riots prompted by the violent beating of Rodney King by LAPD officers. However, for Bill it was the location of some of the best food in the city.

"I want to show you a side to Mexican food in the city most people don't know about," Bill said after collecting me from my apartment. That particular neighborhood seemed to me an unlikely venue for a great meal. But Bill did not seem perturbed and after about half an hour of driving through the streets of Los Angeles he pointed ahead to what appeared to be an auto repair shop.

The forecourt of the garage was illuminated by four white lights, of the sort you might purchase at Home Depot, dangling loosely from a wire. A folding table had been set up at the edge of the parking lot and was being overseen by two tiny women, who were preparing food for a group of Mexican men surrounding them. Even from a distance, I could see that the customers were devouring tacos, and the glorious smell of charred meat was in the air as we approached.

In the center of the folding table, a large and shallow round cornal de acero, or metal dish, had been set up over the flames of a portable burner. The center of the bowl was raised in a convex dome, giving the effect of an upside-down wok. The trough surrounding the dome was filled with bubbling golden liquid in which assorted chunks of meat were simmering away. One of the women was retrieving meat with a pronged fork, cutting it into smaller pieces, and placing them on the hot dome to fry. Bill gave me the rundown of what was available.

"That's buche," he said as he pointed towards a piece of meat that I recognized as hog maw, or pig stomach. "Then there's lengua [tongue], sesos [brain], suadero [brisket], chorizo, and tripa [tripe]." It was a large enough selection that I had to stop to ponder before making a decision. Bill's expert eye, however, had already told him that the buche and lengua looked particularly promising and he ordered two tacos of each for us to sample. The lengua was taken straight from the bubbling dish and placed on a double layer of small hot tortillas, while the buche was tossed on top of the dome to sizzle until it developed a crisp outer coating, before it too was placed upon warm tortillas and handed to us on thin paper plates.

Next to the cooking area, a table had been set up with large plastic containers filled with traditional accompaniments. Bill led the way as we topped our tacos with cilantro, finely chopped red onion, and diced tomatoes. He layered the tops of the tacos with a deep red chili sauce and then completed his task by sprinkling with a few drops of liquid from quartered limes that had been piled high onto another plate.

I followed suit as he folded a tortilla around its varied contents and raised it carefully to his lips. The first bite reminded me of why Mexican food at its best can be so addictive. My taste buds were immediately sparked to life by the combination of the chili sauce and lime juice, then came the crunch of the onions, the acidity of the tomatoes, and finally, the main event, the crackle of the crisp buche between my teeth. I was wearing a short-sleeved shirt and the juices from the succulent meat began to trickle down my arm as I finished taco number one in a couple of bites. Taco number two was just as good. Bill took advantage of my rare moment of silence to tell me more about how these stands operated.

"These vendors are not strictly legal, but the locals set them up to raise extra income." He wiped up the juices from his plate with the last shred of tortilla and popped it into his mouth. "Occasionally they get closed down by the police or health officials, but then they just move to a different location and set up again a few days later. The lights are the giveaway. Whenever you see them, you always know you can find something good to eat." Although I pondered on the health consequences of playing illegal street food roulette, both tacos were so delicious that I was happy to continue eating. My companion obviously had no such qualms and after we handed over $5 to one of the women for our meal, we set off again in search of more guiding lights.

Over the course of the next couple of hours, we stopped at three more stands. Each time, I put myself in Bill's expert hands, letting him order after he had given close inspection and decided what looked best.

"You can find food at these stands from all over Mexico," he declared as we sampled dishes from a variety of vendors selling everything from Tijuana-style carne asada to Puebla-style cemitas. Bill's knowledge of the cuisine and the people of Mexico was seemingly endless, and he seemed more than happy to share it with a relative newbie to the nuances of Mexican cuisine. The evening became as much a very enjoyable lesson on Mexican regional street food as it did a genuinely terrific eating experience, and I was more than a little disappointed when Bill said it was time to head back to West L.A. Before we ended the night, he wanted to make one more stop. This time it was not at another stand, but at a fully functioning taqueria we had driven past on our arrival in South Los Angeles.

"Tripa de leche," he announced as we pulled up in front of the storefront's small serving window. Tripa de leche is different from other types of tripe, which is taken from a cow's stomach. In this case, it is the intestine of a milk-fed calf that has been cooked in its own juices until it becomes crisp. We were already full by this time, but the thought of crisp tripe tacos was enough to help us both to create a tiny bit of extra space in the belly, and I didn't hesitate when the cook slid a paper plate containing two tacos towards us.

In fact, they were the best taste of the night. The crunch of the fried intestines reminded me of the pork chitterlings I have eaten so often during meals in soul food restaurants and it was only the fact that I was so full that stopped me from ordering another round.

It was the perfect way to end the evening, and I returned home not only with a bursting stomach but also knowing far more about Mexican cuisine and culture in Los Angeles than just a few hours before.

However, Bill wasn't done with my education, and on a Saturday morning a few weeks later my phone buzzed with a text message that simply read, "Carnitas?" My response was an immediate, "Yes please."

Bill followed up with more detailed information and told me to meet him at an address in Boyle Heights early the next morning. At the mention of carnitas, Sybil insisted on joining me, and we met Bill at the agreed time. Climbing from the car, I was uncertain as to why we were outside what appeared to be a private home. Bill appeared in the driveway, explaining, "The owner of the house makes probably the best carnitas in the whole of the United States."

He beckoned us to follow as he turned back towards the house.

There was a small covered alley to the side and Bill introduced us to his friend, Romulo "Momo" Acosta, who was busy preparing what is possibly my favorite Mexican dish of all. Carnitas is a dish that uses the fattier, well-marbled parts of the pig like the shoulder, which are slow braised in their own fat along with herbs like Mexican oregano, spices such as chili and cumin, and often, Bill told me, brown sugar, oranges, and even Coca-Cola. The resulting meat is shredded and then fried or roasted until crisp and served with warm tortillas.

"We have some pretty decent carnitas in Los Angeles," Bill told us as Sybil and I peered across to see what Romulo was doing. "But there is nothing close to this. Romulo is a real artisan." The chunks of pork were bubbling gently in lard in cazos, high-sided copper pots that stood over an open flame. The sight and smell was enough to remind Sybil that she had not yet had breakfast, and Romulo's son, Billy, ushered us into the house and seated us all around a small kitchen table.

"Romulo learned how to make carnitas from his father, who was a butcher in Salamanca," Bill said as he explained the background to Carnitas el Momo. "His family has a food truck, which his daughter runs, but some weekends he likes to invite friends to come and eat at his house." I felt truly honored that Romulo had included me and Sybil in Bill's invitation, even more so when he began to fill our table with food.

We began with a bowl of dark red and heavily spiced broth and a slab of meaty slow-cooked pork ribs, both of which brought disturbing moans of pleasure from my wife and nods of approval from Bill. The next delivery of meat arrived wrapped in foil, letting out a billow of meat and spice-scented steam as it was released from its packaging. The contents were the color of burnished mahogany and lacquered with a slick coating of a viscous sauce that I scooped up with a spoon to layer onto a hot tortilla from a basket Romulo had brought to the table along with the meat.

"He doesn't just use shoulder," Bill informed us as he speared a large piece of meat from the package. "This is a real nose-to-tail production." It was definitely different from any carnitas I had tried before. The pork had been gently pulled apart rather than shredded and had a slightly denser, more firm texture, with a depth of flavor that none of the other carnitas even came close to matching. Sybil obviously agreed—by the time she had fashioned and eaten at least half a dozen tacos, her face and hands were covered with sauce. After cleaning up, she agreed with little persuasion when our hosts suggested that she might want to take home a doggie bag so she could enjoy the remains of the carnitas over the next few days.

Bill told us that we still had one last stop before he was done with my education. We followed him in our car as he led us to the corner of Olympic Boulevard and Central Avenue. After a few goes around the block to find a parking space, we emerged to find ourselves in the middle of a busy market populated almost entirely by Latin Americans. The noises, sights, and smells reminded me of the vast La Merced that I had spent so much time wandering through on my only visit to Mexico City.

Bill caught up with us at the intersection of the two streets and pointed to the skyscrapers of downtown Los Angeles that were barely a mile north of our location. "It's incredible, isn't it?" he asked rhetorically. "That so close to downtown Los Angeles, you are to all intents and purposes in a Mexican City." It was an accurate assessment, as just about every conversation except our own was being conducted in Spanish and along each side of the road were stalls selling compact discs of Mexican music and DVDs of films dubbed in Spanish, and, of course, dozens of food stalls. "They are only here on the weekend," Bill shouted above the din of music from the CD vendors, "mainly selling food from Michoacán, Mexico City, and the Puebla regions."

We walked the length of the market, stopping to watch women press fresh tortillas from blue corn masa, warming cheese-filled quesadillas on hot plates, and pouring glasses of brightly colored aguas frescas for their customers. If we had not just eaten the best part of half a pig between us, I am certain we would have contributed to the economy of the market to great effect. As it was, we decided to limit ourselves to one "snack," and Sybil stopped dead in her tracks when she saw a man piping batter into a bath of hot oil. "I want churros for dessert," she announced. After four years of marriage, I knew enough about her to know the consequences if her craving was not dealt with in a speedy fashion. We waited until the stall holder had dribbled a fresh batch into the oil, and then bought a bag of the piping-hot fried dough, allowing him to sprinkle it with a little cinnamon and sugar while it was still warm.

Bill had to leave us at this point, and Sybil and I spent the next hour wandering around the market while we nibbled on the churros and watched people going about their business. "It's not going to be too many generations before all of Los Angeles is like this," she suggested. Looking around us, I couldn't help but agree.

The process is going to be a painful one, as previous generations of Los Angelenos rail against the change in the status quo, but the figures are proving that the process is inevitable, with all the considerable good and some bad consequences the changes will bring with them.

As for me, if it means I can keep getting Mexican food as terrific as I had eaten on these outings with Bill Esparza, the street gourmet of L.A., then I am all for it.

Farm Fresh

I n 2007, I somehow managed to end up celebrating Thanksgiving in the West Coast retirement community for the stark-raving bonkers that is more commonly known as Santa Cruz. I immediately fell in love with the city and with the people who had been kind enough to invite me, and have made it a point to get back there as often as I can ever since.

On a subsequent initial visit, I was fortunate enough to be introduced to a lady named Cynthia Sandberg, who at that point was running a small-scale farming operation on a plot of land just outside the city. She had already built quite a reputation for herself as an expert on heirloom tomatoes and had named the tiny farm Love Apple, after the nickname the tomato fruits had been given on their introduction to Italy, where they were believed to have aphrodisiacal properties. Her sales of tomato plants were already outstripping the potential of the land she had when we met, so it came as no surprise to me when I found out that she was moving to a much larger property in 2010.

This new farm, which she again named Love Apple, was nearly twenty acres in size and situated on land that had previously been a vineyard owned by the comedy duo the Smothers Brothers. She expanded her tomato-growing operation and added other plants to the crop list, produced honey, and started holding classes in the farm buildings she had restored. Cynthia saw herself as much as a teacher as she did a farmer, and these classes still take place every week, covering a wide variety of subjects both culinary and horticultural.

It was one of these classes she had in mind when she contacted me after hearing about my latest travels. "We'd love to have you come up and teach a culinary class," Cynthia said over the phone, "perhaps cook some Indian food while you talk to people about your adventures?" It definitely sounded fun. I love to talk and I love to cook. But, on this occasion, I wanted more. I really wanted to get involved.

"What if I came up to work?"

There was an extended silence on the other end of the line. I could imagine Cynthia's brain whirring as she imagined the havoc a chubby middle-aged Brit might wreak on her beloved plants if he was left unattended for even one moment.

"Well," she replied hesitantly, "you could come and spend some time with the apprentices to show you what working at Love Apple is really like," adding, "We could even find space for you in the bunkhouse."

The first part was exactly what I wanted to hear. The chance to spend some time learning at the feet of one of the most respected names in the new wave of organic and biodynamic farming in America was simply too good to pass up. The second part was a little more challenging, as it meant that I would have to spend the week in close proximity to a group of young people.

Let's take a break here while I let you in on a not terribly well-kept secret. However much I might like to pretend that the stern person you see judging on the Food Network is just a screen image, the truth is that I really am a very grumpy man indeed. Lots of things make me cross. I hate bad meals and bad service; I get quite miffed when people talk in cinemas or push past me when I am in line; I dislike babies on planes, babies in restaurants (in fact babies about most anywhere); and I get terribly upset when people to whom I am paying good money in return for a service (dry cleaning, car repairs, etc.)

don't live up to their end of the contract. I have to admit that I also often find young people incredibly annoying, which is in truth probably as much down to my envy of their youthful energy as it is because of anything they might have actually ever done to me.

I try and regulate this unseemly attitude by keeping away from them as much as possible. But I knew that if I wanted to have the full-on experience at Love Apple Farms, I just needed to get on with it and get the hell over myself. I had no idea that the men and women I would meet during my week at the farm would change the way I think about young people for the rest of my life.

The drive to Love Apple from Los Angeles took about five hours, and I arrived just as the sun was beginning to drop over the horizon, shedding a muted golden glow over the terraces of raised beds that dropped away from the farm buildings towards a tree-lined valley. I had visited the farm a few times before, but had forgotten quite how beautiful it was, and I lost myself in silence for a few minutes to take in the view before darkness fell.

I was disturbed from my reverie by a loud bark and a thudding against my legs as one of Cynthia's dogs came out to check on the stranger standing in front of the farm buildings. Cynthia was not far behind him. "You made it!" she said, giving me a hug. Then she turned towards the farm. "It's beautiful, isn't it? I never get tired of looking at it."

Cynthia Sandberg's story is a similar one to my own. Just as I had given up my job in publishing to follow my desire to "go everywhere, eat everything," so too had Cynthia given up a successful and lucrative career as a trial attorney to follow her passion for farming. Like my own journey, the path had not always been an easy one for her and there had been setbacks along the way, but by sheer hard work and learning as she went, she had grown Love Apple Farms from the small plot she had owned when I first met her to the impressive sight we were both enjoying as the sun set.

"I've invited the apprentices to come and join us for dinner," Cynthia said, "but first I should show you where you are sleeping." I retrieved my suitcase from the trunk of my car and followed her down a shallow slope away from the main farm towards a small one-story building. Inside, there were three cubicles partitioned by dry-wall, each separated from a small communal area by a curtain. Each cubicle contained a bed, a few shelves, and some space to hang clothes. The first two were filled with the personal belongings of the two male apprentices, the third was empty. "That's your home for the next week." Cynthia smiled at the thought of me bunking down in a space the size of a walk-in closet. "Get yourself settled and then come on back up for supper." By the time I had unpacked and made my way to the farmhouse, the rest of the farm's company was already present. Along with Cynthia, there was her garden manager, Stephan, and the apprentices, Claire, Quinn, Adam, and Brenden.

"The apprentices are with us for six months," Stephan explained as we talked over dinner. "The work is hard and we expect a lot from them, but they learn a lot in return." This was not news to me, as before I had arrived I had scanned the slightly stern-sounding requirements on the apprentice application page on the farm's website, where it proclaimed that:

> Love Apple Farms welcomes positive, teachable, non-complaining, situationally aware, get-it-done, take responsibility, clean cut, grateful, drug free, smoke free and hard-working apprentices to the farm.

At the time of reading this, I had thought that since I didn't smoke or take drugs, I could probably fake the rest of it for a week. However, as I was faced with the genuine and earnest enthusiasm of Stephan and the four young apprentices I was already beginning to think that maybe this had not been such a good idea after all. This was compounded when, just as I was considering a third glass of wine, Stephan suddenly announced, "It's time for me to hit the hay, we all have to be up at six a.m. tomorrow for harvest." The others all nodded in agreement and began clearing up the dinner plates in preparation for an early night.

All this was slightly distressing, as not only do I always find that the third glass of wine of the evening is the best one, but when I glanced at my watch I noticed that it was barely past nine-thirty p.m. It seemed far too early to go to sleep, but as everyone else was already halfway out the door by this point, I trudged back to my little cubicle and stared at the ceiling for a while until I finally drifted off far earlier than any grown man has a right to.

I was awake before dawn the next morning. I could hear Adam and Brenden still breathing gently as they slept in the other cubicles, and hoped that they had not been too disturbed by the snoring and unsavory emissions that had been emanating from my part of the bunkhouse during the night. I showered and dressed and went out to explore the farm before the harvest took place. If I had thought it was beautiful by sunset, Love Apple Farms was even more glorious in the early hours, as the sun rose and the fields were washed by the watery morning light. There was no sound but birdsong in the skies, and as I sipped on the strong cup of tea I had made for myself and took in the clean air and the views, I found it hard to recall many places more beautiful that I had seen on the trip so far.

By the time I had drained the last drops of tea from my mug, the others had awoken from their slumbers and had begun to congregate in one of the farm's greenhouses, all looking a little disheveled from the rapid pace at which they had dressed, and yawning as they wiped the sleep from their eyes. Stephan appeared with a list in his hands and placed it on one of the garden benches. Without discussion, everyone picked up their gardening shears, looked at the list, and rushed off in various directions to begin the harvest, leaving me and Stephan standing alone in the greenhouse.

Stephan handed me a brand-new pair of shears. "The most important tool you can have in the garden," he said, adding, "Come on, you can shadow me this morning." He turned around and began walking at a brisk clip towards a raised bed at the far end of the gardens.

In 2008, Cynthia had formed a long and mutually important relationship with West Coast chef David Kinch. He had been looking to find a kitchen garden to supply Manresa, his famous restaurant in Los Gatos, and had seized the opportunity of working with Cynthia to make Love Apple Farms his exclusive supplier. The relationship had worked well and had now grown to the point that every other day the farm would receive a list from the restaurant detailing what produce they needed to be harvested and delivered.

"There are over a hundred lines on the list. That's why we have to start the harvest so early," Stephan told me as he knelt down to cut dainty little patty pan squash from the bed. "It works both ways. They tell us what they want, but we also let them know what's coming to the end of its time and what is going to be growing soon, so they can plan their menus."

I wasn't there to simply watch and listen, however, and Stephan and the other apprentices soon had me hard at work as we made our way around the terraces collecting the very best specimens from each bed, carefully washing them, wrapping them for storage, and marking down on the list that they had been harvested. It was six hours of intense physical work and my back soon began to make alarming cracking noises as I bent over to pluck vegetables from their stalks. It was also, mentally, far harder than I had ever imagined, as David Kinch would not accept anything but the very best ingredients for his plates and Cynthia would let nothing leave the farm that did not match the quality she demanded. Each vegetable had to be chosen at its peak, ready for eating in the next two days, and then snipped with utmost care so as not to damage either the vegetable or the plant. If a vegetable did not come up to scratch, Stephan would reject it and these vegetables would be placed in a pile to one side in the greenhouse for the apprentices to cook during mealtimes. It was as hard a half day's work as I had done in years, and by the time the sun had reached the top of the sky, I was covered in dirt, wringing wet with sweat, and covered with enough nicks and cuts to make a social worker think I had discovered self-harm.

Despite my obvious lack of gardening chops and snaillike pace of working, Stephan and the apprentices could not have been more welcoming and supportive as they guided me around the farm and passed on the information they had picked up during their time working there. "We are coming to the end of our stay here," Adam told me as we plucked green beans from their stems. "I am really going to miss this place." I could understand what he meant. Despite the fact that it had been such backbreaking work, I had really begun to enjoy both the physical effort and the companionship of the young people I was spending time with, neither of which were things I had expected when I first agreed to visit Love Apple Farms.

Once Stephan had checked through all of the harvest to make sure that it was up to scratch, it was packed away carefully into coolers and loaded onto one of the farm's trucks for the short drive to Los Gatos. While he took care of the delivery, the four apprentices invited me to join them for lunch in the apprentice kitchen. It was a simple meal, consisting mostly of ingredients that had come from the farm— eggs from the chickens that milled around in a pen by the entrance, vegetables that had been harvested but deemed not restaurant-worthy by Stephan, and thick slices of excellent toasted rye bread and butter from the local farmers' market. Despite its simplicity, the meal was one of the most enjoyable I had experienced on my travels so far, in part because of the quality of the ingredients and the hole it filled after all the efforts of the morning, but mainly because of the hospitality of the remarkable people who prepared it for me and the conversations we shared while eating it. After less than twenty-four hours in their company, my ill-thought-out prejudices against young people were being chiseled away by their generosity of spirit.

By the end of that first day, my body had stiffened from all the activity. I could suddenly see why nine-thirty p.m. was the bedtime of choice for people on the farm and I was in my bunk and asleep before anyone else had even made the suggestion that it might be time to retire.

Love Apple Farms is run on the biodynamic principle of farming, which has its roots, if you will, in Dr. Rudolph Steiner's philosophy of "anthroposophy." It is quite a complex philosophy that looks at how plants can be grown and the land can be replenished (or even healed) using its own natural resources. It is more spiritually based than just farming on an organic level and really impacts those who follow its practices as much as it does the land they work on.

Cynthia and her team were keen to show me how this philosophy informed everything they did at the farm, and how it was put to practical use in growing what they needed for the restaurant. "There is no better way of finding out than actually doing it," she told me, and over the next few days she had me help her staff with all the daily tasks around the farm. I learned how to sift worm casings that would be used to fertilize the soil, and how to "amend" the raised beds after one crop had been harvested and before another one was planted in its place. I learned how to sow seeds and seedlings into the amended beds, and I learned the natural methods that the farm used to protect those growing plants from bugs. I fed goats and chickens, and even learned about beekeeping while tending the hives that were dotted around the farm.

Most of all, I learned that farming is an unforgiving and nonstop business. Cynthia and Stephan would tour the farm at the end of each day, making a list of what jobs needed doing, and from the moment the apprentices began their work in the early morning they would be kept busy, with barely a chance to take in the breathtaking surroundings in which they were working. And yet, I noticed, they worked not only without complaint but also with genuine enthusiasm, recognizing that the few months they spent as apprentices at Love Apple Farms would give them an opportunity to learn that was available to very few others.

Their enthusiasm and energy were infectious, and after only a couple of days I began to feel less like a visitor and more like one of the team as I naturally fell into the rhythm of the farm. I even began to enjoy the hard physical activity, which was so far removed from my life behind a keyboard or a judging table on television. I spent my evenings with the four apprentices, joining them for jaunts to nearby Santa Cruz and sharing more simple yet delicious meals in the farmhouse with Cynthia. I felt refreshed and rejuvenated, and I was already regretting the fact that I would have to leave so soon to get back on the road. I knew I had plenty of great adventures ahead, but my time at Love Apple had provided a welcome retreat from early-morning flights, budget accommodations, and tiredness cause by constant traveling.

It had also made me appreciate, all the more, just what goes into getting the food we eat to our table. It is very easy, when we are selecting food at the supermarket, to forget just how much bloody hard work farming really is, but my time spent talking with Cynthia about the legacy she was hoping to build with her apprentice program, as well as working with the apprentices themselves, made certain that I would never look at a plate of vegetables in quite the same way again.

Before I left, the apprentices had one more surprise for me. On my first day, I had asked Cynthia if I might be allowed to take some of her prized vegetables back to Los Angeles so I could cook with them at home. She had generously agreed, and had tasked the apprentices with collecting a selection for me. By the end of the week I had totally forgotten all about my request and on my final night had retired particularly early, as I had to be on the road before dawn the next morning.

When I awoke, I left the bunkhouse, my unlikely home of the last several days, and walked out to where my car was parked. Placed by the trunk of the car were bags and trays filled with enough squash, beans, eggplants, onions, garlic, and herbs to start my own farmers' market. Attached to the trays was a handwritten note from Brenden, which read:

> *Simon, we all had such a great time putting all of this together for you and working with you. Stay in touch and come back and see us soon.*

I am not a desperately emotional man, but this last act of kindness touched me more than I would have believed possible a week earlier, and I drove back to Los Angeles knowing that my stay at Love Apple had an impact on me that would last a very long time.

I won't lie to you. I am still a very grumpy man. I still hate bad meals and bad service, I still get furious when people talk in cinemas or push past me when I am in line, and I am still not terribly keen on babies. But, thanks to the apprentices at Love Apple Farms, I am a now a great deal more fond of young people.

Er, sometimes.

Fed, White, and Brew

I f, for some unlikely reason, the Jim Henson Company ever needed to produce a Muppet version of ex–Doobie Brother Michael Mc-Donald, I'll be sure to send them a photograph of Skip Madsen, the master brewer at the American Brewing Company in Edmonds, Washington, to use as a model.

In case any of you doubt my respect for the man, while Skip Madsen may indeed be the spitting image of the crooner of "Sweet Freedom," he also happens to brew some of the finest beer I have ever tasted on my travels around the United States.

Given the huge importance beer plays in the American way of life, it would have been ridiculous for me not to dedicate at least one chapter to visiting one in the new wave of craft breweries that are springing up all over the country. Looking at the American Brewing Company, it was clear that they are very serious about what they're doing, and the name seemed just perfect for a journey about American citizenship.

A mutual friend put me in touch with the owner of the company, Neil Fallon, a businessman who had originally been looking to invest in a distillery but instead had been attracted by the growth figures he saw in the beer trade. As he discovered, beer sales in general may have been declining over the last half a decade as more people moved towards drinking wines and spirits, but sales of craft beer went through the roof during the same time. Representing 7 percent of the total beer market (a total value of nearly $4.5 billion), craft beer gave plenty of incentive for an entrepreneur like Neil to see this as the perfect investment opportunity.

"It's not just about the money," Neil reassured me during our first telephone conversation, "I also wanted to be certain that the beer we made was going to be fantastic." To that end he approached Skip Madsen, a brewer with a legendary reputation in Washington State, and had persuaded him to join his quest to create the perfect portfolio of beer for the new company. He had chosen well. In the nearly two years since the American Brewing Company had been open, Skip had added two more coveted medals from the Great American Beer Festival to the already impressive collection he had amassed during his career, and had created a range of beers that attracted a large and passionately loyal local following.

My original intention had simply been to visit the brewery for an afternoon, maybe get a personal tour of their production facility from Skip, and then sample some of their beers. Neil, however, likes to think on a much grander scale and dismissed this suggestion out of hand.

"You should come and brew a beer with us," he insisted. "If it turns out well, we can enter it in the Great American Beer Festival for 2013 and then you can join us in Denver to see if we can win another medal." No fool, I accepted without hesitation, promising to liaise with Skip between our brief phone conversation and my visit so we could decide exactly what type of beer we were going to make.

Over the next couple of months, Skip and I swapped e-mails, debating what would be the more suitable brew. In the end, after a bit of good-natured haggling, we agreed that we would make an ESB, or extra special bitter, similar to that made by Fuller's, one of my favorite breweries back in London. Skip was even kind enough to agree to my suggestion that we call the finished product Fed, White, and Brew in honor of the book you are holding.

Edmonds is situated about eleven miles north of Seattle, and after completing the short drive from the airport I was delighted to find that the hotel I had booked was actually only a few hundred yards from the brewery. I was not due to begin working with Skip and his brewery manager, Dan, until the next day, but by the time I arrived, it was just past noon. I decided that my early start from Los Angeles had at the very least earned me the right to a quick pint, and so I wandered over to the brewery's tasting room.

The room was empty except for a man who was fiddling around with beer taps behind the bar. As the door closed behind me with a crack, he turned and faced me, giving me a vast beaming grin that I was soon to find out was one of his trademarks.

"You must be Simon," he said in an elongated drawl.

He was wearing blue jeans and a black T-shirt, and his head and face were each covered with a large shock of silvery white hair. I did not actually know what Skip Madsen looked like, but this man in front of me looked more like a brewer than any man I had ever met and I was prepared to hazard a guess.

"Skip?" I asked.

"You got it," he replied, and as he did so he reached for a pint glass and began filling it with an amber liquid. He placed it on the bar in front of him with the words, "Do you want a beer?" If the counter had not been between us, I would have—at the very least—given him a bear hug. Instead, I pulled up a wooden stool at the bar and took a long refreshing glug of the cold beer he had offered me.

It was the brewery's signature Breakaway IPA and, despite reservations I have about this style of beer, I found it to be clean and crisp, with a slightly citrus finish that made it more palatable than the overly hoppy IPAs that often seem to be the norm. I drained the glass in four short gulps, and before I had even had a chance to say, "I rather liked that," Skip had filled another clean pint glass and plopped it on the table.

As I was to find out, Skip Madsen is not one who is ever shy coming forward with offers of beer, and before I finally staggered out of the tasting room some five hours later, I had been taken on several tours of the brewery's entire range. While drinking all that beer made my head spin like a carousel, it also convinced me that I had made a very wise choice in my selection of which brewery to visit.

"I don't like beers to be messed around with," Skip explained as he poured my fifth (or was it my sixth?) pint. "I'm a great believer in the purity of beer and don't like to mess it up by adding stuff just for the sake of it."

It was a philosophy that is very close to my own views on cooking. I am often far more impressed by a chef who excels at making good examples of the classics than by a chef who tries to bludgeon my taste buds with his or her endless creativity.

The brewery had a small range of beers, but all of them were marked by Skip's adherence to the purity of his recipes. This insistence gave each of the beers, despite their very different styles, a remarkably clean taste on the palate, which, he added, "is exactly what I was looking for."

As we drank, Skip filled me in on his personal history, which had seen him travel from being an enthusiastic home brewer in Missoula, Montana, to becoming one of the most respected brewers in the Northwest. I was really looking forward to working with him the next day but realized that his capacity for beer far outstripped my own and that I had better get out while the going was good.

After one final pint of a particularly delicious oatmeal stout, I made my excuses, agreeing that I would meet him early the next morning to begin making the Fed, White, and Brew. I wobbled a little as I stood up from the stool, but steadied myself on the bar and began waddling slowly and purposefully towards the door.

I was awakened early the next morning by the rattling of my

hotel window in a strong wind. Rather remarkably, I felt far more chipper than I had any right to, which speaks more to the effect of drinking very well-made and pure beer than to any sort of iron-man constitution that I might have developed over the years.

Even if I did not have the hangover that I so thoroughly deserved, I did notice that I had managed to oversleep by nearly an hour. I threw on some clothes and hurried over to the brewery to find Skip and his brewery manager, Dan, already hard at work preparing for a day on the beer-bottling line.

After reassuring Skip that he had not done permanent damage to me with his beer-fueled generosity of the previous day, we made our way to the brewery's grain store. To start brewing the beer we had discussed so much and for so long was even more special than I had anticipated, and I felt a genuine thrill as Skip beckoned me to join him in the brewery's grain storage room.

ESB is a peculiarly British style of ale and, although it is produced by a number of breweries in the United States, it is still relatively unknown here. Not to Skip, however, who had already scribbled out the detailed recipe for Fed, White, and Brew onto a large white message board in the brewing room and was overseeing the pouring of the required malted barley down a large grain chute.

People are often surprised to find out that, despite the many styles of beer available, the brews are all basically made using the same method, and have been for most of the nearly seven thousand years that man has been known to produce the world's most popular alcoholic beverage. They also use, with a few variations, the same four ingredients of cereal grains (most commonly barley, but sometimes rye or oats), hops, yeast, and water.

The first part of the process is called mashing. Barley that has been malted (partially germinated to help release its starches) is placed in a large pot, or mash tun, with hot water for about an hour. This releases the sugars (which will be fermented into alcohol) from the barley and also adds that familiar slightly sweet malty taste to the final brew.

After an hour, the water is drained from the mash tun and the grains go through a process known as sparging—a word that comes from an early French word meaning "to scatter." More hot water is passed over the grains to make sure that every last bit of sugar is removed, and then the grains are discarded and the liquid, which is now known as wort, is removed to a clean tank called a boil kettle.

The wort is boiled to make sure that any microorganisms left are killed off, and then hops are added to the proto-beer. The use of hops in beer-making dates back to medieval Germany and, as they were then, they are used to add body, aroma, and flavor to the final brew. The stage at which they are added to the boiling wort determines what their contribution will be. It's here where you can see the real skill of the master brewer in action. Add the hops at the beginning or middle of the boil and it will increase the body of the beer. Add it towards the end and its impact will be on the flavor and aroma.

After about an hour, the wort is cooled down rapidly so that any yeast added once the liquid has been transferred to a sterile fermentation tank will not be killed off by the residual heat. The yeast will eat the sugars that have been released and turn them into alcohol.

Fermentation takes at least two weeks, at which point the beer would be ready to be carbonated and then put into kegs or bottles. That was frustrating, of course, as having been involved both in the creation and the process of making this new beer, I was eager to try it. But good beer can't be hurried, and as a consolation I accepted Skip's offer to come and sample some of the other beers that were nearing completion in the fermenting tanks.

He decanted small amounts of beer from each tank into a glass and, after giving them a good sniff, he took a small sip and rolled it around on his tongue. "This one needs a few more days," he declared about one beer, "but this one is ready to be bottled," he said of another. It was here where I really began to see why Skip is held in such high regard by his peers in the industry. Both beers tasted pretty much the same to me, but his trained palate was able to pick up the minute difference that would separate a good beer from one that met his high standards.

Determined to get the most out of my visit, I spent the rest of the time helping the team with their brewery chores. The day rapidly became one of my favorites of the whole trip so far, not least because every time I stood still for more than about thirty seconds, Skip insisted on placing a full pint glass in my hands.

In the months that followed, I kept in regular contact with Neil and Skip, who told me that they had begun selling the Fed, White, and Brew in the tasting room a few weeks after I had visited and that it had been an instant hit. It sold out almost immediately, so they would be brewing a new batch just for the Great American Beer Festival.

The Great American Beer Festival was founded in 1982 by a former nuclear engineer named Charlie Papazian. The first event attracted just twenty-two breweries. Since then, the annual event in Denver, Colorado, has grown into the largest celebration of beer in the United States and, in 2013, 624 breweries participated, serving more than—wait for it—forty-eight thousand gallons of beer to nearly fifty thousand people. Demand was so high that tickets for the event sold out in less than twenty minutes, so I was delighted when Neil told me that he had sorted me out with a brewer's pass, which not only got me into the event for each of the sessions but also meant that I could step behind the counters to serve willing customers and gauge their reaction to my brew.

On opening night, once customers had shown their identification to prove that they were of legal drinking age, they were given a wristband and a small plastic beaker. They were then free to roam around the hall sampling one-ounce pours of any of the thirty-one hundred beers that were on offer. Not that anyone would be foolish enough to try it (I think), but to put that into perspective, if you were to try all of the beers available, it would be the equivalent of drinking 194 pints.

The hall was split into sections representing different areas of the country, and before I went to take up my position behind the American Brewing Company station, I took the opportunity to wander around the hall and sample some beer before it became too crowded. The scale of the event was impressive, even for someone who has attended the equally huge and fun Great British Beer Festival, and the sheer number of breweries on show reflected the growth that this sector of the beverage industry is currently experiencing. In fact, as more than one person told me during the evening, in 2013, new breweries were opening at a rate equivalent to two a day. It was a staggering number and was probably not sustainable in the long run, but it did prove just how fashionable craft beer and brewing has become.

Before I stepped behind the counter, I wanted to try the Fed, White, and Brew I had created with Skip a few months earlier. I was delighted with the first sip of our beer. Its malty sweetness and a slight citrus note from the hops added towards the end of the process transported me immediately back to many happy nights spent in London pubs. Skip, who was already at work, seemed pleased, and the people who sampled our beers seemed to back up my own response, with many of them standing in line more than once to get a refill on their pours.

The approval of the public would have been good enough for me, but I knew that both Neil and Skip were hoping to see the brewery collect another medal for at least one of the seven beers they had entered in the official festival competition. For Neil, it would give a terrific commercial boost to the brewery at a time when he was planning to expand. For Skip, it would be yet more evidence that he was one of the most highly respected brewers in the country, a fact that had already been supported as innumerable people from the beer industry stopped at our table to say hello and shake his hand.

On the last morning of the festival, I found my friends among a large crowd outside of the Denver Convention Center. There was an expectant buzz about the place as every brewer and their colleagues milled around, waiting to claim the best vantage point for the final award ceremony. Once the doors were opened, we fought our way into the hall and staked out enough seats for all of us.

The room was lined with tables from sponsoring breweries, each of which was offering their beers for the attendees of the ceremony to sample. Despite the fact that it was not yet ten a.m., it would have been rude to turn down their kindness, so Skip and I worked our way around the room until an announcement that things were about to begin sent us waddling light-headedly back to our seats.

The combination of the beer, the heat of the room, and the fact that it was incredibly, incredibly boring to watch as the bronze, silver, and gold medal winners in eighty-four categories were announced meant that I drifted off more than once. I was woken with a rib dig from Skip. "The ESB category is coming up soon," he whispered, adding with some degree of dejection that none of their other beers had been successful in gaining a coveted medal.

It was all down to "my" beer to save the day, and so I sat up straight in my chair.

"And the bronze medal goes to," the presenter announced, "Fed, White, and Brew from the American Brewing Company!" Our little corner of the room erupted with the sort of noise that only slightly drunk and very happy people can make. I am not going to deny it, I even indulged in a high five or two with my fellow winners. Winning anything at all was truly an achievement, and to do it with a beer that I had helped create was astonishing. Skip and Neil were jubilant and insisted that everyone in our party join them up on the stage as they received the medal.

Once the ceremony had finished, we emerged from the hall into the bright sunlight that flooded the convention center. It was almost time for me to say good-bye and head back to my accommodations to pack for my next flight

I was very sad to leave my new friends, particularly at this moment of celebration, but I was thrilled when Neil generously offered to have a replica made of our award for me to hang on my wall at home.

Before writing this chapter, I checked various beer review websites to see what the reaction has been from those who have sampled Fed, White, and Brew. The response has been almost universally positive, which is a testament to the brewing skills of Skip Madsen. However, one of them does describe the beer as "dark and slightly bitter," which definitely proves, in case anyone doubted it, that I had a hand in the process.

Bear, Where? There.

My love of traveling in the United States meant that, long before the Fed, White, and Blue adventure was even a twinkle in my eye, I had already visited every state in the country bar just two, Delaware and Alaska.

To clarify, for me to tick a state off my list I have to have stayed at least one night within its borders and, because just about everything in my life is governed by food, I have to have had at least one meal there. While visiting Delaware was at best a "well, I guess I ought to since I am on the road" kind of decision, a trip to Alaska was one of the first things I scribbled on my Fed, White, and Blue wish list.

I have been fascinated with this second-to-last addition to the United States ever since I was asked to write an essay about it at the age of eleven. Alaska not being a regular subject for discussion among grubby little boys in a small steel and mining town in northern England, I was not entirely sure where it was. Consequently, I recall a very happy Saturday afternoon paging through large atlases and encyclopedias at my local library, as I gleaned facts that have stayed with me to this day.

For example, I can tell you that the state sport of Alaska is dog mushing and that it also has a state fossil (which, just in case you can't live without knowing, is the woolly mammoth). I also learned that the landmass of Alaska is equivalent to about a fifth of the continental

United States, or what the residents of Alaska call "the Lower 48," and that it was purchased from Russia in 1867 for a little over $7 million, or approximately 2 cents an acre, by a chap called Seward who endured quite a bit of undeserved ridicule for his decision.

I also learned a lot about the people. At the time of its purchase, Alaskan residents numbered only about thirty thousand and were primarily from the native Eskimo, Indian, and Aleut tribes. The number doubled towards the end of the nineteenth century when gold was discovered in Alaska, and has continued to grow to the present day, now numbering a "massive" seven hundred fifty thousand. To put it in context, that is about the same as the population of Sheffield, the nearest big city to where I grew up in England, in an area about seven times the size of the entire United Kingdom.

At the time, the sheer scale of Alaska fascinated me. It still does, but its allure has been added to by the fact that just about everybody I know who has ever made the trip has told me that it is the most unbelievably beautiful state they have ever visited and indeed, if they are more well-traveled, is one of the most beautiful places on earth.

I was already deep into organizing my own plans to visit Alaska when an e-mail message arrived from Dr. Terry Simpson, a research scientist and weight loss surgeon from Phoenix, Arizona. We had been barbing amiably for the last few months since we started following each other on Twitter, and I had watched with amusement as Terry used his considerable scientific knowledge to debunk the culinary myths posted by other users. Despite having to deal with people whose lives are in danger because of morbid obesity, Terry does not see food as the enemy like so many of his peers. Instead, he advocates developing a new relationship with food for his patients by teaching them how to cook and make smart choices in the grocery store and in the kitchen.

When Terry saw on Twitter that a visit to Alaska was on my itinerary, he immediately got in touch to suggest I join him and his wife,

April, on one of the visits they had planned during silver salmon fishing season towards the tail end of August. It sounded a great deal more exciting than my own tentative plans, and so I accepted immediately and blocked off the days in my calendar.

Excited though I was to be finally visiting a state with which I had been fascinated since I was a child, I was slightly less excited with Terry's confirmation that we would probably encounter quite a lot of grizzly bears during our visit. He seemed particularly gleeful when he informed me during our first phone conversation, "If we see bears when we are fishing, I don't need to outrun them, I just need to outrun you." Being a city boy, I was not entirely sure just how serious he was.

He kept this interesting form of encouragement up with a constant flow of e-mails every few days and by the time we finally met at Long Beach Airport for our flight to Anchorage, I was just as terrified at being mauled by a vicious eight-hundred-pound grizzly bear as I was excited at the thought of eating salmon that I had caught and cooked myself.

Terry looks like a slightly squished version of Kenny Rogers, which made it all the more implausible when he told me that, as well as containing strong strains of Nordic and Welsh blood in his veins, he is also a quarter Athabascan Indian. He sits on the board of the Southcentral Foundation, a tribal organization that offers medical care to Alaskan natives, and it was this foundation that would be our hosts. As well as staying in their accommodation in Anchorage, our fishing adventure would take place at a lodge owned by the tribe at Cook Inlet. It was inaccessible by land and could be reached only by a short plane ride.

We arrived in Anchorage late in the evening. As we emerged from the airport, Terry looked up at the darkening sky, which was already beginning to drop its rainy contents onto the ground. "This could be a problem," he said. "If this weather doesn't clear up, the plane won't be able to land onto the beach by the lodge and we'll be stuck in Anchorage for the next few days."

I had nothing against Anchorage, but I had come to Alaska to catch salmon and doubted that this city, with a population of less than two hundred fifty thousand, could offer a comparable experience to fishing in the wilderness. I went to sleep with the sound of heavy rain rattling against the windows of my guest room, hoping that the morning might bring clearer weather and better news.

Unfortunately, I woke to the same sound track to which I had fallen asleep. I came downstairs to find that Terry and April had been joined by another member of the foundation, Leanndra Ross, and her husband, Jon, who would be our fishing guide if and when we made it out to Cook Inlet. While they were not able to offer any more optimistic news about our chances of reaching the lodge, they at least softened the blow with the promise of a great Alaskan breakfast.

Jon had set up an electric griddle on the kitchen counter and was ladling batter to make sourdough pancakes, using a starter that he told me was over a hundred years old. Leanndra was cutting chunks of cold butter into a large cast-iron skillet in which she was planning to fry slices of reindeer sausage and deep red fillets of fresh Alaskan salmon. She had also opened a small mason jar and was decanting its contents onto a plate. "This is some of my homemade smoked salmon," she said when I walked over to the counter to take a look. "Everybody smokes their own salmon here," she added, making sure to dribble some of the red oil from the jar over the fish.

It was not like any smoked salmon I had ever tasted before, and I enjoyed it a great deal. The flesh was slightly chewy, almost like jerky, and the taste was deeply smoky and savory. I made a mental note to buy a few jars for me and Sybil before I left Alaska. Terry was also doing his part and had popped the cork from a bottle of champagne, adding its fizzy contents to glass flutes into which he had already poured fresh orange juice.

There are few moods that can't be improved by a good breakfast, and after I had worked my way through three dinner-plate-sized pancakes, two large salmon fillets, several slices of sausage, scrambled eggs, and the best part of half a bottle of champagne, I resigned myself to the fact that we might be stuck in Anchorage for another day.

Just as we began to clear our breakfast plates, Katherine and Kevin Gottlieb arrived at the house. They were the top two executives at the Southcentral Foundation and the ones whose generosity had made it possible for me to visit Alaska in the first place. From the look on Katherine's face, I could tell that the news about the weather was not going to be good. "Today is out," she announced. It was frustrating news for everyone, but it did at least mean that I would have the chance to find out more about Anchorage.

Forty percent of the population of Alaska lives in Anchorage, and yet I couldn't help but think it still seemed like a very small town as my friends gave me the tour. Despite that, I found myself taking rather a liking to it, sensing a very appealing frontier-town energy and a strong sense of pride for the history of Alaskan native culture among its people. I paid a visit to the hugely impressive Alaska Native Heritage Center, where I learned about the struggles Eskimo and native tribes have faced over the last century and a half, and how they have fought to reclaim their languages and their land in the last few decades. It may not have been quite how I had planned to spend my first day in Alaska, but as I fell asleep again that evening, it definitely did not feel like a day that had been wasted.

The weather did not seem a great deal better the next morning. However, Katherine and Kevin arrived at the house bearing new, more promising dispatches, and we soon all rushed to the overnight cases we had prepared in advance and headed straight to the airport.

The plane would only have a brief window of time to land on the beach in front of the lodge while the tide was out, so there was no time to lose. As soon as we arrived at the small local airport, we were all bundled aboard an aircraft just big enough to seat the seven of us and took off immediately for the one-hour flight to Cook Inlet. For the first twenty minutes or so of the flight, the pilot had to fly blind through the clouds, but we soon emerged into clear skies. It was then that the whole of Alaska's majestic landscape began to be unveiled below me and I realized that, finally, I truly was in the biggest state of the Union.

Terry smiled as he saw me gaping out the small window of the plane. "I've seen it so many times," he shouted over the rattling of the propeller, "but I never, ever get tired of it." As I marveled at the lush green vegetation of the land, set against the snowcapped mountains and the flinty blue seas, it was very easy to understand why. I nodded and continued staring out the window at some of the most beautiful scenery I had ever seen, until the pilot began our descent, pointing the nose of the plane sharply down towards the beach.

We made a surprisingly smooth landing, the plane pulling to a stop directly in front of the entrance to the lodge. It had been recently refurbished, Terry told me as we climbed down onto the sand, and a line of smart A-frame guesthouses had been erected around the edge of the camp. Jon Ross led me towards the one that would be my base for the night and handed me a flashlight. If Terry had just been joking with all his talk of grizzly bears, Jon's advice was deadly earnest. "Bears often come into the camp at night in search of food, so if you need to use the bathroom block, wave the flashlight and shout, "No bear, no bear!" in a loud voice. It usually scares them away." After we spent the afternoon digging for clams and preparing an early supper, I retired to my little A-frame, making a very definite note to myself to sleep with my legs firmly crossed.

We were all awake at daybreak the next morning, and after breakfast I rushed to join the rest of the group, who had gathered in the lodge's equipment room. There, Katherine was handing out fishing rods and instructing everyone to pull on fetching groin-high brown rubber boots that would protect us if we wanted to wade into deeper currents. "We only have one day now," she insisted. "We have to make the most of it." I joined the others as we paraded out to the beach, stopping only to catch a brief glimpse of myself in a full-length mirror, looking like a reject from a low-budget S&M movie.

Outside, Katherine pointed towards a row of all-terrain quad bikes that we would use to transport ourselves to the fishing spot she had chosen, where a small river leaked into the ocean.

We chugged along the beach, Katherine leading the way. While the others raced ahead, eager to begin fishing, I drove my quad at a leisurely pace, taking the time to let the fact that I was finally in Alaska sink in. I met up with everyone just as they were parking their quads on the edge of a clearing. We grasped our fishing rods and started to walk towards the prime fishing spots along a path cleared by previous fishermen.

Suddenly Katherine stopped and let out a loud stage whisper. "BEAR."

"WHERE?" I replied, not seeing anything but the rustling of the grass.

"THERE," Katherine whispered again, pointing towards a clearing in the bushes from where a six-hundred-pound grizzly had emerged and was wandering amiably along towards the riverbank, oblivious to the fact that it was causing any concern.

Had it not been for the fact that the bear was no more than fifteen feet away from me, I might have smiled at the fact that Katherine and I had just reenacted an Abbott and Costello routine from the early 1940s. Instead, I stayed rooted to the spot and prayed that I would not have to return to the lodge for a change of underwear.

Kevin, on the other hand, was directly in front of the bear and had to do something. He began to walk slowly but with purpose out of the bear's path, all the time saying, "Hello, bear; hello, bear," in a calm voice so the animal knew that he was there but not of any consequence. After what seemed like a lifetime, but was only probably a matter of seconds, the bear sauntered away from us and towards the water's edge. The whole group emitted a collective sigh of relief and we began to move again towards our fishing spot.

"They are more interested in the fish than they are in us," Kevin assured me as he rejoined the group. "But you have to give them absolute respect and realize that, when they are around, you are no longer number one in the food chain." I took him at his word, and while we fished I spent as much time looking over my shoulder for bears as I did looking at where I cast my line.

It was not my first time fishing, but it was the first time I had fished for salmon. I accepted every bit of advice the others had to offer and was soon casting along with the best of them, enjoying the heat of the sun on my back and the gentle touch of a cool breeze on my face.

The presence of the bear seemed to have spooked the salmon almost as much as it had spooked us, and for the next few hours we all cast our lines into the water with no results. I received more bites from the gargantuan insects that flew around us than I did from any fish and soon began to resign myself to the fact that luck was not with me on this trip.

I was already composing a few "well, we didn't catch anything but we still had a great time" thoughts for the book when suddenly my line became taut and the silvery flash at the end of it told us all that I had hooked a decent-sized fish. I moved back onto the bank and began to reel in my line until a beautiful salmon flopped up onto the shore. It was not Moby-Dick by any stretch of the imagination, but it was my very first salmon catch and at five pounds I knew it would make decent eating when I got it back to Los Angeles.

I must have been doing something right, because less than fifteen minutes later I felt another sharp tug that told me that, this time, I had a big one on the line. It put up an impressive struggle, as indeed

I would have done if I had known what was going to happen to me, but in the end I was able to pull it on to the shore and dispatch it to fishy heaven with a swift blow of a small wooden club. It was a beauty, and as I picked it up to pose for the obligatory photograph with the mountains of Alaska in the background, Kevin nodded in approval.

"It has to be at least ten pounds," he estimated as he placed it with my other catch in a metal keep box to protect it from any wandering bears. Although we kept trying for the next couple of hours, the salmon had quickly cottoned on to the fact that "Simon the Salmon Slayer" was in town and were now keeping a healthy distance from our lures.

Katherine announced that it was time to return and prepare for the arrival of our plane ride back to Anchorage. Before I packed, I had to clean the fish that I'd caught so that they could be flash-frozen and sent on to me at home. I was instructed to do this on the beach, well away from the lodge, to make sure that the smell of the fish did not attract any more bears. Just in case any did become curious, Jon Ross acted as an armed guard, standing over me with a shotgun to frighten them off. As I cut the fish open to clean out the guts, I was particularly pleased to find that each also contained a large sack of luminous orange eggs that would make delicious salmon "caviar" once I had washed and salted them.

The weather had improved dramatically since our arrival, and as the plane took off from the beach I was able to get an even better view of the stunning landscape of Cook Inlet. I was disappointed to have to leave so soon, particularly as the weather had meant that our stay had been such a short one. However, I was delighted that I was now able to put a large checkmark next to the "catch a salmon in Alaska" box on the list of things I had written down at the beginning of the Fed, White, and Blue journey.

A few days later, after my return to the urban sprawl that is Los Angeles, the beauty of Alaska and Silver Salmon Creek seemed a very long way away indeed. I was distracted from my writing by the buzz of the doorbell and opened the door to find my friendly FedEx man weighed down by a sizable box. I took it from him and placed it on the floor of my living room while I went in search of a knife in the kitchen. Finding one, I cut the box open to reveal a care package from my new friends in Alaska. It included the two fish that I had caught, which had been flash-frozen, vacuum-sealed, and packed in dry ice, as well as two jars of smoked salmon and two jars of that bright orange salmon roe that we had removed from the fish on the beach.

I began to make room for all of the goodies in the fridge, already mentally planning what I was going to cook with them, but I just couldn't resist opening up a jar of that incredible smoked salmon and taking out a piece to nibble on as I worked. One taste transported me back to Silver Salmon Creek Lodge. I could almost feel the sun on the back of my head and that breeze across my face. I could have eaten the whole jar, but I knew what the consequences would be if Sybil found out that I had done so. I am greedy, but I am not stupid.

I placed all of my fishy items safely in the fridge and returned to my writing with a promise to myself that it would not be long before I returned to Alaska.

So, silver salmon, be warned. "Simon the Salmon Slayer" is coming to get you.

Grizzly bears, on the other hand, you are probably just fine.

Roasting in Santa Fe

A short history lesson.

In 1846, James K. Polk, the eleventh president of the United States, took advantage of separatist rumblings in what became the state of Texas to launch a full-scale assault on its southern neighbor, Mexico. And, in a war that lasted for two years, the U.S. Army soundly defeated Mexican forces at every turn until Mexico City itself was captured in late 1847 by General Winfield Scott.

The "Mexican-American War," or the "War of U.S. Invasion," as it is still often referred to in Mexico, had serious impact on the future of both countries. The signing of the Treaty of Guadalupe Hidalgo saw Mexico lose rights over almost half its existing territory, while the United States, in a single stroke, added California, Utah, and Nevada to its union, as well as large parts of Arizona, Wyoming, and Colorado. It was a result that many might argue was almost as profound in the history of the United States as the defeat of the British, the signing of the Declaration of Independence, or the Louisiana Purchase. The United States also claimed a sizable part of what is now the state of New Mexico, completing the acquisition of the whole territory in 1853 by means of the Gadsden Purchase. New Mexico finally became the forty-seventh state in 1912.

The reason for this little lecture is to put into context New

Mexico's not-so-distant past, which did, and still does, influence its people and every aspect of its culture, including, of course, its food.

New Mexico has, in my opinion, one of the most eclectic mixes of influences on its cuisine of any part of the United States, taking, as it does, leads from the cooking of the native Pueblo, Mexican, Spanish, and even cowboy cuisines of the immigrants who passed through its lands on the way out West. It all comes together to combine into arguably one of the most exciting and most delicious cuisines in the whole of the country. At its fiery heart is the chili, or "chile," as New Mexicans will insist you call it—and so I will. That benign-looking (as you might think) fruit is used in just about every dish in New Mexico and has the ability to bring pleasure and pain in one bite.

Although you will often read in lazily researched articles that Christopher Columbus "discovered" chile peppers, the most credible theory at the moment is that they originated in the coastal lowlands of Brazil and began to spread around Latin America as they were carried by birds that were able to eat the peppers with no ill effects and dispersed the seeds as they flew. There is evidence that native tribes were cultivating chiles almost six thousand years ago—certainly long before Columbus sampled one and gave it the name "pepper" because the burning he felt while eating it made him mistake it as being from the same plants as black pepper. Traders began to bring the peppers back to Spain, where they were correctly considered to have health-giving properties. From there, they made their way to Portugal, where traders and missionaries brought them to the cuisines of India, China, and Southeast Asia, where they are so familiar today.

There is no archaeological evidence as to when chile peppers first found their way to New Mexico, but the theory that they ended up there as a result of trade between the Pueblo natives in New Mexico and the Toltec Indians of Mexico is most widely supported. The state now grows nearly a third of the peppers eaten in the United States, and even though it has faced strong challenges of cheaper imports from abroad, particularly China, it is still New Mexico that most people probably think of when the chile pepper is mentioned.

Given the isolation caused by the vast distance between Mexico City and New Mexico, it is little wonder that the territory began to develop its own unique culture and unique cuisine, for which it has now become famous, and for which I had already developed such a fondness over my few previous visits to the state. It still, however, retains a very Mexican sensibility, with around 47 percent of its two-million-person population being of Hispanic descent.

It had been over two years since I had last visited New Mexico and I was determined to add it to my itinerary for the Fed, White, and Blue journey in the hopes that I might find out more about its food, how chiles are grown, and how they have become such an indispensable part of every New Mexican menu. As I did my research, one name kept popping up time and again, that of farmer Matt Romero, the self-styled "King of Chiles." I got in touch and he responded with an invitation to come and visit both his farm and the farmers' market he attends in Santa Fe every Saturday morning.

By this time in my journey, I thought I had earned a break from flying and persuaded Sybil to do without our car for a few days, allowing me to make the drive from Los Angeles to Santa Fe in one long, backbreaking day.

I had agreed to meet with Matt early the next morning and was waiting for him, as requested, in the parking lot of a small store on the edge of Highway 68 when he rolled up at the wheel of a large pickup truck. He climbed out of the cab to greet me.

"Thanks for meeting me here," he boomed in a loud, friendly voice. "You'd never find your way to the farm on your own, so it's best if you just follow me."

He was wearing khaki shorts, a bright red T-shirt, and an equally bright orange baseball cap that protected his bespectacled face from the sun. His salt-and-pepper beard parted from its accompanying mustache to reveal strong white teeth in a flashing smile that I was to see almost constantly over the next couple of days. "I've got a lot to show you. C'mon, let's go." He waved me back to my car and I followed him off the paved parking lot down a short bumpy driveway until we arrived at his farm.

Matt Romero began his farming career back in 2004, after several years working as an executive chef. He returned to his native New Mexico to a plot of land that he worked on behalf of neighbors and friends. It had started as a small-scale operation, but over the last nine years Matt had built it up to such a level that he was now the largest purveyor to attend both the local Santa Fe and Los Gatos farmers' markets. "I built the business up on the quality of my produce," he told me as he pointed out across the three acres of land. "I knew from my time in the kitchen what chefs were looking for and I have been working hard to provide it ever since. I sell to all of the best kitchens in town."

He gave me a tour, stopping every few moments to pluck a piece of produce from its stalk and pass it to me. "Look at that," he said, handing me a bulbous shiny eggplant. "And this," he said again, this time tossing me a perfectly formed squash. By the time we had done one circuit of the farm, he had already given me enough produce to feed a family of six for a week. Although I was impressed with all of the vegetables piled in my arms, I was really here to see one thing, the chiles for which he had become so famous. "The land here is so perfect for chiles," he told me as he pointed towards a line of tall trees at the edge of his land. "Just behind those is the Rio Grande. That's where we take all our water from to keep the land irrigated."

Matt grows over twenty varieties of chiles on his land and, as we made another circuit of the farm, he stopped again at regular intervals to pluck peppers from their stalks, tossing them to me to add to my collection. "You have to take these with you to cook with at home," he insisted as we finally completed our tour and he thrust a handful of bags at me in which to carry away my booty. The chiles, with their shiny, unblemished skins, were beautiful to look at and Matt picked up few prime examples to show me the differences between them.

"Red and green chiles are basically the same, but the color changes as they become more ripe," he explained. "Some we pick when they are green and roast before we sell them. Others we let ripen until they are red, then we dry them and use them in our cooking either whole or ground to a powder."

"Each variety has a different name, and each variety has a different amount of heat depending on how much capsaicin is in them." With a motion of his hand, he instructed me to take a nibble of each of the peppers he had laid out in front of me.

"This one is the Joe Parker," he said. "It's very mild, but good and meaty, so it's great for making chile rellenos.

"This one's called Alcalde Improved," he added as he pointed the sharp end of a pepper towards me. "It's one of my favorites, quite a lot of heat." I took a bite and could see what he meant as the warmth began to move across my mouth and my eyes slowly began emitting tears of surrender. The heat soon subsided, replaced with a deliciously lingering aftertaste that stayed on my tongue for at least fifteen minutes.

"It becomes addictive," Matt said as he took a bite out of one of the peppers in his hand. "That's why people in New Mexico eat them with just about everything."

The farmhands who worked for Matt had been busily harvesting the whole time that he had been giving me the tour and had already constructed large towers of black plastic crates filled with produce for him to inspect. After agreeing to meet him at the market very early the next morning in time to see him and his crew setting up, I left Matt to get on with his work, collected my bags of peppers and other produce, and set off back to Santa Fe.

As I headed back along the highway, I spotted the large sign of a restaurant called Angelina's a short way off the road just by Española. It promised "Authentic New Mexican Cuisine" and, as all this talk of chiles had by now set my stomach rumbling, I decided to duck in for some breakfast. I grabbed a booth and, after a cursory glimpse at the menu, ordered the breakfast enchilada. As Matt had told me I should, I asked for it to be served "Christmas-style" and was soon presented with a colorful plate, half of which had been smothered with green chile sauce and the other half with red chile sauce. It was filling and delicious. There was no way that anyone could ever call this elegant food, but the chicken filling, combined with the two chile sauces, reminded me why I am so fond of New Mexican food and set me up for the rest of my day, spent rediscovering one of my favorite U.S. cities.

At five a.m. the next day, long before the sun made its appearance in the morning sky, I found myself walking the two and half miles from my bed-and-breakfast towards the Santa Fe Farmers' Market, located at the city's former rail yards. I am not always the biggest fan of farmers' markets, as, quite frankly, I think there are far too many of them and not enough great producers to keep them supplied. The end result is that they often fill more spaces with stalls selling prepared meals and aging hippies making balloon animals for children than they do really good produce. But the Santa Fe Farmers' Market is the real deal, a proper producers-only market. I could tell even before setup was complete that the day ahead was going to be impressive.

I found Matt setting up his booth at the far end of the rail yard. It was the largest stall in the market by some margin and he had already unfurled a banner reading "Fresh Roasted Green Chiles" and attached it to the top of one of the awnings. As he spotted me, he waved enthusiastically for me to join him.

Matt's chef's eye for plating was obviously coming in useful as he instructed his team where to lay out all of the colorful baskets of produce to best effect.

"I want people to come into the stand and wander around," he told me as he sipped on a cup of coffee that was sending whispers of steam into the cold morning air. "Once they get close and see how beautiful the produce is, you just know they are going to want to buy it."

At the side of the booth he had begun to lay out the star attraction, his display of peppers. Eleven wooden baskets had been set in rows on the concrete, each filled to the brim with a different type of pepper. Attached to each basket was a sign telling customers what type of peppers it contained and just how spicy they would be.

"Here." Matt handed me an apron with the Romero Farms logo printed on the front. "There's no just standing around watching in my stand. Now you are one of the team." I was more than happy to oblige and helped him carry his pepper roaster into position. It was a large cylindrical cage, set in a metal stand with a turning handle on the side. The cage was set above a wide downward-sloping chute into which the roasted peppers would be dispatched so they could be collected and then sorted into one-pound bags, which would be sold for $7.

"They are only four dollars a pound if people buy them raw," Matt told me as he began to light the burner attached to the pepper cage, "but people love to buy them already roasted, because they just can't get the same flavor when they do it at home."

This love of roasted peppers was already obvious even this early in the morning, because there was a small line of people waiting for the first batch of green peppers to come out of the roaster. The flames from the burner began to lick at the side of the roaster, and Matt began to turn the handle at a steady pace, making the peppers tumble inside the cage as their skins began to blacken. "Pepper-roasting is an art form," Matt shouted above the noise of the burner. "You have to get the timing just right. You want the skins to blacken and blister so you get the smokiness, but you don't want them to burn or they will become bitter."

People didn't just want to buy the peppers, they wanted to see them being roasted by the King of Chiles himself and for the next few hours Matt held court at his post, keeping up a constant repartee with his willing audience. Just about every person who passed by his stand stopped to take pictures of him and the baskets of shiny peppers.

"It's theater." Matt beamed as he scooped the latest batch of smoked chiles from the chute beneath the burner. "I don't just want to feed people, I want to entertain them." He tossed me one of the hot poblano peppers, laughing while I bounced it from hand to hand until it was cool enough to eat. I peeled off some of the blackened skin and sucked on the flesh that lay beneath. The layers of flavor that had been brought out by its time under the burner were obvious. There was, of course, the initial smokiness, but once you got past that, there was heat, sweetness, and even a slight taste of citrus that coated the mouth. Once again, it was easy to see why the people of New Mexico have become so addicted to these peppers and why they have become such an integral part of the state's cuisine.

I spent the morning at the market, talking to customers and trying as hard as possible not to get in the way of Matt or the young people who manned his stall. I had to leave sooner than I had wanted, as I had to be back in Los Angeles the next day, with that long drive in front of me. I handed back my apron to Matt, and in return he gave me a bag of peppers that had just come off the roaster to nibble on as I headed home.

"Next time, come back for longer and we'll cook for you," he said with one more of those flashing grins as I shook his hand. As I reached the edge of the market, I looked back one last time. The King of Chiles was already hidden behind another crowd of people, all eager to buy his peppers and watch in thrall as he did his thing.

Back in Los Angeles, I unpacked and went straight to the kitchen to plan what to do with all the peppers that Matt had given me at the farm. I separated them into piles of red and green. The red chiles had already begun to dry out a little and I decided to complete the process, laying them on a rack to finish desiccating in the California sun on my windowsill. Once they had dried, I would smoke half of them and then grind them all in my spice grinder so that I would have both smoked and unsmoked red chili powder.

The green chiles, however, were still looking fresh and juicy and I decided that they had to be used immediately. When Sybil returned to the apartment that evening, she was greeted by the smell of a classic New Mexican green chili sauce simmering on the stove. She dipped a spoon into the pot and licked it with a murmur of appreciation.

"I should probably let you use the car more often," she said as she headed to the bedroom to change for dinner.

It had definitely been worth the drive.

Hook 'em Horns

can still recall my very first time watching a game of American football. It was during my maiden visit to the United States at the beginning of the 1980s. I was barely seventeen and had been invited to stay with relatives, who soon tired of having a teenager around the house and palmed me off to friends who had children of my own age. At that age, I was, to all intents and purposes, a walking gland, and had became rather besotted with one of them, a stunning blonde named Stacey, who had a lilting Texan drawl and also happened to be a cheerleader at the neighborhood high school. When she invited me to join her and some friends at a football game, I leapt at the chance, hoping at the very least that Stacey and I would get to do something altogether unsavory under the bleachers.

Unfortunately, life is never quite that benevolent. Stacey soon became bored with my company and disappeared into the night with a chiseled behemoth named Brad or Josh, and left me sitting disconsolately with her parents to "enjoy" the game. It was impossible. What was happening on the pitch was a total mystery to me. I realized then that you need particular reflexes to watch football, which seemingly only come by being born American. Everyone there appeared to know by instinct and experience what was going on, and at key moments would leap to their feet in unison to be sure to catch all the exciting action. I, on the other hand, had no such training and spent most of my time staring at the bulbous backsides of the doting parents sitting in front of me as they cheered on their offspring. Even when I did manage to get an all-too-brief glimpse of the game, I still did not have a clue what was happening, and by the end of what felt like an eternity I was driven home brokenhearted and holding a very firm conviction that American football was something that I never needed to bother myself with again.

For the best part of the next thirty years I held to that view—until, that is, I met Sybil and moved to America. She rather enjoys her sport and, thanks to much urging on her part, I have now seen more football games than I ever would have thought possible when I was in my teens. While I would still never describe myself as a "fan," my original opinion of football has softened to the point where I can respect the skill and passion that is involved, even if I would still rather watch a game of "proper" football 99.99 times out of 100.

One upside of this begrudging acceptance of American football is that my wife's love of the game has also introduced me to an aspect of it of which I heartily approve, that of the pregame tailgate party. This is something that is almost totally unknown in the UK, in part because the supreme awfulness of our weather is something that makes grilling outside a possibility on approximately two days a year, and in part because the majority of British soccer grounds tend to be situated slap-bang in the middle of cities where there is barely enough space to park, let along set up a cooking station.

The British soccer pregame ritual is something I love. The time in a pub sipping on a few pints of beer while moaning about your beloved team's form, the walk to the match ground with your friends, the chanting of songs from the stands to bait the fans of the opponents before the game starts. These are part of my life and will always remain special to me. But an American tailgating experience takes things to a whole new level. With over fifty million Americans taking part in the activity on any given game day, I was determined to add it to my itinerary.

My first decision was to choose between a professional or college game of football. I knew that both would be enjoyable, but I also knew that they would give me very different experiences. In the end, although I received many kind invitations to attend both, I decided to throw my hat into the college ring for a couple of reasons.

The first was that from as long ago as I can remember, American places of learning have always seemed impossibly glamorous to me. A notion that was fueled by the images I soaked up in my youth watching television programs like *Happy Days* or movies like *Grease* and *American Graffiti*, it's lasted into my middle age as I have visited impressive college campuses across the country.

American schools also were, as far as I could tell, Day-Glo-bright places filled with energetic young people corralled into well-defined tribes. There were the sporting jocks, with their broad shoulders and prized letterman jackets, and the perky cheerleaders, aloof and unobtainable to all but the upper echelons of the American gene pool. There were the nerds with their thick-rimmed glasses and science club projects and, most relevant to me, the outsiders who were just invisible enough to avoid a daily beating but not cool enough to be noticed by anyone who registered more than halfway up the attractiveness scale. When they were not at school, the students were apparently always up to hijinks in malls, drive-in diners, and movie theaters. They were at parties on the beach, indulging in forbidden make-out sessions at school proms, or thinking up exciting ways to raise money for that school trip to Hawaii.

As a child, I lapped up this mythology and often daydreamed of leaving behind my own mundane school life to find myself wandering through the gates of these glorious places alongside button-nosed Sandy or freckle-faced Richie Cunningham and his zany pals. It was hardly surprising that I would have such feelings, as, compared to these idealized visions of American life, my own journey through the British educational system was in truth a gray, flat, and staggeringly uninspiring one.

I am not about to suggest that my school days were in any way Dickensian, or that I was forced to beg for extra gruel and received regular beatings from a sadistic schoolmaster wielding a flexible cane with ferocious intent. In fact, from the age of eleven I went to a rather decent school, which, although part of the UK's flawed comprehensive system, had an excellent academic record and provided me with perfectly sound building blocks for the rest of my life. Oh, I got bullied a bit. In part because I was a rotund child with big ears and mixed parentage, and in part because I was a thoroughly unpleasant little twerp who deserved everything I received, and probably a great deal more. But, on the whole, I passed through the UK school system without any great trauma to use, as so many people do, as an excuse for my failings in later life.

If my time in school served my academic needs adequately, it certainly did not serve my spirit in any way at all. I never found a teacher who made me want to stand on a desk and implore, "Captain, my captain," nor one who convinced me, through teaching methods upon which the school board frowned, that calculus was my true calling rather than the streets. My school never managed to create any level of loyalty in me whatsoever and was more or less forgotten the moment I walked through its doors for the last time.

The same was true of my university. I was fortunate enough to end up at a very good college, this time in London, where the combination of local government grants and generous parental contributions meant I was given free rein to explore one of the greatest cities on earth while studying theology, all with the intent of becoming an Episcopalian priest (and that, dear friends, is a story for another time).

But, no matter how much fun I was having at university, there was always a thought lurking at the back of my mind that somewhere across the Atlantic people were having a lot more fun than I was. It was a notion supported by repeated viewings of *National Lampoon's Animal House*, which not only convinced me (entirely incorrectly, for the record) that doing an uncanny impression of a zit would lead to massive amounts of sex, but also that going to university in the United States was less about books and lectures and more about girls in bikinis and attending frat parties dressed in nothing but a bit of frayed bedding.

The aspect that really stayed with me, long after my time in learning was anything more than a hazy memory, was the fact that American high schools and colleges also seemed to engender a sense of loyalty in their alumni that was never to be found in their British equivalents. Among the British members of my peer group, all of us now on a collision course with our sixth decade, the question of where one was educated only had relevance in the years directly after we left college, a time when résumés had to be padded with academic achievements to cover up for the paucity of real-world experience.

As we grew older, our career successes became far more important than our grades had been, and I would be hard-pressed to remember the last time anybody from outside of the United States ever asked me where I went to school. Where I am from, no one really cares. You are certainly never judged on that basis and, unless you went to one of the elite pairing of Oxford or Cambridge, it would have little bearing on how your professional life progressed.

Yet, based on past experience, if I were to raise the question with my American friends the response would probably invoke a certain misty-eyed staring into the distance on the part of the respondent as they remembered their salad days.

Nowhere does this fealty to an American's alma mater manifest itself more enthusiastically than in the allegiance shown to their school's sporting teams. Most Americans I know love their sport to a ludicrous degree at the best of times, but if you add to this their ability to enjoy it through glasses tinted with the rosy hue of school loyalty, it makes for a power-packed combination.

Once I had decided that it was college life for me, the next big question was, where? I had already attended a few tailgate parties at my wife's graduate school of UCLA, but even though their fans were passionate and loyal to their football team, they were the first to admit that I could and should aim my sights much higher. Once again, I received many invitations from lovely people in places where tailgate parties were taken very seriously indeed—like Baton Rouge, where I had heard that the tailgate parties before the games involving the Louisiana State University Tigers were of legendary proportions, and Oxford, Mississippi, where I was certain I would receive the warmest hospitality at any "Ole Miss" game.

In the end, however, it was an offer to attend a tailgate party before a University of Texas game against Baylor that won out, in part because Austin was already one of my favorite cities in the United States, and in part also because any visit to Texas also presented me with the perfect opportunity to stuff my face with the best BBQ in the country.

My invitation came from Mark Murrell, a realtor and alumnus of the University of Texas, who took the opportunity of each Texas Longhorns home game to hold a massive tailgating celebration. "It's one of the biggest in the city," he told me in typical Texan style during our initial conversation.

The Texas Longhorns hold their games in the Darrell K Royal–Texas Memorial Stadium, one of the largest arenas in the United States. It is named after one of the team's most illustrious coaches, who sadly passed away a few short days after my visit, and hosts over one hundred thousand fanatical fans on a typical game day. Long before kickoff, the majority of these fans will have arrived early to spend their time with fellow supporters at tailgating events in designated spots in the parking lot or in close proximity to the stadium.

This is no free-for-all, I realized as I began to read the pages of instructions for tailgaters on the University of Texas website. Spots are rented out on a first-come, first-served basis, with many of the prime locations being reserved for alumni who have made sizable donations to the university. Once the organizer of a tailgate has acquired their spot, there are pages and pages of rules by which they must abide, which regulate everything from how they secure their tents, park their vehicles, prepare their food, and serve alcohol to their guests. All come with severe penalties for noncompliance, which could lead to permanent expulsion from any further tailgating activities. It all seemed quite onerous on paper, but as Mark explained to me, with the number of people involved it is the only way that it could possibly be organized without complete chaos. "Just wait until you see the scale of it," he promised in his final e-mail, "then you will understand."

On the day of the match against Baylor, I left my accommodation early in the morning to join Mark and his friends as they set up for the party. As I reached the brow of a hill that dipped down towards the university campus, I was suddenly faced with a sea of color that rose up almost to where I was standing and surrounded the stadium for nearly half a mile in every direction. The color was the traditional "burnt orange" that has been worn by the Longhorns since just before the beginning of the twentieth century and is now instantly recognizable to any football fan, particularly when decorated with the logo, a silhouette of the front end of a horned steer.

As I made my way down the hill towards the coordinates Mark had given me, I could see that this wave of burnt orange adorned everything in view. I saw people wearing orange sweatshirts and T-shirts, tents with orange awnings, cars festooned with orange pennants, and banners unfurled above some tailgating parties that already seemed to be well under way, even though it was only a little after seven-thirty a.m. I also saw babies wrapped in orange swaddling and even more than one small dog that had been dressed in an orange coat.

When I arrived at the designated spot, Mark, wearing, of course, an orange T-shirt and apron, was already hard at work. It was indeed one of the largest tailgating spaces in the area and he had already set up an awning with two rows of chairs unfolded in front of a large flat-screen television situated on a stand under the covering of the tent. You won't be too surprised to find out that the awning was orange, as were the chairs. The tables he had erected around the perimeter were being covered with disposable plastic tablecloths that, although white, were emblazoned with the silhouette of the Longhorns' logo, and they were being attached with Longhorns-branded masking tape.

"There's a whole industry built up around tailgating," Mark said with a laugh as he threw me a beer, correctly assuming I would want one even though it was barely eight a.m. As soon as I had cracked the opening of the can and taken my first long gulp, he led me over to show me his prized possession, his smoking pit.

"This is my beauty," he said, tapping the outside of the double-door pit that was already pumping smoke out into the still slightly chilled morning air. "You'll have to excuse me if I look exhausted, I have been up all night looking after the brisket." He lifted the lid to reveal a number of stunning examples, each with a thick dark crust, which had developed over hours and hours of slow smoking. "We'll be feeding well over two hundred people," Mark told me as he closed the doors of the smoker and went to carry on with his preparations.

I took the opportunity to step away from Mark's space and walk around the surrounding area, where other tailgating operations were already in full effect. There were small spaces where families had set up just to spend time together and then colossal setups that had obviously been organized by companies and corporations, with the logos of sponsors on full display and security people doling out wristbands to those lucky enough to be allowed in. Music thumped in the air, and even so long before the game itself, everybody seemed to be having a great time.

As I wandered, my beer was replaced frequently by complete strangers and I was invited on more than one occasion to join other tailgating celebrations. The generosity of the Longhorn fans meant that a walk I had intended to last no more than half an hour lasted closer to three, and by the time I got back to Mark's spot, nearly one hundred people in orange apparel were already congregated and hitting the snack table in a way that I have only ever seen a television crew do on one of their very well-deserved breaks.

Mark didn't seem overly worried that I had disappeared on a walkabout, and hurled another beer in my general direction with a loud shout of "Hook 'em." I had heard a lot of people say those words as I strolled around that morning, and Mark explained that the phrase "Hook 'em Horns," with its accompanying Ronnie James Dio–style horned hand gesture, was created back in 1955 by Harley Clark, then the elected head cheerleader of the Longhorns. It had since become the accepted form of greeting for all University of Texas alumni and one of the most recognizable gestures in sport. I suppose that I could have reciprocated with any of a number of hand gestures that I was familiar with from my time back on the soccer terraces of England, but I really didn't want to bring the tone down.

The crowd at the tailgate kept growing in size, each new guest greeting their host with a shout of "Hook 'em," as they disappeared into the sea of orange already milling about on the lawn space. By early afternoon, most of the two hundred and fifty people Mark had invited had arrived and, just as I was about to be instructed in the fine art of touch football, I was rescued by a loud shout that lunch was being served.

There were loud sighs of appreciation from the line that had formed as Mark took his foil-covered slabs of brisket from the smoker and brought them to the serving table. If I have found one thing that Texans take as seriously as I had found they take their football and tailgate parties, it is their BBQ—and this was very good BBQ. I have been lucky enough to eat BBQ brisket in many parts of the United States, including some of the famous BBQ restaurants in Texas itself, and I can say, hand on fatty heart, that Mark Murrell's brisket would not be shamed if it was placed alongside them.

"I have been doing a lot of research on how best to prepare them," he told me as he began to slice through the dark outer bark with an electric knife. "These are okay, but I am sure I can do better." He was doing himself and his brisket a disservice. Inside the bark, there was a thin layer of light purple which showed where the smoke had penetrated the meat and, beyond that, into the heart of the brisket, the meat was oozing clear juices onto the serving station. I took my rightful place in the line and was soon rewarded for my good manners when I reached the front and was given not only two full slices of juicy brisket, but also a few chunks of burned ends for good measure. I proceeded to work my way down the table, topping up my plate with salads, coleslaw, beans, and other sides, before carefully walking over to claim one of the seats in front of the flat-screen TV, where people were watching a college game that was already taking place in another part of the country.

Soon after, Mark fell into the chair beside me. He looked exhausted but seemed to be pleased with the fact that we were all enjoying the food so much. "So," he asked me, waving a couple of tickets, "do you actually want to go to the game?" I was ashamed to say that, given how much I had been concentrating on my food, I had totally forgotten that there was supposed to be a point to a tailgate party other than eating too much and getting buzzed off ice-cold beer. I apologized for the oversight, but Mark just laughed in response. "Sometimes I am so wrapped up in the tailgate that I don't even bother to go to the game and watch it here on the TV. In fact, for a lot of people, the tailgate is even more important than the sport."

I had suspected that this would probably be the case for me, but given that I had come all this way, I thought I at least owed it to my adoptive homeland to try once more to understand their favorite game. I suggested that we should make the effort, and Mark and I left the party to begin the short walk to the stadium. By the time we fought our way to our seats, the Darrell K Royal–Texas Memorial Stadium was already packed to the rafters with a hundred thousand fans, all in their orange attire. The university band was pumping out something Mark informed me was called a "fight song," which everybody seemed to be enjoying very much, and the cheerleaders were cavorting around the edges of the pitch doing things that I enjoyed watching a great deal more.

The game had already started and Mark pointed towards the giant TV screen at the side of the stadium so I could watch a replay of a brief period of action that was being followed by a long period of nothing of any importance. American football always strikes me as being a lot like sex, where a few seconds of very intense sweaty activity is followed by long periods of analysis, shouting, and recriminations.

I tried my best to be enthusiastic, but by the time the game had reached the halfway stage, I was already losing the will to live and wanted nothing more than another slice of brisket and a cold beer. I looked across at Mark. He didn't seem to be enjoying the game very much; although the Longhorns eventually went on to carve out a victory, the team was putting its coaches and fans through an emotional wringer. Mark nodded at me and we left our seats to make our way back to the tailgate party. I was surprised that so many other people were doing the same, but Mark just shrugged, adding, "I told you, for so many people the game is almost an afterthought."

I stayed at the tailgate party until late in the evening, when the game was long over and people had begun to disperse into the night. I left Mark still seated in front of the television, beer in hand. He gave me one last smile, one last weary horned hand gesture, and one last weary shout of "Hook 'em!" as I went in search of a taxi to take me home.

I suspect that no matter how long I live in the United States, it's unlikely that I shall ever become a fan of American football. But, after a day enjoying great hospitality, far too many beers, and some top-notch brisket, I can say that the tailgate party is one of America's greatest contributions to the advancement of human civilization.

Paying It Forward in Texarkana

From its very inception, the Fed, White, and Blue journey was meant to be a joyous celebration of America through its food, the people who produce it, and the people who bring it to our plates. I hope you will think that I have been at least partially successful to this point. However, if one is going to write about the relationship the United States has with its food, it's never going to be a completely rosy picture. I always knew that there would be darker aspects to experience if I wanted to get a true impression of Americans and the way they eat.

I had already seen some of these less pleasant elements when I encountered the issues of mass production during my time with the beef ranchers of Nebraska. And now, as I drove east along I-30 from Dallas to Texarkana, I knew that I would be discovering more about one of my new homeland's most shameful statistics, the fact that in a country so wealthy and so productive, nearly one-sixth of its population does not know where their next meal is coming from.

Encountering hunger in others is not something that is new to me. The amount of time I spend traveling within developing nations means that I often see crippling starvation at almost every turn, particularly when I am visiting my father's homeland of India. While I have, thankfully, not become totally inured to the misery I see, there are at least clear reasons to explain why so many people might go hungry in these countries. (The main ones being inequitable distribution of wealth, chronic overpopulation, and an infrastructure that is seemingly always on the brink of collapse.) These are not excuses and should never alter the distress any of us should ever feel at seeing a fellow human being in need of food. However, they do, at least, give one a way of rationally explaining why such hunger might occur.

The United States has no such get-out clause. It's a nation that, as of 2013, had a gross domestic product of $15.8 trillion and supplies between 15 to 20 percent of all the food produced in the world every year. As a country of such wealth and resources, the fact that the United States also has over fifty million people, of whom sixteen million are children, living under the shadow of food insecurity should be genuinely shocking. When you add to that statistic the fact that nearly a third of all the food Americans buy each year goes to waste, it tells you that something is very seriously messed up indeed with our food distribution system.

Jill Whittington, executive director of Harvest Texarkana, had read about my journey and was keen for me to see the other side of the American food story. She e-mailed me with an invitation to visit their food bank, suggesting that I might like to help in their daily operations for a few days as she and her staff coordinated the collection of surplus food from restaurants and retailers and then managed its distribution to food pantries and others in the surrounding area.

Rather than suggesting an anonymous local hotel, Jill invited me to stay with her and her family during my visit. It was the sort of generosity I had encountered many times on the journey by this stage, and yet I was still appreciative of how many people in this new country of mine would be willing to open their homes to a complete stranger.

You all probably know this, but it was not until I did my research that I realized that Texarkana is in fact two cities. They are split down the middle by the state line between Texas and Arkansas. The city of

Texarkana, Texas, has a population of around thirty-seven thousand people, while the city of Texarkana, Arkansas, trails it slightly with a population of around thirty thousand.

There is, as one might imagine, considerable rivalry between the two cities, particularly when the football teams of Texas High and Arkansas High clash every year in front of ten thousand people for the ownership of the Battleaxe. And, as I was to find out, people are very keen to let you know from which side of the state line they hail. The two cities do have two things in common, however—a shockingly large number of their population goes hungry every night, and even for those who can afford it the availability of nutritious food is very limited.

"We live in a food desert here," Jill told me during our initial conversation.

The term "food desert" was first used in 1995 in a United Kingdom report into supermarket trends and is now defined by the American Nutrition Association as:

Parts of the country vapid of fresh fruits, vegetables, and other healthful whole foods usually found in impoverished areas. This is largely due to a lack of grocery stores, farmers' markets, and healthy food providers.

In 2011, the U.S. Department of Agriculture issued a food desert locator as part of an initiative spearheaded by First Lady Michelle Obama to battle the problem of childhood obesity. The chart delineated regions across the country that are either low-income or have low access to supplies of healthy food. It makes for genuinely scary reading when you see just how much of the country falls under this banner, particularly when you realize, as I did, just how close to your home some of these places are.

The reasons food deserts exist are many, but the primary one is, of course, money. Supermarket chains have little interest in opening branches in low-income areas of the country, preferring instead to invest in more affluent neighborhoods or large out-of-town super-stores near freeways, where they can draw customers from a wider region.

This creates a fresh-food vacuum in both inner city and more rural areas. Not only do the residents of these areas, particularly those without automobiles, not have access to supplies of healthy food, but the retail space, left vacant by the supermarkets in these regions, is more often than not filled with fast-food outlets, discount stores, and quickie marts that offer attractively inexpensive but highly processed foods containing unhealthy levels of fat, salt, and sugar. The rest of that story unfortunately writes itself, creating that vicious cycle of low income, poor diet, and poor health care which contributes to the epidemic obesity problem that is being fought throughout the United States.

"In Texarkana," Jill told me when I arrived at her house, "about nineteen percent of both cities live in food insecurity." It was not hard to believe. As I had approached the city after my long drive from Dallas, I had seen the strip malls filled with chain restaurants and fast-food joints. I'd seen the dollar stores and the thrift shops, and the small convenience stores, but I had not seen more than a handful of recognizable supermarket branches in my whole trip. "There aren't many," Jill said. "It makes it very hard to shop well if you don't have a car."

The next morning I joined Jill and her team at their twenty-thousand-square-foot facility on the Arkansas side of the state line. My first task, she instructed, was to help one of her drivers, Tarrell, with his biweekly collection of surplus food from two local branches of Walmart. She must have seen the look on my face, because she added, "I know that many people see Walmart as the great enemy, but it's one of the only places that people have to shop locally and they are incredibly supportive. They give us a lot of food."

As Tarrell backed the truck up to the loading dock of our first stop, the door raised to reveal a pallet loaded high with boxes that had been marked out for "Harvest Texarkana Collection." "This is produce," Tarrell said, tossing me a pair of gloves. "Now we need to check out the other departments." Some were more receptive to our arrival and had surplus stocks of canned and dry goods packed and ready for collection. Others just shrugged when we turned up, pointing without enthusiasm towards a few meager items they had thrown in a box. In either event, Tarrell remained good-humored. "It depends on the person in the department. If they care, we'll get lots of food from them; if they don't, we won't."

As I helped him load everything into the back of the container, I asked what would happen to any food that we didn't collect. "It'll just go to waste," he responded, adding when he saw me grimace, "That's why I always try and be friendly and polite so I have a good relationship with the people and they keep the food for us." That had obviously paid off today, as, by the time we had visited both stores, the back of the truck was nearly two-thirds full. "This isn't bad at all." Tarrell grinned as we headed back to the warehouse. We had collected a motley assortment of goods that ranged from frozen turkeys to fresh produce, bottles of soda, and trays of cakes and cookies. "We're not picky," Tarrell grinned. "As long as it's safe to eat, we'll take what we're given."

Back at the warehouse, I left Tarrell to transfer the food we had collected into storage, while Jill explained to me more about the operations of Harvest Texarkana. They began just doing food rescue, collecting unused food from restaurants and distributing it to soup kitchens and shelters so they could use it immediately for people in need. "We still do that, but then in 2005, we became a food bank." She went on to explain that, rather than work directly with hungry individuals or families, Harvest Texarkana is a nonprofit organization whose remit is to collect food from restaurant, retailers, producers, and any other source willing to donate, and then distribute that food to those in need through third-party agencies.

"We have over a hundred now," she continued, "and they come and collect from us on a regular basis depending on how often they open their food pantries to the people who need them." Their distribution network includes churches and homeless shelters, as well as residential centers for both seniors and children.

Jill corrected some of the misconceptions I and many others have had about those who go hungry in the United States. "A lot of people assume that it's just the homeless," she began, "but a lot of the people who need our help are what we call the 'working poor,' that is, people where the husband or wife may have a job, but the other partner is out of work, has been laid off, or has had their hours reduced because of the poor economy. They may not need our help all the time, but may have to come to the food pantry once a month when they have to also pay their rent or make a car payment.

"Then, the food pantries help two of the groups who are most at risk. Seniors are one, as they have so many extra draws on their income. They are often faced with making a choice between eating, heating their homes, or paying for their medication. If we can take the pressure off at least one of those choices, then at least they will be able to keep warm and buy their medicine." It was a sobering thought that so many people who have worked so hard to build the economy of this country, and in many cases served in the military to protect its way of life, are now struggling to eat on a regular basis.

It was just as concerning when Jill told me that nearly a quarter of the children in the ten counties covered by Harvest Texarkana are also classified as suffering from "chronic hunger." Many of them are provided with free breakfasts and lunches at school each day, because their teachers fear that these were the only times they might actually eat. "But then we need to make sure they have something to eat on weekends and during the holidays," Jill said as she led me to a corner of the warehouse where they stored food for their backpack program. "Before the weekend, we put together a small package of food that we place in each child's backpack, so they can have something to eat when they are home." The food has to be shelf-stable, as the child might not have access to a fridge or somewhere to store fresh food. The packages are delivered when the kids are on recess, so they can avoid the stigma of receiving the care packages in front of their class-mates.

Hearing these tales of struggle and hunger was genuinely heart-breaking, but for Jill and her incredible team, it's all just in a day's work. There's little room for sentiment as they deal with the collec-tion and distribution of over 2.5 million pounds of food every year—food that would otherwise almost certainly go to waste and that, from what she had just explained, is desperately needed by so many in Texarkana.

I spent the rest of the afternoon helping the team load food into the cars, trucks, trailers, and minivans of the food pantries who came to collect. I noticed that nearly all of them were from local churches. "They definitely make up the biggest number of our agencies and they are the backbone in Texarkana," Jill told me, adding, "particularly in more rural neighborhoods, where they can be the only place that a community has to come together."

After seeing how the surplus food was collected and distributed, I was even keener to see how the food finally made its way into the hands of those who needed it most. So Jill agreed to take me to visit a number of the food bank's agencies, all of whom have different meth-ods of food distribution and clientele, but all of whom are on the front line of the fight against hunger in Texarkana.

Over the next two days, I visited homeless shelters and churches that use the food bank to supply their kitchens. I was introduced to pastors, social workers, and volunteers in both cities who were working tirelessly to help those in need of assistance. They were all very different in character, but united in their determination to feed those who were in need, whether long- or short-term. They did this not for any praise or glory they might receive, nor certainly for any personal gain, as they were nearly all volunteers, but simply because it was the right thing to do. Meeting them all was truly inspiring, but there was one experience that had a particular impact long after my visit to Texarkana.

One of our stops was at Williams Memorial United Methodist Church, where, Jill told me, they host a weekly meal in the church hall followed by an opportunity for those in need to collect groceries from the food pantry. The meal was already well under way when we arrived, and Jill took me through the building to another meeting room, where volunteers were setting up the pantry in anticipation of what they knew would be a busy night.

"People are allocated access to the pantry on a random basis," one of the volunteers told me. "That way no one can claim that anyone else gets more favorable treatment." Along the walls of the meeting room shelving units had been set up, each filled with a different type of grocery product, from sodas and soft drinks, to dry goods and pastas, to canned sauces, soups, and desserts. I noticed that there was no fresh produce and questioned one of the volunteers as to why they weren't offering food that was more nutritionally beneficial. Her answer was an honest one.

"We just don't have any way of keeping fresh produce, so it would go off. Plus, in a lot of instances, the people we help would not have anywhere to keep it. So it would get wasted anyway." Finally, she added, "We give what we are given to give. If Pepsi donated soda, then that's what we will give. We don't have the luxury of choice." It confirmed what Tarrell had told me on my first day.

Jill, having overheard our conversation, added, "Harvest Texarkana does a lot of food education to try and teach people how to shop and eat well, but sometimes people are in need of calories first and good calories second." It made absolute sense, and made me feel ashamed that I had been dismissive of some of the donated food, having now realized that for many people who would come through the door it was a choice of eating what was on offer or not eating at all.

We finished setting up just as the first arrivals poked their heads through the door of the pantry. Each one was greeted warmly by a volunteer who would guide them around the room, helping them select an allocated number of items from each section, which would then be passed to a central area to be bagged. When they had been on a complete circuit and their bags were full, their food would be carried out to their cars for them by another volunteer.

"In many cases," one of my fellow volunteers told me, "the people who come to the pantry are seniors and they need help getting the food to their cars. But we like to offer to do it for everyone as our way of showing service to our neighbors when they are in time of need."

Jill and I stayed for the whole evening. As I did so, I had an opportunity to see and meet the people who were the recipients of all our efforts and those of food pantries all over the country. Some were old and alone, others were young and with their families. Some were African American, others were Asian or Hispanic, and a few were white. Some were effusive and grateful for the assistance they were being given, while others were quiet, seemingly almost embarrassed that they needed a visit to the pantry to help feed their families. But all were Americans, all were in need, all were treated with respect and dignity—and no one was turned away.

As I made well over a dozen trips out to the parking lot to help load food into the trunks of battered old Nissans, Toyotas, and Chevys, the notion (often promulgated by some of the more odious conservative pundits) that people who ask for assistance are entitled and constantly have their hands out began to leave an even more sour taste in my mouth than normal.

It was an idea that was made even more ridiculous when, on my final trip, an elderly lady whose bags I was carrying reached into her purse to retrieve a crumpled $1 bill to offer me by way of gratuity. I declined, saying that it was my pleasure to help, and she simply replied, "Well, God bless you, then." Cheesy though it might be to admit, as her car pulled away, I had to wipe a small tear from my eye before I returned to the church building. The widow's mite, indeed.

After nearly three hours, the last of the guests had passed through the pantry and the shelves were almost bare. I was there helping for just one night, but I knew that the church volunteers would be there again the following week and again the week after that and after that. "We'll keep being here as long as we need to be," one of them told me as he began to pack away. "Hopefully, there will come a time when we won't need to be here at all." I nodded, sharing his sentiments. Even if, in my heart, I believed that this was an unlikely dream, I agreed with him that one should never stop being willing to help and never stop trying to make hunger in America a thing of the past.

It was an important lesson, one that stayed in my mind when I left Texarkana and drove back to Dallas. I knew that I had learned a great deal during my stay with the amazing people of Harvest Texarkana, including just how hard Jill and her team work to build relationships with restaurants and retailers to make sure they have food to collect and that it is all put to good use. I had also witnessed the incredible spirit of giving and service that was shown by all the volunteers who help in the food pantries, churches, and shelters, a spirit which had inspired me to do even more on my return to my own home in Los Angeles.

But most of all, my time in Texarkana had taught me that hunger isn't just about statistics, however alarming they may be. Hunger is about people. Like the elderly, who have contributed so much to what makes this country great and now need us to make sure they don't have to choose between heat, food, and medication in their later years. It's about the children who can potentially make this country even greater in the future, but first require nutritious meals to feed their bodies and minds, and it is about our neighbors, who like you and me are part of this remarkable American family and from time to time need assistance when things get hard.

Whoever they are, how does the saying go?

"There but for the grace . . ."

Down in the Delta

have to admit that my initial motivations for visiting the Magnolia State had not been altogether positive ones, but rather had been prompted by some disturbing facts about the health of Mississippi's population that I uncovered following my visit to Texarkana.

In 2012, according to the United Health Foundation, the state of Mississippi came in last in a ranking of states by health. This was based on a number of criteria such as life span, number of people who smoke, diabetic population, and levels of obesity. It was little surprise, then, to find that the people of Mississippi also spend a larger percentage of their dining-out budget on fast food (a whopping 62 percent in 2013) than any other state in the country. This goes to explain the state's unenviable numbers of people who are overweight (70 percent) and the even more frightening number of people who are suffering from chronic obesity, at nearly 35 percent of the population.

I also discovered that, in 2013, the U.S. fast-food industry was worth the staggering annual amount of $188 billion. At least a quarter of the population of the United States would eat at least one meal a day at one of the 330,000 fast-food and fast-casual outlets that litter the freeways and strip malls of the country.

While that figure certainly speaks to the unbeatable entrepreneurial spirit that created chains like McDonald's and KFC, it's also a figure that has much darker implications. Although there are chains who aim to provide more nutritious meals for their customers, the primary appeal of fast food, apart from its speed of preparation, is that it is cheap. Supplying food that can be sold cheaply inevitably means that companies have to produce the meals they sell from highly processed ingredients with few nutritional benefits. Cheap, bad food is a particularly toxic combination and there can be little argument that the areas of the United States that have the highest level of fast-food consumption are also the areas of the country that have the worst health records and the most worrying levels of obesity.

After my time in Texarkana learning about food deserts and on researching all of this information about Mississippi, I decided that I would fly down and spend a few days consuming breakfast, lunch, and dinner in a fast-food or fast-casual outlet. As I said, it was not a particularly positive reason to want to visit, and in hindsight it was a bit of a cheap shot at a state that already receives more than its fair share of bad press. But I did think it would give me more insight into some of the food issues faced by Americans that I had discovered on my travels.

Just a few weeks before I was due to travel, I was contacted by Andy Chapman and his wife, Marianna. They run the excellent Eat Y'all and Eat JXN websites, which help promote restaurants all over Mississippi and particularly in the state capital, Jackson. They had read about my adventures and called to invite me to join them for a number of food events that happened to be scheduled for the same time as my planned trip.

When I told Andy that I was already arranging a visit and why, I heard a sigh at the other end of the line. "There is so much more to food in this state than that," he said in an exasperated tone that made it clear this was not the first time he'd had this conversation. It was, Andy told me, often a Sisyphean task persuading people that there was another side to the food in Mississippi than what is reported in the mainstream media, which was one of the reasons why he and his wife had set up their various websites.

"Everybody talks about that side of things, but there is so much more going on," he told me, adding, "Why don't y'all come and visit with us and we can show you that there is some real cooking going on here?" That sounded a much more enjoyable prospect. So I accepted Andy's offer and changed my plans accordingly. The day of my arrival, Andy and Marianna met me at Jackson's tiny airport. "We're going to start with some hunting," he told me as we pulled onto the freeway and headed northwest towards the Mississippi Delta.

Hunting has been part of the American experience since long before the first colonist arrived in the early 1600s, and it is certainly one of the reasons the United States as we know it today exists, as those first settlers would have surely starved if they had not been able to hunt and fish. In fact, it was at this very early stage in the country's history that the freedom to hunt became entrenched as one of the tenets of living in the New World. In England, the right to hunt was retained only by those rich enough to own the land, whereas in the first colonies, hunting was seen both as a right and a necessity, and as such it has remained at the heart of American beliefs ever since.

Hunting, unfortunately, has many faces. Alongside the acceptable aspect of putting food on the table and passing traditions down through the generations has also come the wanton slaughtering of species like the buffalo almost to the point of extinction, along with the senseless killing of beautiful creatures for no other reason than to place their pelts and bodies on display—all of which has contributed to the fact that hunting has become one of the most emotive issues in the United States today, and one about which it is almost impossible for people to have a reasoned discussion.

For my own part, I am not an experienced hunter, but I have to hold my hand up and say that on the occasions when I have been hunting, I have enjoyed it a great deal. I don't actually kill very much, because I am not a terribly good shot, but the animals that I, and the people I hunt with, do kill are killed for two reasons and two reasons only.

The first and most important, of course, is that they are destined for the pot. It is the reason man began to hunt animals in the first place, and the truth is that few things taste as wonderful as food you have caught, grown, or hunted yourself. There are certainly easier ways to fill the dinner plate, but I would always rather eat meat from an animal that has lived a good existence out in the wild and been killed quickly with a rifle or bow than I would an animal that has lived a short, stressful life penned up and then been dispatched with a stun gun or a shock of electricity. Our shameful disconnection from the sources of our food often means that the latter is the only source of protein we have, but if I were offered a choice there would only be one option.

The second reason is less discussed but almost as important, and that is, unpleasant as it may seem, it is sometimes necessary to kill animals. This could happen in situations where animals may pose a threat to people and their houses or on occasions when there are simply too many of the animals in limited space and culling them is the best form of animal husbandry. In either event, it is always better if the animal ends up in the pot, but even if that is not possible, the hunting of the animal may still prove to be the most expedient thing to do. This was, Andy informed me, the case in Mississippi, where the population of wild hogs was multiplying at an alarming rate and destroying hundreds of acres of farmland.

I definitely don't approve of hunting of animals for no other reason than the kill itself. I won't lie, there is definitely a feral thrill one feels when an animal crosses your sights or when you know you have hit a bird in the air. I'm not proud of it, but it is a feeling that is rooted in the most base of human instincts and something over which we have little control. But hunting for the sole reason of fulfilling this instinct is to my mind reprehensible, and the people who do so for this reason and for the trophies they collect to prove their prowess do a huge disservice to the responsible hunters who are a part of a great American tradition.

As I said, very few animals are actually ever put in mortal peril when I go hunting. The real pleasure I derive comes from the time that I, as a normally desk-bound writer, get to spend outdoors, and from the companionship that I find with the people who really understand America's rural traditions. As we made our way through the Delta, I was hoping that it was this kind of hunting and hunter I was going to encounter.

There are times when one is driving through the United States that you begin to feel like you are on a movie set, and this was definitely one of them. I could almost hear the sound of Delta blues playing through my head as the sun began to set over the fields and swamps on either side of the highway.

The Mississippi Delta is an area of the country that has been called "the Most Southern Place on Earth." It earned that sobriquet not for its geographical location but more for the atmosphere I was now experiencing as I stared through the windows. The region still retains much of its culture from the time when the area was the cotton-growing capital of the United States. The cotton industry, which was fueled primarily by the labor of slaves on white-owned plantations, led to the region today becoming primarily African American in population. This is turn led to the creation of both its cuisine and the thing for which it is most famous, of course, its music. The decline of the "King Cotton" and the failure of successive governments to revitalize the area also resulted in crippling poverty and a level of rural depopulation that meant that many of the small businesses were unsustainable and many of the towns where they formerly operated became derelict ghost towns.

We drove through a succession of settlements that were made up of little more than an assortment of shuttered buildings, ramshackle grocery stores with caged windows, and run-down gas stations. I began to wonder if there was going to be anything of note to experience, and continued to stare out of the window until the sun had almost set and the beams from our headlamps were the only lighting on the two-lane blacktop.

I was disturbed from my thoughts by the sound of Andy calling out, "Hey, there's Crews," and flashing the headlights at a man who was seated on an all-terrain vehicle and waving at us from a short direction ahead at the side of the road. Andy stopped the car and turned to follow the ATV down a path that seemed to lead nowhere. We followed for a few minutes through wooded terrain until we finally pulled up in front of an impressive two-story lodge set in the middle of manicured green lawns. The building stood in stark contrast to those I had seen out on the side of the highway and was proof that, while the distribution of it may be hugely uneven, there was still plenty of money to be found in the Delta.

"Crews" turned out to be David Crews, the ebullient resident chef of Six Shooter Lodge. As he showed me to a suite of rooms that was bigger than my apartment, he told me more about the venue for our short hunting expedition. The lodge was built by six wealthy friends from the medical profession, hence its name. It sits on twenty-five hundred acres of prime land which is maintained as a farm, a hunting reserve, and a lumber company. It has played host to judges, politicians, and celebrities, but is primarily used as an escape for the owners and their families.

"I teach culinary courses at the local community college," Crews explained, "but during the season I live here and cook for the owners and their guests. We are going to have something to eat and then we are going to have us some fun." As I was to find out, David Crews likes to have a lot of fun a lot of the time.

Our meal at a local restaurant called Crawdad's consisted of plenty of fresh Gulf seafood: steamed crawfish and shrimp as well as Mississippi catfish and that southern delicacy of deep-fried pickles. The meal was simple, well prepared, and delicious and accompanied by enough beer to set me yawning and declare myself ready for bed.

Crews was having none of it, however. On our return, he disappeared into the lodge, reappearing a few moments later with a huge grin on his face and something that looked suspiciously like an AK-47 slung over his shoulder. "How would you like to give this a try before we quit?"

For the record, if anyone ever asks you if you want to fire off an AK-47 and you have ownership of a pair of testicles, the correct answer is always yes, no matter how tired you may be. Both Andy and I leapt at the chance, and we were soon pumping rounds into the distance as whiskey-drinking southern gentlemen whooped their approval all around us.

I was woken the next morning by a banging on the door of my rooms almost as loud as that of the AK-47, accompanied by Crews yelling, "Time to get up, buddy, time to go dove hunting!" at the top of his voice. As I rolled out from beneath the warm comforter, my shoulder throbbed in agony. A result, I imagine, of the recoil from the mega-weapon I had been having fun with the previous evening. I threw on the same clothes I had been wearing the night before and stumbled into the hallway muttering savage complaints under my breath.

Despite telling me that he had not slept, Crews appeared bright-eyed and eager to get back out into the fields. He led me into the lodge's gun room and kitted me out with a camouflage jacket, boots, and cap, and handed me a weighty Beretta shotgun.

We joined Andy outside and set off towards the prime dove-hunting spot on an all-terrain vehicle, as two of the lodge's hunting dogs scampered behind us, eager to get on with the morning's entertainment. The sky was blue and almost cloudless, the air was crisp and cool, and a welcoming breeze began to blow across my face, waking me up. We didn't shoot very much. In fact, given the number of savage bites that I received from the horsefly population of the Delta, I would dare to say that nature actually came out on top. Despite that, I would have happily stayed hunting to no great effect all day and was more than a little disappointed when Andy told me that we had to pack up and leave for the next stop on our itinerary.

I was cheered by the fact that he told me we still had time for breakfast, as our couple of hours tramping around had brought on a sizable hunger. So, after a quick shower and change of clothing, I joined everyone in the open kitchen of the lodge, where the irrepressible Mr. Crews was busy loading the table with baskets of fresh warm biscuits and plates of shirred (baked) eggs.

As I shared my morning meal with my new southern friends, I was reminded of just why I enjoy hunting so much. For me it's far more about the companionship than the killing, and far more about the scenery than about the shooting. Those birds we had brought down from the skies would be put to good use in meals for the guests at the lodge, but even if we hadn't bagged a thing, it still would have been one of the best ways I could imagine spending time there.

Our next stop was an hour's drive away in Yazoo City. Andy told me that we were going to visit one of the largest catfish farms in Mississippi, which had been run by the Simmons family since the mid-1970s. The owner, Harry Simmons, had grown up in the area and had originally begun farming soybeans before deciding to dig pools in his land and convert to farming catfish. He filled the pools directly from the land's water table and his product became successful enough that in the early 1980s he was able to add a processing plant and start selling under his own family brand name in addition to supplying restaurants.

I was pleased with this addition to the itinerary, as catfish is something that I have become quite fond of cooking with during my short time living in America. It is also one of the few items of fish or seafood for which I believe farmed to be genuinely better than wild. The nature of how catfish feed on the bottom of ponds and lakes means that it can be an ingredient with a very muddy taste if not cleaned and prepared properly. Farmed catfish, on the other hand, is a very clean ingredient that lends itself as a vehicle for a number of styles of cooking. I've used it in everything from the most traditional fried catfish sandwiches to fish tacos and even Thai and Indian curry dishes.

As a good supporter of my new home, I always try and buy American catfish, but it is becoming increasingly harder to find, as Harry explained when he gave us a tour of the farm. "We have the best, safest, and cleanest product on the market," he explained, "but our feed prices are very high compared to our competitors' abroad, so it becomes a real challenge to make any profit when farming catfish." The biggest threat, he added, has come most recently from Vietnam, which in 2013 had been "dumping" a similar species of fish called Pangasius into the U.S. restaurant trade. It was sold at well below market price and often without proper health inspection by the federal authorities, and had caused huge damage to the American industry. Although catfish is a terrific ingredient for the home cook, over 70 percent of the amount eaten by Americans is consumed in restaurants, and this influx of a cheaper but poorer product had had a definite impact on the domestic industry.

Despite this, the Simmons operation certainly seemed to be prospering, and after our tour of the pools and the processing plant, we joined Harry and his family for an excellent lunch of catfish that had been harvested from the farm the previous day. It was a reminder of why I have become a fan of the fish, and I made a note to myself to make sure I used it more when I returned to my home kitchen.

The final stop of the journey was two hundred miles south of

Yazoo. Andy and Marianna wanted to introduce me to Mississippi seafood at a dinner in the coastal city of Biloxi. "Seafood on the Gulf has had some problems recently," Andy told me, making an understated but obvious reference to the 2010 Deepwater Horizon oil spill that jettisoned nearly five million barrels of oil into the waters of the Gulf.

The effects of the spill were catastrophic, particularly on the states of Florida, Alabama, Mississippi, and Louisiana, for whom the wild seafood industry produces a sizable part of their income. The federal government almost immediately declared the event a fisheries disaster for the states involved and calculated that the combined impact of the spill on their economies would be well over $2 billion. For the record, as of 2013, BP estimated the total cost would exceed $42 billion.

Although the fishing ban in the Gulf was lifted in November 2010, there have been lingering concerns about its impact on seafood, not only because of the oil spill itself but also because of the effect of the toxic chemicals and dispersants that were used to clear the oil from the water's surface. The Mississippi Department of Marine Resources and the Mississippi Department of Environmental Quality imposed a rigorous testing scheme to measure the amount of carcinogenic PAH (polycyclic aromatic hydrocarbons) in the seafood caught in their area of the Gulf, and thankfully, by 2013 the levels of such tasty-sounding things as dibenzanthracene and benzo(k)fluoranthene were minimal, and certainly far below the levels of concern cited by the federal government.

Although the science was on its side, the Mississippi tourism industry still had to overcome the fact that the general public was still apprehensive about eating seafood from the Gulf. This dinner, hosted by Mississippi Gulf Fresh Seafood, was part of an ongoing program to convince people that the wild-caught seafood they bought would both come from regulated waters and be subject to stringent testing.

It was still an uphill battle, but one that was being supported across the state by chefs, politicians, fishermen, and people like Andy and Marianna.

When we arrived at the Biloxi Visitors Center, one of the hosts told me, "In fact, if anything good can be said to have ever come from the oil spill, it's that it brought the community together and now the seafood is probably more tested than it has ever been."

Each course of the meal had been produced by a chef from a different local restaurant and was proof not only that the state was bouncing back rather well from one of the worst environmental catastrophes in its history, but that (along with the rest of my meals with Andy) there was far more to the food in the Delta than just fast food.

Despite Andy's best efforts, I felt I really couldn't leave without fulfilling my original reason for visiting Mississippi, and so, after I said good-bye to him and Marianna, I decided to take a break in my journey back to Jackson in Hattiesburg, a city that offers one of the greatest proliferations of fast-food and chain outlets in the state, at the point where I-59 and U.S. Highway 98 intersect.

I found a cheap motel nestled between a batch of the usual suspects and spent the next three days eating nothing but hamburgers, pizza, fried chicken, and chain-restaurant Mexican food. This rather foolish activity didn't really achieve much apart from giving me chronic constipation (enjoy the image) and making me slightly queasy for the following week and a half. But it did at least allow me to add the Taco Bell XXL Stuft Burrito steak (880 calories and nearly 36 grams of fat, for the record) to the list of Icelandic rotten shark meat, Mongolian fermented horse milk, and deep-fried Chinese rat as the nastiest things I have ever eaten. I do it so you don't have to.

Feeding the 500

My career as a food writer has given me the most incredible opportunities to meet interesting people and do interesting things. I never know what each new day will bring, and every morning I wake up and check my e-mails, excited to see if there have been any invitations to dinner or requests for magazine articles that will require me to pack a bag and set off on my travels one more time. I do realize, however, that not everyone has these opportunities and always make an effort to be grateful for just how lucky I am. If I ever needed reminding of this, it happened during a visit to Florida, where I found myself standing next to one of the greatest legends of American sport while a short distance away a melee of people clamored to take pictures or even just to catch a glimpse of him.

It had all begun with one of those e-mails I mentioned. It came from my friends at Smithfield Hams in Virginia. I had visited them at their home office a few months before in order to sample some of the country-style hams they make from their peanut-fed hogs. When they heard about my upcoming trip and plans to become an American citizen, one of my contacts there told me that they might have something interesting for me to experience. I took their promise with a large piece of salt-cured pork, not because I did not think it was genuine, but because I knew how busy they all were and expected the offer to be forgotten the moment I left Virginia and they went back to their real lives.

They did not forget, however, and when I read the e-mail, I was delighted that they had remembered me. It turned out that Smithfield Hams is the main sponsor of the Richard Petty NASCAR team, and they wanted me to join them at the upcoming Daytona 500 event in Florida.

Even though I knew almost nothing about NASCAR itself, what I did know was that I simply could not turn down the opportunity to attend one of the biggest sporting events on the calendar. Smithfield's only caveat for my attendance was that I would help prepare a meal for Richard Petty's crew of mechanics before the race began. It seemed a fair enough demand and I was more than happy to accept, particularly when they told me that my good friend from the Food Network, Michele Ragussis, was also on the invitation list and that we would be working together in the kitchen.

Before I flew down to Florida, I knew that I would need to do some homework about both NASCAR and Richard Petty, realizing that it would probably not be looked upon favorably if I approached a racing legend and said, "So, what is it you do?"

Richard Petty is NASCAR royalty. His family has been involved in this sport—which, as Rick Houston puts it on www.nascar.com, "has its roots soaked to the very tip in moonshine"—since its foundation, and even though he retired from driving in 1992, he is still one of the most familiar and well-respected faces on the circuit.

NASCAR's history is well documented. Even a Brit like me who was raised watching the more sophisticated and glamorous racing of Formula 1 has heard the stories of how moonshiners in Georgia, Virginia, and the Carolinas souped up their cars in order to outrun local revenue officials. They soon began to race these cars against each other, primarily for bragging rights, and by the end of World War II there was an unofficial circuit of race meetings that was already drawing sizable crowds.

This loose collective of drivers, promoters, and spectators officially came together in the late 1940s under the auspices of one "Big" Bill France, who wanted to create something more organized to protect the interests of everyone involved. And so, in December 1947, a meeting was held at a hotel in Daytona Beach, Florida, at which the National Association for Stock Car Auto Racing (or NASCAR, as we know it today) was officially born. The first Daytona 500 race took place approximately two months later and is now held at around the same time every year, having become the most prestigious race in the sport.

NASCAR has since those early days become one of the biggest spectator sports in the United States. The thirty-six-race series, particularly the final ten races of what's known as the Chase for the Sprint Cup attract huge live crowds and millions of television viewers. Although the organizers of NASCAR have tried to spread their wings both nationally and internationally, it is still a sport that remains very close to its roots in the South and prides itself on the close connection that exists between those who compete in the races and those fans who come to watch them.

Richard Petty is part of the greatest NASCAR dynasty. His father, Lee Petty, was one of the original stars of NASCAR, and his son Kyle only recently retired from the sport after a successful career. Neither of them could touch Richard, however, who is known to one and all as "the King" because of the two-hundred-plus wins which brought him seven championships and seven victories at the Daytona 500. He now runs his own team, Richard Petty Motorsports and it was for the members of that team that I would be cooking on the day of the Daytona 500.

This would not be just a case of turning up and making whatever we wanted, however. Once we received our invitations, Michele and I were asked by our hosts to submit our suggested menus so that they could pass them under the eyes of the team nutritionist for approval. "The race puts a huge draw on the energies of the pit crew and the drivers," our contact told us. "So we need to make sure that they are fueled properly, just like the cars."

In the weeks before the race, Michele and I fashioned a menu that we thought would make a filling meal for approximately thirty hungry racing folk. Once we had made our final selection we sent it off for approval, along with a list of ingredients and equipment we would need. Michele and I arrived in Daytona the day before the race ready to prepare the hopefully enticing menu below.

Hong Kong Pork Chop Sandwiches
Bacon Cuban Sandwiches
Asian Red Cabbage Slaw
Bacon Creamed Corn
Tri-Colored Potato Salad
Tomato and Cucumber Salad
Candied Bacon Treats
Mixed Berry Cobbler

If you have ever seen Michele on any of her appearances on the Food Network, you will know that she is not a reticent character and that she likes to promote her beloved New England at every opportunity. She is also one hell of a good chef and one of the funniest people I know. I was certain that, whatever else happened and however well our food was received, the day was going to be a whole lot of fun. This was confirmed when we arrived at the racetrack early in the morning on the day of the race to find that our transport for the day was to be a golf cart that had been redesigned to look like a cartoon pig along with an oinking horn that Michele took childish delight in pressing on every occasion it was needed, and far too many when it wasn't.

Our meal was going to be served at the team's RPM hauler trackside, but the food would have to be cooked at another trailer some distance away and then transported when the crew was ready to be served. It also meant that we had to prepare our sizable feast in a tiny kitchen that was slightly smaller than a gentleman's handkerchief.

I was not sure that this was going to be possible, given that the kitchen was barely big enough for the two of us to fit into and only had a tiny stovetop on which to prepare food. Michele, however, was such an experienced chef that she didn't seem in the least bit fazed. "I've cooked for many more people in far smaller spaces," she said encouragingly when she saw the look on my face. I decided that it was probably best to stop whining and start cooking. Guided by someone who has overseen professional kitchens for most of her adult life, I was able to get all of my dishes prepared just in time for the pig-shaped golf cart to come and transport us to the trackside two hours later.

Our route to the track took us through a large open space that was filled to capacity with motor homes and tents. "People don't just come here for the race," one of our hosts told us. "They come for the whole weekend and this campsite becomes a fully-fledged community for a few days." The tents and motor coaches were a motley assortment, with those in the cheapest spots farthest away from the racetrack forming their own shantytown that reminded me more of the slum districts I had seen in developing countries than the campgrounds at a sporting event in one of the richest countries in the world.

Outside the battered trailers and ramshackle tents we passed, crowds of people were showing signs of early heavy-drinking activity and chilling out to the laid-back strains of southern rock music. They raised their glasses at us in salute as we passed in our pigmobile, hollering out when they recognized Michele's signature spiky blond hair. She happily returned everybody's greetings with oinks from the golf cart's horn. "They call this the Redneck Riviera," our friend told us. "We always say, what happens in here, stays in here."

The closer we got to the track, the more impressive the motor homes became. Right by the perimeter of the track enclosure, we drove through an area reserved for the team owners and drivers, which was filled with the most lavish trailers I had ever seen. They were all at least twice the size of my small apartment back in Los Angeles and cost, we were told by our driver, into the hundreds of thousands of dollars to purchase and kit out to specification. "The trailers are transported from racetrack to racetrack during the season," she told us, "and the drivers and owners all have their own private planes to take them to each destination."

Once we reached the RPM, the driver of the Richard Petty team bus came out to help us set up for service. It would normally be his job not only to take care of transportation, but also to prepare meals for the crew. Although he was happy to be given the day off from that part of his task, he was keen to help and shouted instructions over the fierce roar of the engines. We soon had all of the food laid out on long trestle tables, and finished just in the nick of time. We had barely begun to place out the last of the serving dishes before the crew broke for lunch and began to hover around the serving tables. Michele barked for them to "come and get it" and, not needing more than one invitation, they began attacking the food like a descending horde of pillaging Norsemen.

The crew had been working since the crack of dawn and from the noises of approval they made, they certainly seemed appreciative of a good hot meal after their morning's labors. It was obvious that some dishes were received more favorably than others. The pork chop sandwich was a big hit—people returned two or three times to ask for more. The bacon Cuban sandwich too received lots of thumbs-ups as people chewed their way through the gooey delights of pork and cheese. Michele's warm tri-colored potato salad flecked with dill and celery was by far the hit of the day and was so well received that the three serving dishes we had prepared were emptied in less than five minutes.

Unfortunately, my Asian slaw was about as well received as a fire in an orphanage. The crew steered clear of the slaw as if it carried the mark of death. I felt slightly crushed, until Michelle pointed out that the berry cobbler I had just placed out for dessert had almost entirely vanished and that someone was cleaning the bottom of the cast-iron pan in which it was cooked with their fingers to get the last of the juice.

As we came towards the end of service, Richard "the King" Petty arrived to sample our food with the team's driver, Aric Almirola. Like a great general, he had waited until all of his troops had been fed before coming up to collect his own food. He had also spent a great deal of the last couple of hours signing autographs for faithful fans, many of whom were now taking the opportunity to snap pictures of him as he stopped to eat.

"He is known as one of the most approachable people in the business," one of the crew members told me as I also grabbed a bite to eat from what was left on the table. "He realizes that this is a sport that the fans built." He laughed, adding, "We had to hire someone to play the bad guy to come and drag him away from fans so we can get him to do the media we need him for on race days."

I was surprised that the fans were allowed to come so close to the team trailers, but the same crew member explained, "It's a fan-based business and they can buy special passes that allow them to come and wander among the teams. They know not to get in the way and we know that they are the only reason we are here. It works." It was a far cry from the more elitist Formula 1 event I had once attended, where a very strict division was enforced between the drivers and the "great unwashed," who were kept at a distance.

After we had finished serving lunch, I dragged Michele to join me for a wander around the track. It was a decidedly blue-collar crowd, which was unsurprising given the origins of the sport, and it would be easy, if one were so inclined, to poke fun at many of the people we saw. But I have to say that I loved the atmosphere and that Michele and I received among the most hospitable welcomes I was to experience on my entire trip, from folks who had traveled from all over the South to get close to their heroes.

And they got very close indeed. As the start time for the race approached, the powerful stock cars began to emerge from their haulers and take their places on the grid as their famous drivers came out to inspect them one last time. I was amazed that, far from being shunned from the track at this important time, spectators were allowed to get up close and personal with the cars and the drivers. Even the megastars of the sport, people like Danica Patrick and Dale Earnhardt Jr., whom even I, a NASCAR newbie, had heard of, made time to take pictures and sign autographs despite the frantic throngs of press who clamored for their attention.

A message bellowed out of the crackly PA system announcing that it was time for the singing of the national anthem. Everyone in the racetrack, which was now filled to capacity, turned to face the Stars and Stripes, which were unfurled at the top of a large flagpole. Our hosts warned us that this was a part of the annual event that was taken very seriously indeed by the NASCAR crowd, but they really didn't need to. As an American citizen, Michele is as proud of her country as anyone I have ever met. As for me, I had also been in enough situations during this journey to know just how reverential Americans can be about their national anthem to treat it with the respect it deserves. On this time of hearing, the anthem definitely had more resonance than it might have done at the beginning of my travels around the country.

It was time for the race to begin and Michele and I were led away from the track towards the pit lanes, where each team had a tower from which they could watch the whole track. We were ushered up a slightly shaky ladder into the Richard Petty pit tower, directly opposite the finish line, and given seats along with a set of headphones through which we could hear all of the different team managers instructing their drivers as the race began.

The cars set off with a roar that even through the headsets made me shiver. It was a real "pinch me" moment as I thought how fortunate I was to be watching one of the most famous sporting events on earth from the pit tower of a team owned by its most illustrious competitor. The honor was not lost on me and I knew that there would be thousands of people across the country who would have given everything to swap places with me even for a few seconds.

As for the race itself, I have to be honest that after a few laps I turned to Michele and raised my eyebrows slightly. I knew from doing my homework that the race was five hundred miles in distance and would take over four hours to complete. Impressed as we were with the whole setup, that's a hell of a long time to spend watching as very fast cars blip by every couple of minutes. I was far more interested in the work of the crew and leaned over from my seat to watch them working in the pits. They were all in nonstop motion below us, readying fuel tanks and new tires for rapid changes when the cars were called in by the team managers. It was obvious that all the calories they had consumed during the lunch we prepared were being put to excellent use, and my respect for them was even greater than it had been before.

A number of other spectators in the tower had second thoughts about remaining there for the whole four-plus hours and gestured for me to join them as they descended and walked back to the team enclosure. While the race itself was obviously the main attraction, there was still plenty going on around the track. I decided to go for a wander among the fans who had spent their hard-earned cash to come to support their favorite racers and were watching the races in bars and on big screens near the tracks. A few of them recognized me as I ambled along and inevitably pressed a beer into my hand, asking me how I was enjoying Daytona. I truly began to understand why so many people had told me that NASCAR was a sport that, more than any other, existed because of its fans.

Shamefully, I'm not sure that I could even recall who won the race if you put a gun to my head. But looking back, the outcome was actually the least important part of what had been a very special day where I had met many extraordinary people. I was hugely honored to be asked to cook for the Richard Petty team, particularly alongside such a terrific chef as Michele, and I had been even more honored to actually spend time with the King himself.

If anyone was to ask me my opinion about NASCAR, as I write nearly a year later, I would tell them two things I know for certain. That NASCAR fans are the best in sport and that NASCAR pit crews really, really hate Asian slaw.

Conclusion

I slept soundly on the flight back from Florida to Los Angeles, only awoken by the sharp crackle of the PA system as the captain announced our descent into LAX. It was a little after nine a.m. and I could see that the infamous I-405 was already fender-to-fender with traffic as we passed over it. I felt a slight wave of depression wash over me as the wheels screeched on the tarmac, realizing that this extraordinary journey was now coming to its natural conclusion. Between the planning and the execution, it had taken up nearly two years of my life. Now that it was done, I was filled with trepidation about what the next stage of my life would entail.

One thing I did know for certain was that I would have much more time with my patient wife, Sybil. I was excited to see her and knew that she would be in the cell phone lot waiting for my call to come and collect me at the terminal. If the journey had been physically tough for me, it had been just as tough for her, but in a very different way. While I dealt with the joys of early-morning flights and living out of a suitcase, Sybil contended with my regular absences from our apartment and life together for the last year. Although she had been unfailingly supportive of my quest right from the very beginning, I was certain that she would be thrilled the journey was finally over, if only because it meant that the laundry would now be done on a regular basis and that dinner would be on the table when she came home from work.

As soon as we arrived back at our apartment, I unpacked and showered as she put on the kettle for tea. I threw on a T-shirt and my favorite pair of ratty shorts and sank down into the welcoming Simon's-ass-shaped sag on the couch with my laptop and pile of notebooks. Sybil knew that I wanted to capture my thoughts about the end of this journey while they were still fresh in my mind and, with one last patient gesture and a hot cup of tea, left me to my own devices.

Just on the numbers alone, my Fed, White, and Blue adventure had been an impressive one. I had been on the road for a full year. In that time, I had taken over one hundred flights and had slept in two hundred different beds. I had visited thirty-nine states and by doing so had completed another bucket list dream of visiting every state of the Union. Along the way I had filled a dozen notebooks with my musings and taken over five thousand photographs of the places I had been and, of course, the food I had eaten. I had also amassed a colossal pile of books, pamphlets, leaflets, and newsletters on everything from cheese making in Wisconsin to catfish farming in Mississippi. More amusingly, I realized as I looked upon a teetering pile of clothing Sybil had created in the corner of the living room, I had also managed to curate a remarkable collection of apparel given to me by different organizations in every part of the country.

There were over a dozen baseball hats, including one now signed for me by Richard Petty during the Daytona 500. There was an array of vests, T-shirts, sweatshirts, aprons, and oven mitts, all given to me as mementos by the kind people I met along the way. I laid them out on the dining table, each one in a position equivalent to the state from where I had been given them, on the map. There were very few gaps, a testament to both the scope of the journey and the generosity of the people I met along the road.

And that was the key to it. The numbers were indeed very impressive, but as with all of my travels, this journey to discover my adopted homeland had been about two things: eating amazing food and using that as a way to meet amazing people. As I looked through my notes and photographs and at the multicolored pile of clothing, I knew that from that vantage point the journey had been a complete success. I was also certain that no one could ever call into doubt that I had given America a fair shot at showing me what it means to become a citizen through its food and people.

The slightly desperate squeaking of my bathroom scale as I stepped onto it after my refreshing post-flight shower confirmed that America had also truly delivered on its promise to feed me well. As I scrolled through the images of food on my laptop, the memories of the people, places, and incredible tastes came flooding back to me. The Shabbat meal I ate in Kansas City; the communal meals I shared with a bunch of bright-eyed twentysomething apprentice farmers in Santa Cruz; the lobster roll in Rockport, Maine; the clam fest while hanging with the Rebel and the Bay Rat in Egg Harbor Township, New Jersey; the ethnic feasts in the Bronx; the late-night Korean blowout shared with the Seoul Sausage Company boys; the Alaskan salmon; and, of course, all that BBQ. So many great meals that even thinking about them now as I write makes my head spin and my stomach rumble.

That's not to say for a moment that everything I ate along the way was good. I am still suffering the intestinal fallout from the meals I endured at the chain restaurants I visited in Hattiesburg, Mississippi, and my memories of the wretched breakfasts I scarfed down out of necessity at buffets in cheap hotels, or the grim snacks I settled for at airports, are not what you might call fond. Despite these minor aberrations, I am delighted to say that the Fed, White, and Blue journey was a genuinely positive dining experience.

However, this journey was supposed to be just as much about nourishing my soul as well as feeding my body. I had set out on a quest to break bread with America—not just to have brief meetings where I turned up, helped out for a few hours, and then buggered off. I desperately wanted to make lasting connections with the people of America and, by doing so, find out more about the country that I hoped would be my home for the rest of my life. One glimpse at my e-mail in-box or at the dozens of texts on my cell phone convinced me that I had achieved my goal. Over the last year, I had met as wide a cross-section of the population as ever I could have hoped for when I first sat down and made my wish list. But I had done a great deal more than that. I had also created a beautiful extended network of people, many of whom had become my family. A family which, much like America itself, is filled with people of different races, politics, and religions but who are united both in their love of their country and the unending generosity they had offered to a wandering individual.

I thought of my many new friends: Terry French, the Rebel Chef, who used food to climb back from the brink of depression; Jamie "the Bear" McDonald, who eats ridiculous amounts of food to fill a college fund for his kids; Skip Madsen in Edmonds, Washington, who collaborated with me on an award-winning beer; and Frank Soukop and his family, who gave me such an impressive introduction to celebrating the Fourth of July. I thought of the many chefs who had opened their kitchens to me; of AJ, the young Filipino chef who fed a host of my crazy in-laws; and the boys from the Seoul Sausage Company, who still insist on calling me "Uncle Simon." I thought of Matt Romero and his chile roaster, and Terry Simpson, the weight loss surgeon who took me fishing in Alaska. Then there were the good people of Harvest Texarkana, who work ceaselessly and without glory to feed the hungry in America's biggest food desert, and Mark Murrell in Austin, who showed me what tailgating was all about. Bill Esparza, who introduced me to the underworld of Los Angeles street food, and Cynthia Sandberg, who allowed me to apprentice with her at Love Apple Farms in Santa Cruz. So many people, so many new friends, and so many great memories. Even if I had not had a grander purpose for my journey, the foundation of this new extended American family would have made it all worthwhile.

But, quite apart from making new friends and gaining fifteen pounds, I had set myself a task to see what it means to be an American, and while I knew from the start that my journey would never give me a definitive answer, looking back I felt quietly pleased with what I had accomplished over the last months, particularly as it had all begun with just me on this same couch armed with nothing more than a telephone, a laptop, and a completely blank sheet of paper. I may not have succeeded in getting to every part of the country that deserves attention, nor did I get to do all the things I set out to do when I first wrote down my initial list. But it would take a very savage critic to suggest that I had not given it my very best shot.

If you recall, on the first day I started planning the Fed, White, and Blue journey, I wrote the word "AMERICA" in large letters at top of the first page in my otherwise empty notepad, in part to remind me that this trip had a purpose. Now, at the end of the trail, I read through the list of words I had created. I began to circle the ones that really stood out as illuminating something about my adopted country.

Diversity
Immigration
Opportunity
Meritocracy
Freedom
Reinvention
Contribution
Rights
Responsibility

These might have been just words on paper when I first wrote them down, but they were brought to vivid life as I traveled and were reinforced by what I had experienced, both the positive and the negative.

I have certainly seen just how diverse America is both geographically and ethnically. I stared in awe at breathtaking landscapes as I crisscrossed the country from Miami to Seattle and Maine to New Mexico, and I had been fortunate to cross paths with so many of the more than one hundred and fifty ethnic groups that make up the American population.

I've also seen the positive impact immigration has had on every aspect of American life, from the day the first Pilgrims staggered ashore after fleeing religious persecution in Britain to the day I inherited my own menagerie of crazy but beloved Filipino in-laws. Each wave of arrivals has enriched American culture, and I have tasted how they have all seasoned the melting pot that is American cuisine.

Unfortunately, I also saw the polarizing effect that fear of more recent immigration has caused among an ill-informed section of America's population—people who seemed entirely oblivious to the irony of being able to cite their lineage in exact percentages ("I'm one-quarter German and one-tenth Cherokee") while wanting to deny others the chance to experience the incredible benefits and opportunities that living in America might offer.

And, if proof were even required that America genuinely is the great land of opportunity and reinvention, I needed only to look in the mirror and see the chubby reflection of the fifty-year-old expat British publisher who has been allowed to carve out a career as a TV food critic on his move across the pond.

I realized as I sat on the couch with my cup of tea that becoming an American was definitely going to be a two-way street. If I was going to take advantage of the rights of being an American citizen, I would also have to be subject to the responsibilities it demanded. I didn't think for one second that anyone would expect the slightly doughy mass that is typing this book to go to war on their behalf, unless they are hoping that the enemy will die from laughter, but I've been convinced that becoming a citizen of any country, particularly one as vibrant as the United States, can never be a passive experience.

It also occurred to me that while the travels for this book were at an end, my travels of discovery in America most definitely are not. There are still plenty of places left to visit, plenty of invitations I have not yet had the chance to accept, plenty of people still to meet, and plenty of great food still to be discovered. I fully expect that, money and wife willing, I shall be carrying on the Fed, White, and Blue adventure until the good Lord calls me home, or at least gives me a heart attack as a warning to slow down a little.

I had been on the sofa for a couple of hours by this point, and was plucked from my deep thoughts by the sound of Sybil calling from the other room. She was summoning me to join her and catch up with all of the TV shows she had recorded while I had been on the road. I had not been away so long that I had forgotten the phrase "happy wife, happy life" and willingly obliged. Her patience during the last year deserved far more than my attendance during a few episodes of *Revenge*. She is, after all, the very reason I came to this country in the first place.

Before I went to join her, I picked up my pen to add just one more word to that list under the heading "AMERICA" I underlined it twice with thick black lines, closed my notebook, and went to join the most important person in my life for the next stage of our great adventure.

Just in case you are interested, that last word can be found on the next page.

Home.

EPILOGUE

Civis Americanus Sum

At two p.m. on September 17, 2014, I became a citizen of the United States of America.

A little over one month before, I'd navigated my way smoothly through the final naturalization interview and had departed the rather bleak field offices in downtown Los Angeles, clutching a document explaining what to expect on the day of the oath-taking ceremony. Although I was pleased to be reaching the final stages of the journey, I was slightly disappointed to find out that it wasn't going to be the quite intimate, small-scale event I had anticipated when I began the process some two years earlier.

When the big day finally arrived, I found myself elbowing my way through 3,215 of my closest "friends," hailing from 148 nations at the Los Angeles Convention Center, as I sought to find Sybil, who had been obliged to use another entrance as I registered. We snagged two seats in a prime location and, during the short time before the event got under way, sat to take in the convivial atmosphere as everyone, me included, prepared for one of the biggest days of their lives.

Things became more solemn as the presiding judge addressed the crowd, deemed that the court was now in session, and asked us to stand, raise our right hands, and recite the oath of allegiance. We stood and, following her lead, announced in one voice:

"I hereby declare, on oath, that I absolutely and entirely renounce and abjure all allegiance and fidelity to any foreign prince, potentate, state, or sovereignty of whom or which I have heretofore been a subject or citizen; that I will support and defend the Constitution and laws of the United States of America against all enemies, foreign and domestic; that I will bear true faith and allegiance to the same; that I will bear arms on behalf of the United States when required by the law; that I will perform noncombatant service in the Armed Forces of the United States when required by the law; that I will perform work of national importance under civilian direction when required by the law; and that I take this obligation freely without any mental reservation or purpose of evasion; so help me God."

Anyone who knows me well will tell you that I am not a particularly sentimental man. However, even though I was only one among thousands of others sharing the same experience, I found the ceremony to be far more moving than I had ever imagined possible. I will even admit to surreptitiously wiping a small tear from my eye with the sleeve of my suit when Sybil had turned away for a second.

In hindsight, I think the presence of so many people, from so many different backgrounds, actually added to rather than detracted from the significance of the event. I was able to witness the joyous celebrations of all the participants and their families and, once it was announced that we were now "official," I realized that while my journey from frequent visitor to permanent resident to citizen had been a unique one, so, too, had each and every one of theirs.

There were participants from every continent, both a testament to the appeal and benefits of owning an American passport and to the multicultural nature of the City of Angels. Some may have come to escape political or religious persecution; some for economic opportunity, for them and their families; and others, like me, because they fell in love. Whatever their origins, and for whatever reason they arrived on these shores, they had all now been given the rights and had accepted the responsibilities of citizenship and were greeting the news with loud whoops of celebration, very American high-fives, and impassioned group hugs.

As for me, my reserved inner Brit still needing some training on how to enjoy myself, I was satisfied with giving Sybil a gentle hug and informing her that her previously much-used threat to "have you deported" every time we had an argument no longer carried any menace. She was now stuck with me.

I would never go so far as to describe the whole experience as sacramental, but the ceremony definitely provided a pleasing sense of closure. It was not only a natural end point for this book, but also meant that I could begin to think about my plans for the future. Even, if at this point, I had no idea what those might be, I hoped they would at least continue to include travels across the United States, where I could share many more conversations and delicious meals with my new fellow countrymen.

Whatever happened in the long term, a sharp tug on the slightly damp sleeve of my suit reminded me that in the short term, things were going to remain very much the same.

"I'm hungry," Sybil informed me in a tone that made it clear that my new status carried little weight when pitched against the growing chasm that was forming in her stomach. She smiled and linked her arm through mine as I replied, "Let's go and have an early dinner."

What better way for one of America's newest citizens to end the journey?

ACKNOWLEDGMENTS

This book could easily have been twice the length it is and yet it still would not have given me enough words to cover all my experiences during the last year. I hope that those amazing people who are mentioned in these pages will accept that fact as both my thanks and a sign of just how unendingly grateful I am for their invitations, their kindness, and their ongoing friendship.

I also hope that those who were just as kind and who have become just as good friends, but who are not mentioned, will understand that this is down entirely to a lack of space rather than a lack of appreciation for the generosity they showed me. Mentioned or not, all of these people are now part of my new American family and I consider it my duty to them to become the best citizen I can.

I would like to thank my manager, John Tomko, and all at Rain Management for their continued support in my second life career and I would like to thank everyone at William Morris Endeavor for remembering that I exist when they have far more important clients to look after. I would particularly like to thank Eric Lupfer of the WME Book Division for beating me up until I crafted a proposal that made a publisher go, "Mmmm, that might be interesting." Without his efforts and sage advice this book would not have happened.

During my first career, I worked for Penguin for nearly ten years. The fact that this book is being published by Hudson Street Press, an imprint of that same house, makes me feel like I am coming home, and the extreme professionalism and author care shown by everyone I have met there during the last two years reminds me of why it remains one of the world's great publishers. I would particularly like to thank Christina Rodriguez for her enthusiasm during my journey and for her guidance during the editorial process. Books are very much a partnership between author and editor, and I could not have hoped for a better partner. Also, high words of praise must go to Dave Cole for copyediting the manuscript.

I would like to thank Alton Brown for his extraordinarily generous offer to donate a foreword for *Fed, White, and Blue*. The opportunity to work with a man of such stature and such intellectual curiosity on a regular basis has been one of the true highlights of my time in the United States. I am honored that he allows me to call him "friend." I would also like to thank my attorney, Allison Aquino-Silva, from the legal firm of Aquino and Loew, for helping make my journey through the U.S. immigration system both speedy and painless.

I would like to thank the many resources I turned to for historical, culinary, and political information during the writing of this book. A list of these books, websites, and podcasts can be found in the bibliography, and I strongly recommend you seek them out as reliable and enjoyable sources. If I have failed to credit anyone or made any errors, the fault lies with me and I shall be only too happy to make corrections in any future editions of this book.

Finally, I want to thank my family for their constant support and my beautiful wife, Sybil, whose agreement to marry me started the journey to write this book and who remains the best thing that ever happened to me.

Top Ten Best Eats of the Journey

It is, perhaps, a little unfair of my editor to ask me to list the top ten tastes from my journey. There were so many terrific meals along the way that I could give you a hundred choices without touching the sides. However, I do know how you (we) Americans love our rankings, so on the understanding that if you were to ask again tomorrow the answers I would give might be totally different, here you go:

Lobster roll—*the Pearl Restaurant, Rockland, Maine*
Pleasant Ridge Reserve cheese—*Wisconsin*
Carnitas el Momo—*Boyle Heights, Los Angeles, California*
Smoked salmon—*Alaska*
Kare-kare—*Salo-Salo, West Covina, California*
Roasted green chiles—*Santa Fe, New Mexico*
Fed, White and Brew—*Edmonds, Washington*
A salad made with just-picked produce by the apprentices at Love Apple Farms—*Santa Cruz, California*
Fresh clams—*Egg Harbor Township, New Jersey*
Saint Louis ribs—*Phat Jack's, Lincoln, Nebraska*

SELECTED BIBLIOGRAPHY

Although *Fed, White, and Blue* was never meant to be a history book, I hope that you found some of the fascinating facts I uncovered about the United States to be of interest. If so, I would recommend you check out some of the books, podcasts, and websites I turned to when I did my research.

I would also like to point you in the direction of the websites of many of the people and organizations I met along the way, which provided me with a lot of insight during my journey.

General

http://civilwarpodcast.blogspot.com/
A Century of Restaurants, Rick Browne (Kansas City, MO: Andrews McMeel, 2013)
Aquino and Loew, immigration and nationality law specialist—http://www.aquinoloew.com

Masarap: Delicious

Salo-Salo Grill—http://www.salosalogrillwestcovina.com/

You Heave, You Leave

Bears Smokehouse—http://www.bearsbbq.com/
Wing Bowl Official Site—http://wingbowl.cbslocal.com/

The Baron and the Bronx

Baron Ambrosia Official Website—http://baronambrosia.com/
Garinet, information on all things Garifuna—www.garinet.com

A Pilgrim's Progress

Plimoth Plantation Official Website—www.plimoth.org
Wampanoag Tribe Website—www.mashpeewampanoagtribe.com/

On a Roll in Maine

Davina Thomulasa Blog—http://forknplate.com/
The Pearl, Rockland—http://www.thepearlrockland.com/

Minnesota, Nice

Grand View Lodge—http://www.grandviewlodge.com/
Brainerd Chamber of Commerce—http://www.explorebrainerdlakes.com/

Freezing with the BBQ Brethren

Phat Jack's BBQ—http://phatjackslincoln.com/
Kansas City Barbecue Society—http://www.kcbs.us/

From Pasture to Plate

Nebraska Department of Agriculture—http://www.nda.nebraska.gov/
University of Nebraska, Lincoln Animal Science Department—http://
    animalscience.unl.edu/anscextensionmeatscience
The Nebraska Club—http://www.nebraskaclub.net/
The Greater Omaha Packing Company—http://www.greateromaha.com/
The Nebraska Beef Council—http://www.nebeef.org/default.aspx
Beef: The Untold Story of How Milk, Meat, and Muscle Changed the World,
    Andrew Rimas (New York: HarperCollins, 2009)

Pressing the Shabbat Reset Button

Yosef Silver's Blog—http://www.thisamericanbite.com/
Vaad HaKashruth Kansas City—http://www.vaadkc.org/
Kansas City's Kosher BBQ Contest—http://www.kckosherbbq.com/

SELECTED BIBLIOGRAPHY

Whey Out in Wisconsin

The American Cheese Society Inc.—http://www.cheesesociety.org/
Uplands Cheese Company—http://www.uplandscheese.com/

K-Town Rocks

The Seoul Sausage Company—http://www.seoulsausage.com/

North of South of the Border

Bill Esparza's Blog—http://www.streetgourmetla.com/

Farm Fresh

Love Apple Farms—http://www.growbetterveggies.com/

Fed, White, and Brew

The American Brewing Company—http://www.americanbrewing.com/
The Great American Beer Festival—http://www.greatamericanbeerfestival
.com/

Bear, Where? There.

Terry Simpson—http://www.terrysimpson.com/
Southcentral Foundation—https://www.southcentralfoundation.com/

Roasting in Santa Fe

Matt Romero—http://mattromerofarms.com/
Santa Fe Farmers' Market—http://www.santafefarmersmarket.com/

Hook 'em Horns

University of Texas Tailgaiting—http://www.utexas.edu/parking/parking
/specialevents/tailgating/
American Tailgater Association—http://americantailgaterassociation.org
/news/history-tailgating-time-honored-tradition/

Paying It Forward in Texarkana

Harvest Texarkana—http://www.harvesttexarkana.org/
Feeding America—http://feedingamerica.org/

Down in the Delta

Eat Y'all Website—http://www.eatyall.com/
Six Shooter Land and Timber—https://www.facebook.com/SixShooterLand
    AndTimber
Chao Photography LLC—http://www.chaophotography.com

Feeding the 500

Smithfield Hams—http://www.smithfieldmarketplace.com/smithfield_hams
Richard Petty Motorsports—http://www.richardpettymotorsports.com/
NASCAR—http://www.nascar.com/

Simon Majumdar is a world-renowned broadcaster, food writer, and author who has spent the second half of his time on this planet trying to fulfill his ambition to "go everywhere, eat everything." This journey has taken him to all fifty states and to dozens of countries around the world. He has written two previous books, *Eat My Globe* and *Eating for Britain*. And his latest book, *Fed, White, and Blue*, catalogs his journey to American citizenship in 2015. Simon is a well-recognized personality on the Food Network, regularly appearing on shows such as *Iron Chef America*, *The Next Iron Chef*, *The Best Thing I Ever Ate*, *Cutthroat Kitchen*, *Extreme Chef*, and *Beat Bobby Flay*, and has also appeared as an expert commentator on National Geographic's *EAT: The Story of Food*. He lives in Los Angeles.